The Psychology of Myth, Folklore, and Religion

Leo Schneiderman

Nelson-Hall nh Chicago

Library of Congress Cataloging in Publication Data

Schneiderman, Leo, 1925-
    The psychology of myth, folklore, and religion.

    Includes index.
    1. Psychology, Religious. 2. Mythology–
Psychological aspects. 3. Folk-lore–Psychological
aspects. I. Title.
BL53.S34   291'.01'9   81–9471
                                    AACR2

ISBN 0–88229–659–0 (cloth)
ISBN 0–88229–783–x (paper)

10 9 8 7 6 5 4 3 2 1

Contents

Acknowledgments

S EVERAL BASIC texts and translations of key myths, legends, and stories were consulted in the preparation of this work. References to Greco-Roman myths (chapters 3, 6) are largely based on Robert Graves' *The Greek Myths* (1955). Although the author does not necessarily subscribe to Graves' Great Goddess theory in all its details, he is in essential agreement with the thesis that matriarchal and totemistic forms of religion were the forerunners of historical religions throughout the world. Frazer's *The Golden Bough* (1922) has also been consulted freely, even though its assumptions are every bit as controversial as those of Graves. Both works are extraordinary in the scope and richness of the materials presented as well as in their implications for understanding the prelogical sources of modern religious systems.

References to Ramakrishna's writings in chapter 4 are based on *The Gospel of Sri Ramakrishna* by Mahendra Nath Gupta ("M"), translated by Swami Nikhilananda, and published in 1952 by the Ramakrishna-Vivekananda Center in New York. The primary source for information about Ramakrishna's life was Christopher Isherwood's *Ramakrishna and his Disciples* (1965).

The text which served as a basis for the analysis of the cycle of legends centering on Jason and Medea (chapter 6) is E. V. Rieu's 1959 translation of *The Voyage of the Argo* by Apollonius of Rhodes.

The History of Herodotus, edited and translated by George Rawlinson, provided the basis for the discussion of ancient Egyptian religious beliefs and practices associated with the cult of Osiris. Until the advent of modern archeology the writings of Herodotus constituted the only source of information about Osiris. In general, archeological findings confirm the accuracy of Herodotus' descriptions.

Chapter 7 is based on R. T. H. Griffith's monumental translation of the Ramayana (1870–1875), as well as a contemporary description of the Ram Lila festival by Norvin Hein, which appeared in *Traditional India: Structure and Change* (1959) under the editorship of Milton Singer.

The five fairy tales which provide the text for chapter 8 were compiled by the Comtesse de Ségur in the mid-nineteenth century and published under the title *Nouveaux Contes de Fées.* The book has gone through many editions in French; a representative modern edition was published in Montreal in 1945 by Editions Variétés. The first English translation was probably made by Mrs. Chapman Coleman and her daughters and appeared in Philadelphia in 1869 under the Porter and Coates imprint. For the present purpose, the author relied on two twentieth century translations, an anonymous one published by the Penn Publishing Company in 1920 in Philadelphia under the title *Old French Fairy Tales,* and Virginia Olcott's *Princess Rosette and Other Fairy Tales* (Philadelphia: Macrae Smith, 1930). Of special importance in influencing the author's interpretations was P. Saintyves' *Les Contes de Perrault et Les Recits Paralleles* (Paris: Librairie Critique Emile Nourry, 1923).

Two texts provided the foundation for chapter 9: F. W. Bourdillon's translation *Aucassin and Nicolette: A Love Story* (London: Kegan Paul, Trench & Co., 1887) and his facsimile edition of the manuscript *Cest Daucasi & De Nicolete* (Bibliotheque Nationale, fonds francais 2168). This edition was published at Oxford by Clarendon Press in 1894.

The author wishes to express his gratitude to the *Psychoanalytic Review, Literature East and West,* the *Journal for the Scientific Study of Religion,* and the *Connecticut Review* for permission to reprint chapters 1–7 and 9 in modified form.

Introduction

THIS BOOK is an attempt to apply the conceptual tools of psychoanalysis, anthropology, and folklore to the analysis of selected topics in religion, such as mysticism, ritual, sacred myth, and folklore originating in archaic religion. The prevailing theme is that religious symbols, rituals, and myths reflect the terrifying and inspiring contents of the unconscious. This view, derived from psychoanalysis, is by no means novel; what is new is the effort to apply this theory to myths, folktales, and mystical experiences that hitherto have not been studied by means of an interdisciplinary approach.

I believe there is a special urgency in carrying out such an analysis because the legendary symbols and motifs of both Western civilization and the East are rapidly losing their vitality, and even their meaning, in the face of profound social change. These symbols and motifs gained currency because they conveyed the significance of human hopes and fears that were often too overpowering to express directly. Now, before we have lost touch entirely with the distinct frame of mind that created the magical dramas, narratives, and rituals of the past, it is necessary to try to translate that frame of mind into language that modern man can understand.

Obviously, the task is more difficult than mere translation. Mythographers, storytellers, ancient wizards, masked initiators, and others who were the vehicle for preserving the folkways of the past often had no more insight into what they were expressing than the modern reader. They used symbols that had been passed down to them by tradition, and these symbols at no time possessed a precise meaning. This does not mean that the symbols used in myth and folklore represent a defective system of communication. They are rather to be thought of as a code for conveying shared feelings, images, memories, and desires, but a code based on the still obscure laws of prelogical thinking.

Of course, we moderns are not strangers to prelogical thinking, based as it is on wishful thinking and the residue of infantile fears and hatreds. But we are impatient with ancient writings or sacred dramas because they seem not to speak to the human condition as we know it. In some measure, this impatience is justified because historical changes have altered the conditions under which men live. In another sense, however, as Erich Fromm and others have pointed out, the existential conditions of life remain unaltered. I refer to the crises of birth, separation, adolescence, marriage, and parenthood, to say nothing of the critical events of sickness, death, catastrophe, and conflict that are inseparable from human experience. It is important to reconstruct how ancient man experienced the world and how he dealt with his feelings in relation to existential challenges, because we face the same challenges.

Although modern man is, due to the growth of technology, more effective in dealing with existential crises than our forbears were, human hopes and fears remain constant. Myths, folktales, sacred dramas, and rituals provide a picture of how man dealt with the demands of the outer world and of his own human nature, demands that have not changed materially, although their scope has been considerably enlarged. For example, Western man has never ceased to strive for a progressive view of social evolution.

Hand in hand with this aspiration, we see the gradual emergence of the concept of ethical monotheism. I do not think this is a historical coincidence. As men struggled toward an optimistic (not to be confused with messianic) view of the future, the concept of God likewise changed in the direction of increased emphasis on the benevolence of the Deity. By examining the religious beliefs and practices of ancient man, we can form certain hypotheses as to how the conception of God has undergone modification.

This is the purpose of chapter 1, "The Birth of Demons." It argues that the contemporary eclipse of God in the Western world is related to a phase of deep pessimism through which we are now passing. Ancient man also experienced periods of diminished faith and even hostility toward his gods, but on a periodic basis related to the cycles of the seasons. For modern man, the consciousness of God's presence as a benign force depends on the ability to repress—i.e., ignore or unintentionally forget—the knowledge of actual evil and suffering. When it ceases to be possible to overlook unpleasant realities psychoanalysis speaks of a failure of repression. Something of this sort seems to be happening in our time.

The evidence for this assertion is as follows. Instead of passively bemoaning the fact that the era of endless progress has come to a halt in the shadow of nuclear war, environmental pollution, civil strife, diminished energy resources, worldwide hunger, mass unemployment, and uncontrolled inflation, we see a dramatic resurgence of interest in the occult, in messianic religions, and in the polytheistic religious systems of the Orient. Outside the West, particularly in India and Japan, revivalism, often with political overtones, is a real force. It is a force, moreover, that is ambivalent toward modern technology and the cult of material progress. This kind of reaction to man's tragic circumstances has much in common with ancient man's periodic destruction of old gods and their replacement with new ones for the purpose of quickening the forces of nature in the service of life-renewal. I am not sure of the extent to which ancient man's impulse to slay his gods periodically was due to a failure of repression; although, as I suggest in chapter 1, unconscious resentment caused by initiation experiences may have been a factor. In the case of modern man, I believe there has occurred a gradual expansion of consciousness, leading to the tragic realization that progress is far from inevitable. Corresponding to this insight, men begin to rediscover a multitude of exotic gods who represent the wish to escape frustration and despair, as well as a horde of demons who personify evil. Thus, the achievement of ethical monotheism is far from guaranteed, and the conception of God as omnipotent and benevolent is threatened.

It is no accident that the decline of traditional religion, particularly in the West, has been accompanied by a reawakening of interest in mysticism. Although mystics have often been adopted by established churches, they tend to appear on the scene at times when social cohesion is at its weakest and when men find it increasingly difficult to find security through participation in traditional institutions. The alternatives to sharing collective representations are either to suffer outright alienation; or, more indirectly, to undertake the search for God alone and unassisted, either outside the framework of conventional worship or, more commonly, on the fringes of established religion. This is what chapter 2, "The Mystical Quest," is all about.

In chapter 2, I argue that as long as men remain under the spell of repression—i. e., so long as they are unable to admit to themselves that they have terrible misgivings—conventional religion suffices for them, and they carry on their dialogue with God somewhat impersonally as if He were a remote but benign father figure. When repression fails and doubts and confusion force their way into consciousness, certain individuals become more insistent in the demands they put upon God to reassure them of His love. At the same time, these individuals—would-be mystics—begin to look more closely into themselves. Some of them, perhaps those who are destined to set an example for others, do not hesitate to descend into the private hell of their unconscious, searching for the dark side of God and the fullness of God, as well as for the signs of His benign presence. By means of his voyage into his unconscious a true mystic succeeds in penetrating the disguises of God, experiencing Him as the spiritual counterpart of the objective world, and not as a mythical hero or as the magisterial judge of the universe. This discovery makes possible the sincere love of God, without reservations and without exaggerated affirmations of love by way of reaction formation. Perhaps the present interest in mysticism as a way of life based on spiritual discipline may give people the courage to respond wisely and compassionately to the critical challenges of our troubled times.

Although people rarely have made the connection between mystical experience and individualism, I believe we are dealing with similar psychological needs in both instances. A mystic who tries to attain a sense of oneness with God or with the universe is paradoxically an individualist who is not content to relate himself to society on its terms. He seeks a response from the divine Other, a sign, a vision, a token of love that society is unable to give him. The mystic guesses that society does not value individuals as such but is instead an arrangement for perpetuating a type of human being. Hence his preference for God conceived as the divine companion to each living soul.

In chapter 3, "The Cult of Fertility," I analyze the relationship between the collectivity and the individual, advancing the thesis that society seeks to subordinate the individual to its purpose, which is nothing more than self-renewal. The instrument for self-renewal is the cult of fertility, as powerful a force today as it was in remote times.

The cult of fertility is opposed to the demand by individual human beings that they be allowed to live their lives as if they had some significance. Moreover, the cult of fertility, as applied to relationships between men and women, stands in the way of a wholehearted love relationship based on companionship, sex, and shared responsibility. In place of these criteria of intimacy, the cult of fertility substitutes a sole obligation, the obligation to perpetuate the species. In the name of fertility—essentially a sacred, magical function, overvalued by the collectivity—sex in particular has been placed under a set of complex taboos in an effort to keep the function of fertility strictly within its sacred context. Thus, the cult of fertility is symptomatic of the age-long struggle between the demands of the group and the need for human intimacy. Apart from the fact that the cult of fertility is irrational, being grounded in sympathetic magic, it is obviously a major factor in producing overpopulation, along with famine, social upheaval, and general backwardness. But these results are not surprising because the cult of fertility is based on the sacrifice of human lives as the necessary price for the preservation of the species, in a manner analogous to the prodigal laying of eggs by insects with the consequent destruction of many individual eggs by the forces of nature. Is it necessary for man to emulate the insects in order to survive as a species?

Chapter 4, "Ramakrishna," might logically follow the chapter on mysticism, since it deals with the life of a modern Hindu holy man. However, I have placed it deliberately after the chapter on the cult of fertility. This is because the reigning obsession in the life of Ramakrishna, at least during his early years as a mystic, was his preoccupation with the Hindu goddess of fertility, Kali. The turning point in Ramakrishna's life came, I believe, when he began to recover from a chronic psychosis, of which the most important symptom was his inability to differentiate himself from his mother and his mother surrogate, the goddess Kali. So long as the mystic remained identified with the fertility goddess, even assuming a female identity for a number of years, his mystical quest remained one-sided, although his defenders tried to justify his transvestism on philosophical grounds. It was only when Ramakrishna began to relate to his disciples as individuals, and was no longer under the compulsion to cling to the statue of Kali as if she were a person, that he was able to find a middle ground between absorption in a sort of cosmic consciousness and self-expression as a responsive individual. In making the transition from selflessness and mystical detachment to active involvement with his disciples, Ramakrishna demonstrated the human potentialities of mysticism, and provided the foundations for an important social movement that was carried to fruition by his disciples.

Chapters 5 through 9 are concerned with myth and folklore and are understandable within the broader philosophical framework provided by the first four chapters. Chapter 5, "The Myth of Osiris," draws certain parallels between the Egyptian cult of the dead and primitive initiation rites, and seeks to call attention to their common focus on symbolic death and resurrection. My emphasis is on the motif of passivity and psychological mutilation which is so much a part of ancient man's outlook on the world and which is akin to modern man's destructive alienation from his own vital potentialities.

Similarly, in chapter 6, "Jason and the Totem," my concern is to show that man's life-denying tendencies are rooted in his unconscious identification with the totemic monsters that our ancestors conjured up as objectifications of their primordial fears. Although Jason succeeded in gaining possession of the Golden Fleece, his tribal totem, it was the demonic power of the totem that came to possess him and, above all, his consort, Medea. I view Medea as a figure linking the phase of totemism in ancient Greece with the later stage of matriarchal religion, long before the cult of Zeus gained ascendancy. My intention is to show that religious and moral evolution proceed by overlapping historical stages and that every advance carries with it remnants of a savage past.

Chapter 7, "The Ramayana and Ram Lila," elaborates on the theme of creation and destruction developed in the early chapters. Based on the Hindu book of scripture and the sacred drama associated with it, this chapter endeavors to show the intimate link between the cult of fertility and the cult of death. My analysis of the Ramayana is concerned not only with the adventures of Rama, the hero, who is an incarnation of the great god Visnu the Preserver, but also with the role played indirectly by Siva, the Destroyer. I believe that Siva, who combines phallic characteristics with his death-dealing role, is represented by the monster Ravana, who is the chief villain in the Ramayana and the abductor of Rama's wife, Sita. Sita is above all an earth-mother, not essentially different from Siva's wife, Parvati. Thus, the Ramayana, ostensibly a document devoted to Visnu, can be seen as a vehicle given over to the interplay of the creative principle, Sakti, as embodied by Sita the earth-mother, with the life-denying principle, as represented by Siva and his surrogates.

Chapter 8, "Female Initiation Rites," starts with a collection of French fairy tales and proceeds to develop the hypothesis that the stories are derived from very ancient, perhaps prehistoric initiation rites based on totemism. It is customary to assume that Western myth and folklore are relatively free of totemic references. As I tried to show in the chapter dealing with Jason and Medea, this assumption is patently false. In chapter 8, I carry the argument a step further and assert that even modern fairy tales, edited for the moral instruction of children, are derived from the most primitive layers of European civilization. The stories analyzed in this chapter provide a series of allegories of female initiation. The tales cover a complete cycle of initiation crises—spiritual death, exile, esoteric instruction by dead ancestors in totemic form, rebirth, and adulthood followed by marriage. A theme running through all the stories is that the ordeals of initiation cannot be overcome by independent action, but require supernatural assistance. As a result of repression, the cruel and frightening elements that once figured prominently in these narratives, and the rites which they probably accompanied, have been filtered out, producing seemingly innocuous cautionary tales.

Scholars rarely approach the courtly tales of the Middle Ages and the Renaissance as anything but sophisticated precursors of the modern short story or novel. In chapter 9, "A Medieval Love Story," I continue to probe for primitive sources to explain the basic plot as well as the incidental and often irrational details of Aucassin and Nicolette. This cant-fable blends folkloristic motifs and erotic themes. These motifs include references to local religious customs associated with May Day, iconographic tableaux, the use of unconscious symbolism founded in folk experience, and other nonliterary components. The tale, on the surface a polished and amusing love story, seems to be a symbolic narrative relating the rites of passage of an adolescent boy and girl. The modern, irreverent features of the story derive, I believe, from a spirit of playfulness combined with defiance of adult authority, of sexual taboos, of religious conventions, and of the norms of a warrior civilization. This spirit of playfulness is in turn understandable as an expression of unconscious wishes that have attained partial expression through the medium of the narrative.

Taken as a whole, the present volume never deviates from its basic position, namely, that modern man is much closer to his psychological origins in the primitive past than is generally suspected. This note was sounded briefly by Frazer and others in the early years of this century, but was quickly muted and replaced by modern anthropology, with its singleminded devotion to contemporary, rapidly disappearing preliterate cultures. Similarly, in psychology, Freud, Jung, Otto Rank, and others did not hesitate to lay bare the archaic substructure of the modern mind, but academic psychology bypassed them in favor of other pursuits thought to be more fully in keeping with the spirit of scientific inquiry, as opposed to speculation. Modern folklore study likewise has turned its back on the remote past, and has placed major emphasis on collecting local and regional narratives, songs, and customs without taking the trouble to do more than abstract out common motifs on a rather superficial basis.

Against this background of neglect of important sources of insight into the foundation stones of modern civilization, I have written this book to remind the reader that contemporary man has a mind that was formed in the neolithic past. With this mental equipment, the great mass of humanity has to cope with the problems of an endangered planet, buttressed only by the wisdom and moral example of a small number of innovators. It is my hope that the essays contained in this volume also will open new paths of inquiry into mythology and folklore, religion, and even the popular culture of our time, as depicted by the mass media, literature, art, and the many other means by which the human spirit expresses itself, scarcely mindful of its storied past.

1

The Birth of Demons

With each enlargement of the tragic sense a new god is born. This is to say that the gods that hold sway for a certain time and in a certain place correspond to man's limited comprehension, not of metaphysical reality, but of the concrete realities of social life. As man becomes increasingly aware of the countless actual conditions of his existence, he must redefine the symbolic meaning of his gods in the light of his new insights. If the old gods reflect conditions of life that have been altered, or if they are found to represent too narrow a vision of the real, then they are no longer psychologically satisfying and must be replaced. Hence it is, in mythology as in real life, that over and over again, the god-king must die.[1]

The gods and the divine priests and kings who are thought to embody them on earth suffice only for a short time, as long as they reassure us that they symbolize in their divine being a balance between the various aspects of social reality, as it is understood at the time. The moment man becomes aware that his own destiny is no different from that of other men within his growing ken and that to the knowledge of his own suffering is to be added the tragic freight of the sufferings of others, hitherto unknown and outside the circle of empathic response, he transcends the symbolic limits of his gods and is ready for a fresh revelation.

From this vantage point, one can no longer share the general view that the mortality of the gods, one by one and in their separate guises, is brought about for the purposes of sympathetic magic, that is, to insure that the magical powers of the deity will be preserved when they are at their fullest.[2] Nor is it conceivable that divine kings must die only so that their subjects or devotees may incorporate their virtues, thereby identifying themselves with their totem in an indissoluble way. Such interpretations leave out of account the strange fact that, for the gods to be preserved, they must first be killed. What is the motive that prescribes such hostile devotion? Are there no other ways of preserving the magical efficacy of gods and heroes? Is not their reward out of character with their merit? It is at this point that one begins to recognize that we are not dealing, after all, simply with the intention to preserve a divine essence and to share in it, however deep the unconscious sources of such motives may lie. The divine king must die because he has failed; the scope of his powers is no longer congruent with the scope of man's everchanging view of himself and his world. In brief, the gods must ever be created anew so that they will be truly in accord with man's changing image of the conditions of his existence.

But why is it precisely among primitive peoples that one finds the greatest dissatisfaction with the reigning king, the symbol of magic power? How is it that those people who are least cognizant of the rest of the human community, and who are least capable of transforming their own world on the basis of new experiences and insights, are the most prone to turn against their deities? The above argument would seem to lead straight back to a theoretical construction along the lines of sympathetic magic, and to discredit our thesis that hostile motives underlie the destruction of the gods or their surrogates. The answer to this question may be found first, possibly, in distinguishing between the dissatisfactions of primitive man and those of his modern successor or his technologically skilled contemporary. Second, it may be helpful to recall the concept of ambivalence insofar as it is an integral part of primitive man's emotional response to his priest-king.[3]

As to the first explanation, one can say at the outset that, however well-adapted primitive man may be to his environment, his control of nature is most unsatisfactory. Even when he is convinced that through magic he may bend nature to his will, it is hardly to be supposed that the result of his spells and incantations will answer to his expectations. In other words, primitive man has every reason to feel that his environment is unpredictable and dangerous, and that his best safeguards—even from his own point of view—do not guarantee him that events will take place as he wishes. At best, he can rest content with the assurance that he has taken the necessary magical precautions against disaster by following the approved formula. But, beyond ritual, he can only wait with uncertainty and dread. To the extent that magic cannot accomplish its purpose, however one may rationalize its failure, the lot of primitive man is a hard one. His dissatisfaction, whether conscious or otherwise, must be no less intense than that of his neurotic counterpart in the modern world, but for different reasons. Insofar as the fate of the priest-kings or godly surrogates is bound up with a capricious and froward natural environment, it must follow that the god-king has to die by way of penalty for nature's default. In this sense, the high mortality rate of the gods among the primitives is based on the inability of the deities in question to adequately symbolize a secure reality. These gods represent a vision of reality that is as unsatisfactory as it is incomplete. When primitive man sacrifices his totemic incarnations of the gods, he pursues his quest for a better answer to the same old vexing uncertainties. The expected regeneration of the gods, in the sense implied here, is no mere rebirth, but a hankering for a new revelation, and a search for a new god.

A second factor that would seem to enter into the primitive version of the drama of the killing of the divine king is the dual nature of the gods; they are at once precious and dangerous because of the power that emanates from them. Because they are powerful they are to be feared. Such fear is compatible with love, one would imagine, as long as the gods bring good fortune. But when things go wrong, it is not hard to see how fear can turn to hate, thereby insuring not only the replacement of a god, but his absolute annihilation.

The relationship between divine failure and consequent rejection of the deity is enhanced by still another influence in the life of the primitive devotee. This influence makes itself felt at least as early as the phase of formal initiation during adolescence, and may be viewed as a consequence of the older oedipal ambivalence, at this point revived and directed toward the officiating elders, now disguised as monstrous gods. In effect, the initiation experience, with its combination of cruelty and exploded mystery, cannot help but produce in the novice that same mixture of love and hate which seems to be the motivating force in the case of the fathers themselves. In the case of the latter, the ambivalence is directed toward the members of the younger generation and includes as one of its main components a fear of incestuous rivalry by the burgeoning youths. At the same time, insofar as the fathers, together with the medicine men, reveal at this crucial point the awful emptiness of the mystery, and the fact, moreover, that it is a sadistic hoax, they betray their own contempt for, and indeed, their disbelief in the deity who is the alleged recipient of the initiation sacrifice. As for the young candidates, it is hard to see how they can avoid hating the very deity whose worship demands so much of their substance, and whose appeasement yields them no natural powers they did not already possess, and no social rights they might not have gained by force. Now, too, they know that the totemic monster is powerless without the help of human agents. Yet, in spite of the pain suffered, or, more likely, because of their humiliation, the initiates are exalted paradoxically, ennobled by their very debasement, and made over into men by having been unmanned!

The oedipal resolution implied in the surrender of the initiate to the authority of the fathers is not any more binding or permanent than the resolution of the earlier, childish oedipal struggle. It is true that in both instances, the boy is compelled by fear of overpowering force to identify himself, or to seem to identify himself with his paternal rival, and the deity in whose name that force is applied. It is equally true, no doubt, that we are confronted by an act of authoritarian "identification with the aggressor" in both instances. An important difference exists, however, between the earlier and the later attempts at oedipal resolution. This difference seems to point to the possibility of a very close link between initiation rites and the mortality of primitive gods. Whereas the resolution in early childhood of the oedipal struggle through identification with the father's role may leave a residue of repressed hostility toward the father, there is no need to posit an element of contempt, as well. The reaffirmation of the fathers' power through divine sanction, dramatically exhibited upon the occasion of the puberty rites, is another matter. Such power is seen to rest on a spurious foundation. The "mystery" so long hidden from the knowledge of the growing boy turns out to be no mystery at all, and it is evident, at last, that the gods speak, not with voices of their own, but by means of "bull-roarers" and other stage "props." Similarly, the power of the gods to punish is seen to inhere in their all-too-human agents. Both the alleged successes and failures of the gods reflect the strength and weaknesses of the fathers, priest-kings, medicine men, sorcerers, etc. This much the initiate has been able to glimpse, and to repress quickly in the midst of his tortures.

In the future, then, the gods, as well as the elders, will not have such an easy time of it! The failure of the gods invites, as a first reaction, the impulse to hold their human surrogates completely responsible. But more than one alternative is available to the initiates, now grown to the estate of full manhood: The first possibility is that they can revenge themselves on the medicine men and leave the feckless god intact; or else, they can blame the *deity* for his own failures, and invent a new and better object of worship, one who will be powerful enough to execute their collective will. Why, then, are the devotees unable to act on their first impulse, knowing what they do, and having so many old scores to settle with their paternal adversaries? Why do the priests outlive the gods? Possibly, man has invented sacrificial worship to deflect his hostility away from both fathers and priests. Instead

of sacrificing the latter whenever the gods fail, the devotees let
out their anger at the totemic victim. Have they not made a sort
of peace—the peace of repression—with the generation of the
fathers and the priests? Also, the primitive initiate has now entered into an incriminating blood covenant with his elders, and
shares fully their guilty knowledge that all gods are men. That
which is good in the fathers and the *human* ancestors must be
preserved: that which is hateful is dissociated and becomes an
attribute of the *totemic* ancestor alone, in addition to his positive
qualities. In this way, the devotees succeed in incorporating the
magical strength of the totem, while retaining the right to destroy
the totemic god whom they hate unconsciously because the mali-
ciousness of the fathers has been displaced onto it. Unhappily for
the fate of the gods, the human weakness and duplicity of the
fathers has also become a part of their nature, foreshadowing their
eventual eclipse when repression fails following some disaster to
the tribe.

I have not dwelled, so far, on the possibility that, in the case
of primitive man, gods are replaced because they do not adequately symbolize the growing complexity of man's insights into
himself, or his expanded sympathies for his fellow men. This
omission is dictated by the supposition that primitive man, as long
as he maintains his isolation from the rest of mankind, is incapable of extending the range of his sympathies. As a result, his
endless succession of gods need be projections only of his dissatisfaction with his condition in brute nature. Primitive gods can
correspond only to primitive perceptions. It remains for historic
man to be dissatisfied with his gods for more subtle reasons—
namely, that they symbolize man's imperfect condition in society.
With each fresh discovery of the wretchedness of that condition,
a new, and conceptually more elaborate god must be envisaged.
When the sum total of tragic insights into man's fate mounts up
unbearably, a single unitary god can no longer symbolize them
adequately but must fall apart so that from one god many are
born.

It might be objected that polytheistic god-making is a primitive
psychological process and cannot follow logically or historically
the more abstract phase of monotheism. After all, does not

polytheism rest on syncretism, the earliest form of concept formation and the least satisfactory? Does not syncretism, particularly
as applied to the combining or dissolving of gods (or their component traits) involve the indiscriminate apposition of irreconcilable
qualities? How can such a hodge-podge mode of symbolizing
divine attributes possibly take the place of monotheism, with its
relative conceptual clarity and single emphasis? Surely monotheism is the historical product of much painful selectivity, of a long
process of filtering out incompatible and unacceptable elements
to produce the triumph of a single unmoved mover.

My contention is that monotheism represents an achievement
of enormous and unstable equilibrium, hovering not between
belief and disbelief, but between the syncretic experience of
polytheism on the one hand and the dualism of God and Satan
on the other. As polytheism represents the confounding of man
and god, so, as I will attempt to show, the division between God
and Satan stands for the dissolution of the psychological bond
between God and actual man. Between the polarities of polytheism, with its magical union with and participation in a world
experienced as ethically good or bad, and dualism, which admits
finally that man himself is a mixture of good and evil, stands
monotheism. Now God stands alone as the ultimate reality whose
nature is goodness. From this it follows (who can deny that the
logic is forced, but psychologically compelling?) that the world is
good, and that man, created in God's image, is also good.

This being so, God no longer has to contend with man and his
possible dissatisfaction, since the tragic circumstances that might
give rise to discontentment simply do not exist. It must be admit-
ted that this reassuring position, in which both extrinsic and
intrinsic evil are denied as facts of life, can be maintained only
as long as man contains himself and refrains from contending
with God. Insofar as man cannot be expected to hold back his
reproaches indefinitely, given the cruel imperatives of his existence, one might guess that monotheism really represents a
phenomenological ideal. Such an ideal can be approached at
times, but always briefly, and only within the context of favorable
historical circumstances.

The stability of the monotheistic concept may be viewed as a

function, among other things, of man's ability to sustain a consistent view of reality. To put it negatively, to arrive at a vision of
one God, beneficent and loving, we must put out of awareness all
that reminds us of our mortality. The psychoanalytic concept of
repression, defined as the incomplete forgetting of painful insights, may be invoked as the mechanism by which one transcends
mortality and arrives at a perfect knowledge of the good. We
repress all those mischances and all those fears that our ancestors
symbolized as gods or demons, hoping thereby to control them,
or at least to neutralize them. The more successfully man has
learned to repress his fatal knowledge of the presence of evil, the
closer he has come to formulating the idea of a perfect God. Any
significant breakthrough into consciousness of the fulness of
man's tragic experience is a sign that the repressive mechanism
is not working perfectly. Surely, the very altar of God must trem-
ble when man weeps, for every tear may nourish the dormant
seeds of the syncretic gods of polytheism, those embodiments of
the multifariousness of good and evil. Repression acts to screen
out the disturbing sources of dread and unrest and so sustains
man's unitary vision of the real.

The trend of thought that we have followed up to now can only
begin to appear reasonable if one grants two related assumptions
that the author has made, perhaps gratuitously. The first assumption is that God symbolizes reality; the second assumption is that
God, from the standpoint of monotheism, symbolizes only the
good, and not the bad.

As to the first assumption, one could no doubt defend the thesis
that God, far from being solely an extension of reality as perceived
by man, is an expression of certain longings for that which is
better than the real, namely, the ideal. Viewed from this lofty
vantage point, God represents a standard toward which man may
struggle. This interpretation is a cogent one because, if man were
concerned only with reality, or more precisely, if man were content merely to acquiesce to the real, he would have no need for
God. The necessity of God's existence is dictated by the very
failure of perceived reality, by the realization that what is actual
is also imperfect, and even destructive of man's happiness and

well-being. According to this line of reasoning, man's hope must shift inevitably to what is potential, transcending finite reality, and culminating in the object of all hopes—God.

My answer is that the ideal is conceivable only in the light of man's historical experience of the real. Such ideals as the brotherhood of man, or the inner necessity of carrying out deeds of loving-kindness, or any number of other visions of the good are precisely that—visions. Insofar as ideals remain unfulfilled in the world of actual events, their substance remains undefined, except at the shallow level of verbalisms. Such ideal traits as are attributed to a divine being do not extend imaginatively beyond man's finite experience of what is possible. In this sense, it may be said that divine beings symbolize, above all, the world of appearances, that is, the tragic reality of man's historical experience. If the gods are sought after because they seem to hold out promise of a better life, now or later, it is only some alleviation that the supplicant must have in mind. That which we envisage as a divine transformation of our apparent destiny is no more than learning to look at our fate in a new way. Similarly, if the gods are emulated for their good qualities, let us confess that they are more often the models for a formal devotion and imitation, and it is left to a handful of prophets and saints to enter into a sincere dialogue with God. In short, I believe it is correct to assume that the gods are perceived with extreme realism, and that their transcendant qualities are not appreciated to any great extent.

The second assumption, that God symbolizes only the good and not the bad, may sound at first as if I were seeking deliberately to impoverish the complexity of the idea of God, and to replace Jehovah with Pollyanna. Moreover, I would seem to be in open contradiction with the point made above, namely, that the gods symbolize tragic reality. But we come now to the heart of the matter; the more we strain to think of God as symbolizing the good, the more impossible our task becomes, because we know that there is so much evil in the world. Yet, we have no recourse but to strive for a self-consistent, unitary conception of God, if our belief is to be authentically in one God. Besides, God cannot be accommodated to the reality of evil without depersonalizing

Him altogether and making of the Deity a non-ethical, detached sort of world spirit. The closer one attains to monotheism, the more relentlessly one is oppressed by the inner contradictions of a god who is seemingly on the side of man, but allows him to fall into the pit with every step. One reads about such confrontments of the actuality of pain and suffering in the lamentations of Job. Similarly, one discovers in the teachings of Buddha a courage of despair that will not yield to any facile interpretation of man's place in the scheme of things.

Both prophets, each in his own way, have come face to face with the god of monotheism and have turned away from their fatal confrontation confused and embittered. How can the beneficent god of monotheism be the source of both good and evil? Hinayana Buddhism likewise turns away from the world of the senses—that life that never ends in total and blissful extinction, but starts ever anew in the agonizing anticlimax of rebirth. In rejecting worldliness, the ironically compassionate Buddha also rejected ethical involvement in the affairs of men. The glimpse of monotheism that Buddha had been vouchsaved was an experience of the tragic realism of things—if God can be detached, then man must be detached. The best one can hope for is to mitigate suffering by asking for little and cheerfully accepting less. This solution is not unlike that recommended by the philosopher-slave Epictetus, who advised, in effect, that the more one expects of God in the beginning, the greater the need for tragic stoicism in the end. Thus, the conceptualization of one God, self-consistent and beneficent, must end either in heroic despair or in the birth of dualism.

Dualism can be defined as the realization that God has not displaced the Devil. It is the understanding that there is so much work to be done, so much mischief to be accomplished, that one cannot leave it all to God. The greater the saliency of God as the exemplar of goodness, the greater the need to force into a separate unitary mold the awareness of evil. It is only as the repressive process is perfected historically, that the idea of a good God is evolved, and the idea of evil attaches itself to the person of the Devil. The repressive mechanism succeeds at last in making evil something that is extrinsic to the nature of God. By implication, man may now flatter himself that evil is something external and peripheral to his nature—but this is not the place to elaborate on this point.

It might be said by way of criticism that I am using the terms "good" and "bad" as if these categories corresponded to manifest events in our collective lives. That is, we see our gods as symbols of good only insofar as our own fortunes are concerned, that is to the extent that we are "successful" or "unsuccessful." Are good and evil to be reduced to such petty things? We are cautioned by de Rougement to avoid such an equation on the ground that what is manifestly tragic may have a larger and more impersonal significance that is good, rather than evil, from the standpoint of the human race.[4] In this interpretation, good and evil are viewed against a long-range ethical and historical perspective, transcending the immediate import of particular events.

While recognizing the abstract intention of the above view, we cannot help but fix our attention on the concrete psychological reality that we call "evil," or "bad," or "tragic." What is humanly tragic in our little lives is forever tragic and forever lost. That historically desirable consequences may flow out of the failures of the past does not negate the obdurate fact that life has said "No" to us with apparent finality.

But, to repeat, God has not displaced the Devil; He merely toys with him. This presumed relationship signifies the almost complete repression, or selective ignoring, of malevolent actions and experiences in man's history in favor of an overwhelming sense of the fitness of things, and of the superior poignancy of goodness over badness as a conscious experience.

Unhappily, the Devil is not content to remain a nonentity. In fact, his very appearance on the scene betokens that all is not well with monotheism. Briefly, the invention of the Devil is already a sign that things have gotten out of hand—God is no longer alone but has a partner. It is but a short step from the classic dualism of God and Satan to the baroque diversity of polytheism.

At this point, we must be prepared for the rejoinder of all those who see in polytheism not the fragmentation of God but only devotion to the acknowledged semblances of an underlying and unitary spiritual reality. This philosophical interpretation stems from Hinduism and is said to be consistent with the doctrine of spiritual monism. Generically, then, the polytheistic or syncretic forms of religious experience can be viewed in the same light as monotheism—as a less pure expression, perhaps, of the Divine Essence—but partaking of that Essence nevertheless.

However satisfying the above interpretation may be philosophically, it seems to be in error as a psychological explanation. It is no secret that Siva is more real and more vivid than Brahma. The very concreteness of the gods of polytheism sets them apart from the abstract God of monotheism, by whatever name he is called. Similarly, the personalized character of the collective gods—whether they be Zeus and his inner circle, or primal Visnu and his associated deities, or the members of any other pantheon—is in every way different from that of the one God of monotheism. The essential distinction remains to be stated, however. The collective gods are both more human and more inhuman than the one God. We have remarked that the one God must have difficulty comprehending within his benign nature all of the malevolence that inheres in man's historical experience. Hence the Devil as helpmate or, more precisely, scapegoat.

But, despite his formidable capacities, even the Devil is unequal to the task of symbolizing fully the range and intensity of man's tragic experience. One is driven, at last, to conceptualize a multitude of demons. These deities, we suggest, are not reflections of a solitary immanent radiance. They symbolize, instead, the death of the spirit in the face of a crushing environmental fate. With each little death, Kali adds a token to her garland of skulls. Her consort, Siva, also wears a necklace of skulls and a skull in his diadem.[5] These ornaments are relics of demons that have been slain; they symbolize the triumph of good over evil. How ubiquitous evil must be. It must be confronted and slain over and over again. Nor is there any certainty that the good gods will not turn into the very demons whom they pursue. Kali herself was destined historically to become the goddess of the cult of *thugee*, and so, the recipient of innocent human sacrifices. As for Siva, is it so startling, after all, that upon slaying the elephant-demon, he dons his flayed skin and dances his darkly serene pavanne? When the gods bedeck themselves as devils, man can no longer be sure of the ground upon which he stands.

Of course, we have spoken all along as if the God of monotheism were conceived as an idea, but obviously this is the exception and not the rule. Religious experience is by its very nature emotional and intuitive; its function is to console. Who can doubt that the universal appeal of religion derives from its powers of consolation? Likewise, if one is to comprehend what evil is all about and to realize the force that it exerts, the Devil cannot be viewed as a mere idea or as an abstract concept for subsuming all evil. But, to recognize this is not to remove the real obstacle— that the gods are mortal. On the contrary, the one God whom we invoke by our passionate longing for reassurance is the most vulnerable, the most perishable of all. The more we humanize the one God of monotheism, the more we insure our ultimate alienation from Him. Now He has the power to disappoint us as no depersonalized First Principle or remote Creator of the Universe can disappoint us. In fact, once the process of personalization begins, the unitary conception of God is threatened; it disintegrates with every wish that remains unfulfilled. Such is man's selfish and dependent nature, one might say. No. A truly living God, who issues from the heart and not from the head, like *Athene,* must expect to die when the heart bursts.

It is not so serious with the god-demons of polytheism. No sooner is one slain, than another arises to take his place. Those who believe in many gods are wise, and know that life is hard and full of suffering. Consequently, they have been able to create imaginatively a symbolic devil for every evil fact. They have repressed nothing, forgotten nothing that is distasteful to recall. The actuality of famine, disease, and infant mortality—to mention but a few of the more conspicuous reminders of nature's intransigence—is inseparable from polytheism and occurs as part of the same cultural complex. In other places, where the surface of experience has been somewhat smoothed over by technological advance, concealing the potential menace of the natural world, the hosts of demonic adversaries are dismissed as being no longer a threat. The battle appears to be over, and the standard of the one God is planted in the field—now no longer embattled—proclaiming eternal peace. To be sure, the Devil is still acknowledged to be at large. But how diminished he has become. What an object of ridicule he presents, with his horns, and other animal features. How theatrical and unreal he appears in his stage costume. In effect, it would appear that the Devil and his hosts have been routed thoroughly.

If only the world of nature were the sole source of mortality, one God, immutable and unshakable, would suffice as the beneficent symbol of a technologically well-ordered world. I have said not a word, however, of the obvious hell on earth that man is capable of creating. I am speaking now of the unnatural hell—the old, familiar, man-made hell of unjust social conventions. The devils who are the proper symbols for man's imperfect and often inhuman institutions and practices have not yet been conjured up by the imagination—Dante notwithstanding. Their names are still in the process of formulation, as we grope for those epithets that will convey an appropriately ominous tone. What, after all, is the fitting personalized symbol for universal war? What symbol —other than the outworn mark of Cain—can one apply to the German murderers and their gas chambers? The little, familiar devils who have begun to fade during the past few hundred years will hardly do. What can they know of the new damnation, with their old-fashioned pitchforks and tongs?

You say that in spite of human suffering, there is no need for many gods and demons, that the one God, in his all-embracing compassion, will suffice. But what if the fallen ones, called before the Divine Presence, should say, in their ghostly voices, "The dead do not salute thee!"

2

The Mystical Quest

A<small>T THIS</small> point in time we see on all sides a quickening of interest in mysticism—not merely as a subject for disinterested inquiry but as a form of experience to be sought after in its own right as something valid and significant. I wish to explore the reasons behind the search for heightened spiritual consciousness, taking into account not only the reasons put forward by would-be mystics, but also the very human motives that impel people to go beyond the limits of ordinary experience. If we take the mystic at his own word, ignoring his psychological needs, we will be left with purely symbolic explanations that speak of searching for Union with the Absolute, or Self-Surrender, or Perfect Love. These are essentially metaphorical ways of expressing goals which also can be expressed in terms of basic human needs, such as the need for security or the need to escape the frustrations of everyday life. I do not mean to approach the mystical quest in a spirit of reductionism but to suggest that mysticism can be understood, in part, in nonmystical terms.

It is not only a question of identifying the psychological needs that serve as a starting point for the mystical quest; it is also a question of recognizing the conditions of modern life that create the need for supraconscious forms of experience. The need for mystical experience may be the result of disillusionment with conventional religion, modern technology, and even familiar social and material gratifications.

I have deliberately omitted reference to artificial sources of mystical experience—those dances, fasts, self-tortures, auto-intoxications, yogic exercises, and so on by which abnormal states of consciousness may be induced. These are obviously no more than techniques, and may be employed for a variety of motives. Though sanctified by tradition, their connection with mysticism is adventitious and leads easily into the error of attributing esoteric motives to the mystic because he is often impelled to alter his normal conscious state by extraordinary means.

Hallucinatory and other abnormal experiences that are the outgrowth of a psychotic process must likewise remain outside the scope of this discussion, insofar as they are symptomatic of what William James has called the "divided self" and what we now recognize as autonomous expressions of the unconscious. If the mystic, like the certified psychotic, hears voices and sees visions, these automatisms are not the start of his ascent—or descent—but the terminal point of a process that began with his response to human voices, consensually real and objective, and his perception of human faces, no less tangible.[1] In either case we are dealing with a symbolic transformation of the environment, but with this difference, that the psychotic objectifies his conscious state, even in its most subliminal forms, while the mystic swallows the entire cosmos and assimilates it to his interior world, so that the cosmos becomes "thou," and the mystic becomes "I."

What useful purpose will be accomplished by attempting to relate the mystic to his human condition? I believe that it is only through an understanding of what the mystic brings to his sacred task that one can begin to see what he brings back with him from his journey to the center of his being. The two burdens, the one heavy like a soldier's pack, the other infinitely light, are closely related. Everything depends on the quality of this transposition, for the successful completion of the mystic's quest involves nothing less than the temporary abrogation of the profane state of becoming, and a taste of the joys of being.[2] The state of being, like the spiritual condition of grace, and much like the dynamic state of *bodhi*, or "deliverance," cannot be achieved unless something is left behind. This worthless remnant of his profane existence the mystic tries with all his heart to leave behind him, knowing that he cannot achieve deliverance unless he overcomes the sense of duality between himself and the "other," be it conceived as empty void, as in the tantric tradition, or as an extrahuman model or personal god, as in occidental terms. It remains to be considered whether what he brings back from the regions of the suprasensuous is better than the tasteless bric-a-brac that was abandoned.

Along with the assertion that mysticism arises out of motives rooted in the human condition, I must make explicit still another supposition. This is the expectation that mysticism in its perfected form, as in its origins, will continue to have much in common with certain desacralized orientations to life which do not resemble the unitive life in the least. The nonreligious analogues of mysticism may be described in general terms as belonging either to the quietistic or the ecstatic extremes of profane feeling and behavior. Quietism of a nonmystical character may be thought of as including the many forms of acquiescence to the externally imposed routines of work or recreation, as well as to the internalized demands of traditions. Whenever such assent is given gratuitously, an act of self-surrender is consummated, thereby gratifying needs similar to those which lead the mystic into making a comparable gift of his autonomy. It is the same with profane experiences of extraordinary excitement which take the form of a flight into the world of the senses. I believe that such flights into "reality" parallel the ecstatic ascent of the religious mystic, who, with eyes opened wide yet seeing nothing of the temporal world, begins to contemplate the presence of God in man. In either case the sense of exhilaration begins with the feeling of spiritlessness, the faithlessness of the mystic's dark night of the soul, and leads finally to the exhaustion of the spirit.

There is a side to mysticism that makes it difficult to relate that frame of mind to the human condition, with its implication that men are creatures living in situations that they have not wholly created. It is the mystic's vocation to generate an experience, or more accurately, a relationship that involves an Uncreated Other, and which therefore leads to a transvaluation of the creaturely state itself. Does this mean that the mystic has overcome his awe of God? The fear of God is felt in the light of one's own powerless- ness—precisely the sense of being a creature—and if this reveren- tial awareness of a transcending power is weakened through the mystical act of approaching God to the uttermost limit, and even merging with Him, what has become of the usual relationship between divine master and mortal servant? By the abundance of his selfless love, and in his forgetfulness of his own ego, the mystic may lose the feeling that he is a finite being, and be transposed to an altogether different plane. Perhaps the mystic has the ability to change his fear into great love, which, as he comes to see it, is his ruling passion. To say, however, that one can love and fear God at the same time, is to sum up the essentially nonmystical attitude of ritual devotion, in which prayers and other symbolic, partial acts of self-abasement are offered as tokens of love.

The mystic, of course, has gone far beyond such piecemeal sacrifices. He is ready to offer himself in love, expending his spirit in a holocaust of desire, and holding nothing back for himself. This way of putting an end to the experience of dualism assumes the proximity of God; it presumes to draw God into the human vortex and to make Him immanent in the heart. It is not that the mystic wants to make God a party to the human condition, but rather that he wants to cross the line into a supra-human world in which one is not only more than a man, but scarcely less than a god. The mystic gives himself wholeheartedly to God because he wants from the Supreme Being much more than a dispensa- tion, or a sense of communion, or a sign of the divine presence; the mystic wants nothing less than God himself.[3] Unlike a ritual- ist, a mystic unfortunately cannot have it both ways. Either he leaves behind his personality, his senses, and even his conscious striving to get close to God and loses himself in the divine ambience, like a holy catatonic who is mute and unresponsive to his own flesh; or he absorbs God into his own being, turning clay into cosmos. Either way, the ego turns against itself, repudiates its Adamic nature, and tries to become something other than the finite self. In brief, the mystic loses himself and departs from the human condition just as surely when he ventures into the Divine Abyss, taking flight toward the remote presence of the other, as when he looks for God in the corners of his heart.

From the standpoint of mysticism, there is of course no danger in losing the finite self, since there exists instead the radiant promise of finding the undiscovered true self, the primordial self, unconfined as yet by conscious reason, and therefore filled with the presence of the divine irrational, which leads one to whisper confidently, "This is what I feel!" In this same unconscious self is contained Lossky's entire "world as organic whole." Here the mystic arrives at the perception of the great causal principle, the first and only absolute, because it is his will to contemplate that which is one, which is nonmanifold, and which is the basis of all material and psychic harmonies.[4] Without fear of shipwreck, the mystic makes his voyage in a sea of archetypes which are for him beacons of light and not shoals of emotional self-indulgence. He is not afraid of drifting beyond the reach of consciousness, of self-criticism, and of practical morality. Indeed, the further he removes himself from the rational plane, the more he feels at home; he finds his freedom in that region of apparent calm where the ego sleeps, enchanted by the siren wisdom of the unconscious.

It was in the unconscious, perhaps, that the original covenant with the perfect other was made by the old Adam—the very same covenant that the mystic is eager to renew, as if to make up for his ancestor's sin. I say the "unconscious" because this is the region in which the binding force of religion is greatest. Here the mystic has a chance of tying together the fragments of profane experience and reconstituting them as pure essence, because the unconscious does not admit of differentiation. On the conscious plane, the mystic's ego refuses to resolve itself into a single reason to explain its being. That is only natural insofar as the conscious ego is committed to an endless variety of covenants with the actual world. These covenants reflect the many purposes which the ego confuses with its own motives, although they are in reality designs imposed by the conditions of society.

The irreligious man and the man who is religious in the conventional sense both differ radically from the mystic because they are enmeshed, not in their own unconscious and its imperious demands, but in the unexamined purposes of the hierarchically ordered external world. The collective unconscious, which forces its compulsions on the collectivity under the guise of freely chosen pragmatisms such as statesmanship, policy, public opinion, and division of labor, is the flux from which the mystic is determined to detach himself.[5] In his own unconscious is located the archetype of grace, the condition in which God offers his saving presence as a gift. Although it is no part of the mystic's psychology to think that his own freely given gift of his ego is the basis for expecting reciprocity from God, he is nevertheless a party to precisely such a covenant—gift for gift, epiphany for selflessness.

The mystic is in a position to surrender the myth of his private consciousness, whereas society cannot suspend its collective myths; that is, society cannot suspend its historically formed character. Nor is society conceivable as an organic whole in quite the same terms as is one's personal unconscious. Society is the web of other people's conscious and unconscious conventions; above all, it is the disjunctive legacy of the dead ancestors, whose surrogates we call the authorities. If the mystic would sever his connection with one part of the social structure—say, the family or the polity—it will assert its claim somewhere else. Other people and the institutions which they animate permit only partial alienations and withdrawals, as well as only muted revelations of their finiteness. Therefore, the mystic cannot speak for other people's illusions; he cannot tell God that he abjures the world because the world will not let go of him.[6] The mystic can relinquish only what belongs to him—his own splinter of consciousness which pierces him by its futility, and his unconscious wishes which have the power either to betray or to regenerate him.

Society has nothing of its own that it can give up as an expression of collective mysticism. Its holocausts consume its human

members, burning out the mortal interstices of the social order
by means of wars and persecutions. The husk remains, however,
its roots sunk in the past and drawing nourishment from the many
layers of ashes deposited there. Society never surrenders its tribal
or national ego which it cherishes above everything else, and
which, hoping to conceal its true nature, it calls by other names
which may suggest spirituality and even otherworldliness. In response to the idea of the transcendence of God, society offers the
presumed fact of its own self-sufficiency, so that all of its collective
prayers add up simply to asking God for a more complete realization of its generic form. In a very real sense society destroys the
concrete human intermediaries which are its only link with God,
and its only hope of transforming itself into a heaven-on-earth. It
might be said that society seeks to possess its members whereas
the mystic wants to be possessed by something other than the
social order.[7]

I suppose that if the time ever comes when society allows itself
to be possessed by its members, it will be ripe for a collective life
of the spirit, including the experience of collective mysticism. In
the meantime, it is not possible to graft the private experience of
mysticism onto any but the most fluid of established religious
conventions. It is perfectly true that mysticism has developed
historically in relation to established religious traditions. It is a
question of whether these traditions have helped the mystic approach directly to the object of his love, or whether they have
interposed themselves between God and man, preventing what
Plotinus described as the "flight of the alone to the Alone."

Whether the mystic seeks God in the world as interpreted
through institutional religion, or whether he reaches out toward
the Infinite, blinded by his own inner light, it is more than an
academic question to ask whether he will find God in everything
or declare that he does not discover him in anything that is merely
determinate. To look for God in everything is, of course, a form
of pantheism; it requires of the mystic that he learn to see objects
in a loving way, searching out their inner secret which is their
divinity, even in the midst of ugliness and depravity. Is this
tantamount to saying that the mystic, in his search for imma-

nence, arrives at holiness by libidinizing everything? What is the source of his limitless psychic energy? From a psychoanalytic standpoint it is hard to see how it is possible to love a multitude of objects without withdrawing affection from some other object or objects. Is it the self that is devalued, thereby liberating the ego from the burden of its own enhancement and causing self-love to be changed into cosmic altruism? Some will say that it is not possible to love others without self-love and that to be indifferent to the self is to be cut off from the sources of empathy, which begins in the subjective knowledge of suffering and makes the response of compassion a possibility. Thus, to turn away from the self, to be dead to the self, is to be insensitive to others. It follows that the mystic who would find God in everything must start by looking for God in his own being.

Of course, what he finds within himself will determine not only the value to be attached to his identity, that is, whether he will love or hate himself, but will also have a decisive bearing on his attitude toward other creatures. Let us say that the mystic finds within himself certain tendencies that he recognizes as signs of God's grace, namely that he is disposed to loving-kindness rather than its opposite, and further, that he himself has intrinsic worth precisely because he understands that he was made in the divine image. Theoretically, he is now ready to love others and, indeed, to embrace the whole world. He has felt the presence of the indwelling Deity and knows that others, too, have been touched by the divine spirit. The trouble is that self-love—call it the love of God-in-the-self or call it demonic possession—has a way of spending itself, of turning into self-righteousness so that there is little good-will, much less love, left over for others.[8] If this is true for those who love themselves and who see in their own linea-ments the semblance of their Creator, how much more true must it be for those who, looking inward, find therein the Devil, who does not interdict self-love in the slightest degree? Must one love the Devil, too, seeing that he sits sometimes at the center of the self, and is a part of creation, like every other entity that derives its being from an indwelling spiritual force?[9] Pantheism knows neither good nor evil, but avows simply that God is in everything.

Only God can emanate from God. It is the mystic's duty to penetrate the disguises of God and to find in the midst of creation the Uncreated Other.

Paradoxically, the Uncreated Other whom the mystic seeks is at the same time the real man, the ontological man who is concealed in the particularity of anthropological man and whose actions are the improbable disguises of God. To achieve his aim of finding God in himself the mystic must first of all dissolve the microcosmos which he calls the self, turning the ordered cosmos of his personality into the chaos that existed before man fell into time from eternity. It is a question of seeking regeneration by courting spiritual death in regression to the primordial unborn self. True mysticism must regard consciousness itself as a barrier to its aspirations, since consciousness leads to differentiation, and the condition for union with God is de-differentiation, in which man is taken outside himself and out of history, thereby becoming a part of the eternal flux. This flux is the very opposite of Hegel's self-perfecting movement of history by means of which universal reason is thought to carry man toward his own full realization within the context of a perfected earthly kingdom. The mystic swims in boundless space and does not progress through time at all. He is at the center of his own spiritual stillness which (paradoxically) is agitated, though it is an aspect of the eternal flux. He approaches a state of dynamic tension in which he hopes to live in eternity for a moment.

Perfectibility developed out of an enlarged consciousness can be no part of the mystic's desire. Instead, he is bent upon the diminution of the ideal of perfectibility and the dismantling of all the usual anthropological and cosmological landmarks that seem to lead to a more perfect world order. In the place of order the mystic wants to experience spiritual chaos to take the place of normal consciousness. To arrive at an undifferentiated state of consciousness it is necessary to suspend all ordinary actions, as well as ordinary thoughts and imaginings. Beyond the interruption of these processes mysticism implies above all the willing acceptance of powerlessness. It is for this reason that mysticism is a thing apart from the quest for yogic power. The essence of yogic discipline is the subordination of consciousness to the will, so that the yogin can concentrate his attention in a highly selective manner, liberating himself from illusion—that is, from bondage to the profane condition.

Mysticism's way is precisely the application of the ascetic's hard-won gift of directed consciousness to the goal of self-submergence or powerlessness. Nor is this a negative goal. The road to liberation from illusion can be traveled only by those who give up the desire to have power over anything in order to avoid being possessed by the object of their desire. It is an error even to continue to possess one's own identity—or any identity—because the retention of any vestige of the self leads inevitably to the reinstatement of the acquisitive ego, that ignoble slave to the world of appearances. Nothing less than complete spiritual chaos clears the way to undivided concentration on God.

Yogic self-mastery, taken by itself, involves a type of voluntary discipline of which the result is the enhancement of the ego and an intensification of its hierarchical power over the senses and the contents of consciousness generally. The aggrandizement of the self through yogic self-control therefore results in a deliberate imperturbability and cannot provide the basis for the condition of maximum permeability, or de-differentiation. The yogin in the ultimate condition of *samadhi* is not fully open to God as much as he is sealed off from the unceasing demands of selfhood and the painful illusions of profane existence. It is only because the yogin presumes to choose God that he falls short of mysticism's highest attainment. With all his lucidity and his capacity for integrating the loose ends of his experience into an organic totality, the yogin cannot force God to enter his phenomenal field, cannot, in short, impel the grace of God. God manifests himself last of all to the yogin because of his very deliberateness, his confidence, his determined asceticism, his undaunted spirit.[10] Only when the spirit is exhausted and the unquiet chaos of pre-creation is reflected in the mystic's heart, does the Creator show himself. It is at that instant that He recreates the mystic and turns him momentarily into a new Adam. The yogin in *samadhi* is transfixed and serene like a god, but the mystic trembles in his stillness because he is afloat on suffering, knowing that God may leave him in his unregenerated state.

How far removed, then, is mysticism from the facile wish to return to the security of the womb? Even though the mystic empties himself of a lifetime and waits to be reborn, it is clear that he waits for God to bring him back to life, not as he was before, but as he ought to be. Mysticism, regarded as a kind of private initiation or ceremony of renewal, is based on the knowledge that the self cannot be reconstituted without first sojourning in the limbo of pre-creation, and that only there can a valid initiation into the divine mystery take place. Does this mean that the mystic tries to force an entry into heaven on the assumption that paradise itself is the other time and place? Alas, as in all initiations, one must first descend to meet the chthonic gods in hell. Strange to say, these false gods, these monstrous gods, these totemic creatures hold the keys to heaven as surely as they hold sway over the nether regions.

Why should it be necessary to shake hands with the Devil or his malignant surrogates and to be initiated into the secrets of hell before one can turn his eyes heavenward and hope to see through the veil of illusion? I must explain that the chaos of pre-creation is not at all the void that we so readily imagine, or rather, cannot imagine. It is natural, of course, to assume that God created the world out of nothing. But what if he created the universe out of the primordial stuff of chaos? What if we assume that before the beginning there were other starts, false beginnings, other creations whose organizing principle we presumptuously call chaos, and what if the beginning that the merely religious man has in mind has nothing in common with the first principle toward which the mystic hopefully turns his face? Perhaps the conventional beginning of creation is only the outermost boundary in time of that chaos that existed before man invented his own more highly ordered but egocentric chaos which is history.

Is it a contradiction, after all, that to receive the grace of God in mystical communion it is necessary to go down into the depths and to seek the intercession of the demonic forces? The mystic, fully knowing the logical absurdity of looking for God in the dark underground places of Osiris, of Pluto, of Satan and the other fallen princes, descends nevertheless, and with each step deeper into hell, his faith grows. Mysticism dares to strip away the layers of spiritual evolution and to start at the beginning of religious consciousness, before the enthronement of God. The conventional religious mind shrinks from any contact with the precursors of God, and insists upon the abrogation of history as well as the repression of prehistory. From this tendency is born the error of attributing to God a sort of modern personality who can be approached by the right combination of love and charity, or of faith and reason, or of doctrine and fellowship.

Mysticism does not ignore these human ideals; indeed, it regards them as indispensable starting points for the unitive quest. But the mystic's God is a tragic God who sees and has seen everything, who feels and has felt everything, and who bears witness to the facts that man exists and that his existence is tragically significant. The roots of such a God are in the depths of time and space and passion. Even if he has no sense of history, the mystic knows that he cannot meet God on the Rialto, or in any other context of man's choosing, unless God chooses to reveal Himself. Nor can he expect to find God only within the context of his modern religions of the last few thousand years. The mystic must be prepared to find God in the most unlikely external places and in the most improbable reaches of his own psyche, realizing that the soul of man is the center for all the epiphanies of God, and that each man is his own Osiris and his own Horus, his own Siva and his own Rama.

Mystical experience is nothing less than the deep awareness of the historical other, and also, therefore, the psychological Other —the God who animates every recess of the awakened soul, who on one level of consciousness we know as God, and on another, as fallen angel or devil or simply as pagan gods. By entering fully into the private hell of his own unconscious; by confronting death, cruelty, immorality, and everything else that is opposed to life; the mystic either finds God or becomes psychotic. The only thing that can save him is the fullness of his experience of God, who signifies His presence by the saving archetypes of life—birth and rebirth, love, compassion, creativity—as well as by the archetypes of death. All of these manifestations of divinity are contained in man's unconscious, but only the mystic dares to pray to God with the knowledge that God is not what he imagines Him to be, but what his unconscious feels him to be.

Can the mystic love God when he senses that He is more than the familiar, beneficent deity and that His divinity has its shadows as well as its incomparable radiance? The proper test of the mystic's sincerity of purpose is the way in which he goes on loving God in the midst of his diabolical disguises. Not to know the dark side of God is to remain in ignorance of the human heart itself. The mystic fails of his purpose—nay, is unworthy of his purpose —if he wishes to draw close to God by repressing the knowledge of God's infinite nature. Those who declare that they love God and are bent upon losing themselves in ecstatic contemplation of His goodness and of His goodness only, reveal that they are acting in bad faith. It is an act of supreme self-deception to imagine that it is possible to love whole-heartedly a god who has been censored by one's own fastidiousness and denatured of his cosmic, supra-ethical, nonhuman powers. The psychoanalytic concept of reaction-formation carries the meaning that too ardent an expression of love may conceal a great deal of repressed hostility. The sincere and unreserved love of God is possible, therefore, only if the dark side of divinity is allowed to emerge from the unconscious. Otherwise, the mystic's passionate strivings will be diverted from their proper channels by the irresistible pull of his own reservations about God. Once deflected from their aim, the mystic's positive yearnings will be transformed into the caricature of love—into a sort of magnificent reaction-formation that leaves untouched the unconscious life-denying residue of divinity. The mystic's reservations about man likewise will remain unmodified, and his unresolved hatreds and fears will persist, so that his love of God will be purchased at the dear price of his hatred of man. In other words, the mystic can love God only if he realizes that God is what He is, just as he can love his fellow man only if he acknowledges his human mystery.

The inability to experience human love as a reflection of divine mystery necessitates in many instances a search for God in the hope of finding a perfect love that is unblemished by human weakness. This is the mystic's dilemma. The attempt to reach out to God, to love Him, to be lost in Him, is bound to fail if the mystic is in flight from his own humanity. But he has to start somewhere. If he starts from a position of withdrawal, unable to love others and unable to commune with others, he takes God as second best. It is more difficult to cultivate a mystical attitude—the attitude that God counts more than anything else—when one is in full harmony with other people, and accepting of the world as it is. By giving up earthly love in the moment of its full realization, the mystic affirms that God is his chief concern rather than his last resort.

Substituting the wide encompassing love of God for the specificity of human love holds still other dangers for the mystic. Chief among these perils is the risk that his own spontaneous emotions will undergo a leveling process and that he will be unable to respond to concrete human situations in a personal way. The same psychological process that can change the impersonal cosmos into the immediate, focused awareness of God's personality, can also lead to a profound impoverishment in the mystic's perception of human personalities, obliterating individual differences, and changing men into the objects of a diffuse pity. No less than the need to love God in an exclusive way is man's need to love specific persons in a personal, rather than an abstract philosophical way. As God becomes more and more real, everything else becomes correspondingly unreal and banal.

To make matters worse, the mystic has no guarantee that he will be able to break through the mythic and cosmological frames of reference that stand between himself and the divine object of his love. Love that is not directed to a specific object is an expression of indiscriminate desire, capable of seizing upon any object and subordinating that object to its own willful pleasure. If the mystic cannot go beyond his apprehension of God in terms of some mythical prototype or other, he is lost, imprisoned by metaphors, and entangled in his own narcissism. In reality, the mystic has to be his own myth-maker because the God who moves through sacred myths is obscured by the penumbra of the marvel-ous, and the marvelous easily becomes the object of an infatuation which is at bottom narcissistic, reflecting the devotee's need to vicariously glorify himself. Myths have a way of overshadowing their substance; though they seem to be the vehicle of the gods, they have the effect of eclipsing the gods by their grand and seemingly arbitrary design.[11] The mystic is the opponent of the traditional myth-maker because the reality that the former seeks is in constant danger of being contaminated with the symbols of the myth. Not that these symbolic arrangements are empty; rather they place the gods in opposition to spiritual death, thus making them the one-sided champions of life-affirmation in the face of adversity. The mystic knows that his God is beyond life or death, beyond victory or defeat, and that the mythic symbols recount the natural history of man rather than the supernatural history of God; God is outside of history in a more radical sense than the myth is outside of duration.

The mystical love of God is very different from loving the haunts of God, the "atmosphere" of God, the man-made stage settings for God. The mystic's God has no need of these props, but the ordinary religious man knows and requires only the back-drop for the divine drama; to be sure, he is in love with the drama itself, but knows little of the author of the play, who is his own author as well.

It is not difficult to mistake the extra-human heroes of sacred mythology for the likeness of God. In fact, it is in the nature of things for historical and quasihistorical heroes to be assimilated to a divine prototype. Mysticism will have no part of such hero-worship because God is not a hero, but the judge of heroes. But the mystic distrusts the mythical images of God for still another reason—he sees the inevitable connection between sacred and profane myths. Secular myths—the myths of the conquering hero, the great statesman, the founding fathers, the utopian soci-ety, the powerful athlete, the Periclean age, etc.—may well be-come sacred in time, when they have been purified of their cir-cumstantiality, that is, of their non-archetypal content. In the meantime, they generate their own debased mysticism, taking men outside themselves and placing them in exhilarating accord with their surroundings. The sort of hero-worship that is intrinsic to nationalistic enthusiasm illustrates the perverse character of profane mysticism. Whatever may be said for nationalism as a force for overcoming merely tribal and regional loyalties and thereby expanding the conception of humanity, its overriding defect is its xenophobia. The illusion of brotherliness, of shared destiny, and of mystical solidarity and the suspension of critical judgment as directed toward one's fellow countrymen all derive their emotional charge from the assumption that there is an "enemy" who sooner or later will have to be destroyed. The ecstatic extremes of nationalistic passion, with their publicly and privately expressed love of an inspired leader, their hysterical massed demonstrations, and their outbursts of fury against the "enemy," bear a resemblance to mystical self-divestiture. The sacredness of the experience of extreme nationalistic fervor is evident in its compulsive, deadly serious character and in its obsession with suffering or inflicting death. Nationalism is the prelude to that sacred duel which we call war, precisely as mysticism is a prelude to confronting the Divine Other, not in a spirit of contention, but with an attitude of total surrender.

In our time, the growing cult of certain forms of sport seems to suggest a search for mystical experience in nonreligious terms. Such activities as flying, parachuting, swimming underwater, automobile racing, and mountain climbing provide certain individuals with something more than a sense of excitement, danger, novelty, or accomplishment. Insofar as the sportsman loses himself in the immensity of nature or experiences an extraordinary kind of "aloneness," he is a mystic on wheels, as it were, moving through that portion of nature which is still the unconditioned other, untouched by man, unknown, undomesticated, and fresh from the Creator's hand. Clearly, this is not mysticism in practice because God does not figure in these journeys away from the center of the self; He cannot be found at the tops of mountains, as in olden times, nor does He reveal himself under the sea. The risk-taking sportsman is his own profane hero, and his feats become the themes for modern myths. Mysticism understands that the sportsman is not looking for a revelation, and that the myths that he engenders, like all profane myths and like the myth of nationalism in particular, express man's striving to take God by storm and to overturn Him. Unfortunately, the same is true of religious myths, and, knowing this, the mystic has nothing to fall back on but his faith.

The faith of a mystic is both his crown and his greatest weakness. I say his crown because the mystic lives in perfect confidence that God's grace will not be withheld from him forever, no matter how far off it may seem and no matter how long it may be denied. Perhaps every true believer shares this faith in the recurrence of grace, but the mystic is unique in that for him the absence of grace is an all but unendurable trial. He has known the depths of love, and the withdrawal of God's love is felt as catastrophic,[12] even though the intellectual side of his faith insistently tells him, "soon, soon." The mystic has the faith of a lovable child who, though scolded and neglected for the moment, knows that his father will welcome him back with complete forgiveness.

The mystic's weakness nevertheless consists in his compulsion to break down the taboo about getting close to God, a taboo that applies to everything sacred. Most men fearfully maintain the prescribed distance from the holy, believing that too much intimacy with the holy may lead to death. Only the mystic dares— because he has to dare—to test the limits of God's patience by the appeal of his own charity. The mystical crisis of faith involves a loss of faith in the self because the mystic knows that he is not worthy to trespass on God. The religious institutions of society reinforce the feeling of unworthiness. On the one hand, they seem to invite participation in the holy by means of ceremonials; on the other hand, they circumscribe the holy as an object of independent introspection, laying down rules and formulas for meditation. To be obsessed with God and to pursue the obsession in idiosyncratic terms is invariably a violation of the convention that religious communion in any form must be in keeping with certain norms.

Society does not accord the same recognition to private obsessions that it grants to popular myths, and it is for this reason that the love of God is dangerous and produces guilt, even in religious communities. The search for the divine companion is by its very nature a repudiation of community and of the usual norms that place a limit on spontaneity, thereby trapping the spirit in the quagmire of other people's expectations. For the mystic has had enough of earthly fathers. The tasks imposed by them have all but exhausted his spirit; as a last resort, he calls upon his Heavenly Father, his firm friend, to give him a sign of His healing presence. I do not wish to suggest that mysticism is merely the search for a supra-mundane father figure. The mystic's God is more than a projection of the archetype of the wise old man whose good counsel triumphs over death. The God of mysticism is man's last resort, the one remaining membrane that separates him from the world of man-made things and that prevents him from becoming one of those things.

It is not only the secular world that presses heavily upon the mystic, but also institutional religion, which, more and more, becomes for him a shadow of the profane world. Religion continues to provide a limited setting for the mystic, but, true to his vision, he bypasses the self-appointed keepers of God and sacrilegiously clutches at the wing-tips of God, saying, "Answer, answer, God. Help, please!" This is no ordinary prayer because the mystic's entire life is an orison, and God finally descends and enfolds him forever in His prayer-shawl.

3

The Cult of Fertility

THE MYTH of the sacred marriage of Acca Larentia to the god
Hercules,[1] which tells of a union between a courtesan and a
statue, is only one of many similar accounts whose derivation is
to be found in ancient fertility rites. These rites—whether celebrated as the nuptials of the king and queen of May[2] or as the
sacred marriage of the sun and earth[3] or as the union of Zeus with
the goddess Demeter[4]—have been widely interpreted as efforts to
maximize the fertility of nature, crops, and livestock by means of
sympathetic magic. In all such enactments, including those not
yet wholly symbolic, in which both principals are human or in
which an entire community participates without restraint, it is
evident that the expression of sexuality is encouraged as something sacred.

It would seem that we are confronted with a ritual—and a
prototypical one—which, far from effecting the repression of its
underlying impulse, permits the public gratification of a private
wish. Evidently, nothing has been interdicted, and, in the interest
of fertility, everything that is unthinkable, even for archaic man,

is allowed to manifest itself in the open. If this is truly a case in
which sublimation is not called for, in which no forbidden wish
stands in need of being denatured by ritual transmutation, then
we must admit of a very serious limitation on the general theory
of sexual repression unless there is a special reason for the repression of sex in everyday life, related specifically to its expression on
the secular or profane plane. This is my point of departure from
the point of view of psychoanalysis, which interprets sexual repression in the light of civilization and its demands for instinctual
renunciation, whether of oedipal strivings, or pleasure-seeking in
general. My contention is that everything in the archaic world
and much in the modern world which is not ritual, not sacred, not
mystery, not designed to accomplish the renewal of nature, and
not, in the deepest sense, irrational or magical is perforce taboo.
Since the promotion of fertility is a primary focus of primitive
religious life, just as the prospering of man on the profane plane
of existence remains a central concern of contemporary western
religions, it can be justly argued that sex qua sex—that is, sex
divorced from fertility—is taboo and therefore subject to repression.

Simply stated, it is the aim of all ritualists to preserve and renew
the natural and social order by means that are unnatural if one
disapproves of them, or supernatural if one believes in them,
thereby insuring a world without end. The ritualist fecundates the
earth with sacred offerings and impregnates the wind with prayers. He does not need to repress anything because he is guilty of
nothing, even in the midst of his saturnalia, even when he is the
lord of misrule or the king of the bean.[5] He is innocent because
he wishes only to make things grow and multiply. Why, then,
must he go on being ambivalent about sex, which is after all the
way to make things multiply? It is because sexual activity outside
the sacred grove and away from the recesses of the sanctuary
demonstrates that man can renew himself and that all living
creatures are fertile in their own right, without benefit of holy
sprinklings, lighted torches, sacrifices, incantations, or other extrinsic means. It is for this reason that even lawful sex remains a
sort of sin, expressing man's willfulness and disobedience to gods

who are felt to be the sole legitimate underwriters of fertility.

In addition, there is the danger that sex, if unrepressed as a fact of profane existence, will bring into being the blasphemous thought that man might be his own creator. In the matter of fertility, it would then be a case of the gods proposing, but of man disposing through his autonomous sexuality. Since such a conclusion runs counter to the conviction that the universe constitutes a magical order which can be fecundated only through the intercession of supernatural agents, we arrive at the central dilemma of the ritualist: How to convince oneself that fertility—which is what primitive religion is all about—is good but that sex is bad, because sex is an affront to the gods and constitutes a standing threat to turn men into gods by disclosing that men can be as creative as the invisible others.

In dealing with his own sexuality, the ritualist finds himself in the anomalous position of the Cretan nymph Britomartis, whose divine mistress was no less a personage than the goddess of birth, Artemis. It was the fate of Britomartis, who was a fertility goddess in her own right, to flee from sex, manifested in the person of Minos, who loved her.[6] If a ritualist is successful in repressing the consciousness of sex, he will arrive at the same symbolic resolution as Britomartis, who escaped from Minos by jumping from a cliff and landing in the nets of fishermen. The religious symbolism of the nets in this connection is clear from Frazer's description of sacred marriages between virgins and fishing nets, or, more precisely, the spirit of the nets.[7] Britomartis remained true to her primordial generative function; we cannot doubt that the fishermen's catch was greatly augmented through her coming into contact with the nets, though the legend is silent on this score. In like fashion, ritual catches sex in a net, substituting the symbolism of fertility for the real thing.

The historical transformation of legendary earth-mothers into virginal goddesses on the model of Athene provides similar testimony that sex and fertility do not mix. In her pre-Hellenic incarnation, Athene was connected with fertility rites and retained maternal characteristics for a long time thereafter.[8] Why, then, in a later legend, did she resist the impassioned Hephaestus,

defending her chastity with a spear?[9] Why does Athene come
down to us at last as a goddess of wisdom and morality? What a
long road the goddess has traveled, raising herself from the very
earth to the celestial heights of abstract wisdom. The requirements of sacred ritual are specific; world-renewal cannot be directly furthered by sexual means, but only by sublimation. In her
most blameless and awe-inspiring form, Athene becomes the embodiment of a whole society, sustaining its peaceful arts no less
than its warlike designs, and generating life on the sublimated
plane of social and cultural continuity.

As an object of ritual veneration, the perfected Athene served
to reassure her worshippers of the continuity of their magical
relation to nature, society, and the gods. In this way, each worshipper remained powerless to discover his own actual or potential
contribution to the creative process. This is an illustration of the
principle that archaic religion demands that man serve his gods
both selflessly, through mystical self-surrender, and by magnifying
the egos of the gods to the point where they and they alone create,
sustain, or destroy the universe and the communities of men who
dwell therein. Apparently even Athene, that paragon of goddesses, was not entirely deserving of the repressive demands that
were made upon her devotees.

I am not referring here solely to her character as a war goddess,
in which her destructiveness appears in a legitimate and patriotic
form, but rather to the legends that portray her as vile tempered
and assaultive. One moment she is portrayed as beating the satyr
Marsyas because he presumed to play upon the flutes she had
discarded; again, in a fit of jealousy at Arachne's skill at weaving,
she struck that proud maiden on the forehead with a shuttle and,
after preventing her from hanging herself, turned her into a
spider.[10] Athene had been shown a cloth woven by the Lydian
princess. It was a faultless work of art depicting the love affairs
of the gods, and Athene tore it up in anger. There is another way
of looking at this legend, with its surface manifestations of petty
rivalry and gratuitous injury. The exchange with Arachne is an
encounter between two distinct modes of being, not the human
as contrasted with the divine, but the truly feminine as distin-

guished from the sexless. First, it is interesting that, in reproaching the far-famed Lydian maid, Athene initially assumes the form
of an old woman and, in warning Arachne to submit to the
superior genius of the goddess, speaks scornfully of the young
woman's blooming years. Here, Athene clearly symbolizes an
attitude of hostility toward youth, and, prophetically sensing her
intention, Arachne affirms both her autonomous will and her
womanliness.

The weaving contest between goddess and mortal woman includes a striking contrast in the themes which the two contestants
chose to illustrate in their respective cloth designs. Athene's design is crowded with scenes depicting the majesty of the gods, and
their acts of vengeance against presumptuous mortals. Its motto
might well have been "Do not aspire beyond the bounds of
human life." On the other hand, Arachne's subject matter is
given over to the intrigues of male deities disguised as animals
who make love to mortal women. In these liaisons, the fertility
function of the gods is no longer uppermost and threatens to lose
its sacred character. Instead, profane love based on sex is plainly
in the ascendant. It is no longer a matter of vestal virgins acting
as nature's handmaidens or of gods bestowing their gift of life on
nature in a more or less impersonal way. It is as if Arachne had
said to Athena that she was her equal, not only in spinning, but
also in her capacity as a young mortal woman such as even the
gods might desire. As sophisticated as Athene has become, she is
still very much a fertility goddess; she is patroness of the once
orgiastic Thesmophorian festival and, as such, is unable to give
her approval to sex without ritual warranty.

The legend of Arachne provides still further evidence of tension between the divine aim of fertility and the mortal desire for
self-assertion. It is significant that not only mortal maidens are
drawn from near and far to marvel at Arachne's handiwork; the
Naiads desert their streams and fountains to come. The nymphs
and virgins of the plain witness the altercation between Athene
and Arachne, and, finally, when Athene discards her crone aspect,
the maidens adore her and withdraw their support from the now
clearly sacrilegious Arachne. Poised between two modes of being,

the nymphs choose the closer approximation to non-being, obedience based on repression. The connection between these spirits and the goddess Athene is a very old one. They knew her in days of old when she was still the undifferentiated mother goddess presiding over the mystery of birth and when she performed the same office as Artemis; when she was Astarte; when she was Hathor; and when she embodied the principle of fecundity while they, her priestesses, participated in Dionysian rites. Now everything is changed, and only the unfortunate Arachne permits herself to think that sex exists. For this failure of repression she was turned into a nonhuman spinster.

Of course, it could be argued, in direct contradiction of my assumption, that Athene became a virginal goddess only after she had served as a fertility symbol, and that she had belonged to the category of virgin mothers from the earliest historical period, before men understood the connection between sex and the production of offspring. However, to accept such an explanation is to fly in the face of compelling evidence that the service of fertility goddesses was sustained by the dramatic tension of sex, and that the significance of such rites derived in no small part from the ceremonial transformation of profane sex into the holy mystery of propagation.

The worship of the Phrygian mother of the gods, Cybele,[11] both in her Asiatic homeland and in Rome, provides a striking illustration of the role of repressed sex—indeed, sex entirely extirpated—in the interest of promoting fertility and hastening the advent of spring. The sacrifice of their virility which the priests performed at the great annual festival of Cybele and Attis (her divine lover) served as an affirmation of their guilty wish (the beginning of their undoing) to possess Cybele after the manner of mortal men. That the unsexed novices bestowed their more-than-symbolic gift alike upon Attis and Cybele strengthens the suspicion that theirs was partly a guilt offering. It was perhaps intended to placate the male deity for having dreamed in their frenzied excitement of serving their goddess the way that their ancestors had served her—through direct sexual expression. Once they had come to their senses, the subsequent function of the

eunuch priests was to make themselves the instrument for quickening the union of god and goddess on a seasonal basis.

It is interesting that the wounds which the priests inflicted
upon themselves were in imitation of their dying god, who had
unmanned himself. The blood which the priests shed on his
behalf was designed to revive the jejune nature god so that he
could come together with Cybele. Thus, the priests accomplished
with their blood that which they could not accomplish with their
seed. Against the carnival background of the Hilaria, the enforced
chastity of the priests has its exact parallel in the transformation
of early fertility goddesses into virgins of the type of Athene, who
remained undefiled in their shrines while the festival of the Thes-
mophoria was in full sway and the crowd threw phallic pine cones
into the caves of Demeter.[12]

We know, or at least may surmise, why the Phrygian satyr,
Marsyas, was struck down by Athene. It was not merely because
he had played upon the flutes she had discarded. It was because,
humble shepherd that he was, he had enjoyed the friendship of
Cybele, had played his pipes in honor of the great mother goddess, and, Attis-like, had died on the pine tree, sacred to Cybele.
In Marsyas, Athene had recognized the violet-bedecked god who
presided over the Day of Blood; she had smelled out the old
fertility god and had punished him in her prudish way.

What about the possibility that the self-mutilation of the
priests of Attis, like the slaying of Attis himself by a boar and like
the slaying of Tammuz and Osiris (by a sow with tusks), was
symbolic of the unstable position of the sacred priest-king in
societies still in transition from matrilineal kinship structure? Cer-
tainly, such an explanation is more straightforward than my assumption that we are dealing in such instances with the repression
of sex as a means of keeping the function of fertility strictly within
its sacred context. It would be a mistake, however, to overlook the
centrality of the motive of anti-sex which is present in such
blatant form in the myths that have grown up around the many
vegetation gods and the male lords of creation in general. Uranus,
for example, was castrated by his offspring, the Titans. It was
mother earth herself, the embodiment of the principle of fertility,

who had armed the Titans with a flint sickle. Through no fault
of his own, Adonis too was gored to death by Ares in the form
of a wild boar, because Ares was jealous of Aphrodite's love for
the handsome youth. While scheming to make love to the nymph
Daphne, a priestess of mother earth, Leucippus, disguised as a
girl, was shown to be an imposter and was slain by a company of
mountain nymphs.[13]

On a much grander scale, the theme of anti-sex is elaborated
in the many instances in which Hera places herself in stubborn
opposition to the unfaithful Zeus and attempts to frustrate his
illicit plans; at other times, overcome by jealousy and spite, she
visits her destructive anger on Zeus's unfortunate partners in sex.
Even Aphrodite, the goddess of desire, felt constrained to conceal
her affairs from her nominal husband, Hephaestus, the lame
smith-god. What could be more ridiculous than the spectacle of
the adulterous Aphrodite caught under the fine bronze net that
Hephaestus had made expressly for the purpose of trapping her
in the embrace of her lover Ares?[14] Surely, if anyone had a right
to commit adultery, indifferent alike to considerations of legality
or fertility, it was Aphrodite, who was born for love. A similar
paradox is seen in the character of Apollo, whose syncretic nature
permitted him to be a god of purification and an advocate of
moderation as well as a philanderer with a special penchant for
nymphs.

The Greek myths are filled with the sexual adventures of gods
and mortals, escapades in which the aim of fertility is absent.
They stand in marked contrast to the fully evolved Apollonian
religious rites with their decorous tone. The cult of Apollo, advancing on a tide of repression, tamed the orgiastic celebration of
Dionysus and replaced the ecstatic sexuality of the latter cult with
the measured divinations of the essentially urbane Apollo. In a
sense, the myths became the residue of anarchic and profane
sexuality which had been filtered out of the increasingly symbolic
and sublimated rituals. The sacred rites remained fertility centered, as in the Eleusinian mystery,[15] the object of which was to
mimic the seasonal perpetuation of nature through the ceremonial death and resurrection of its initiates. The process of symbolic

rebirth—in this case hastened by the performance of magical acts the exact nature of which remains unknown—was not so much a matter of salvation as of self-perpetuation through mystical union with certain sacred and perhaps totemic substances. In spite of its later ethical accretions, the Eleusinian mystery religion remained a ritual quest for the mother goddess; the mother goddess' magical powers of renewal, rooted in nature, were capable of being released only through the will of the gods.

I wish now to take up the question of the psychological meaning behind the persistence of the fertility motif in religion. Ritual preoccupation with fertility, whether disguised as Mystery, or as the passion of the desolated Tammuz, or in whatever form, always has an impersonal nonhuman significance, of which the theme of anti-sex is but a single, though important, expression. In essence, the obsessive concern with fertility is so archaic as to be presocial, in the true meaning of the term. From a modern point of view, one might be tempted to speak of the rites of spring, the festival of the harvest queen, the sacramental eating of corn gods, or any other custom of this sort as expressing in symbolic form man's sense of responsibility to his fellow men. In effect, by earnestly involving himself in the drama of resurrecting dead nature, the ritualist seems to be saying that he cares for others, and wishes to secure ample food for all. But we have no right to ascribe such ethical motives either to archaic man, or to his modern counterpart. The face of the fertility seeker is turned away from other human beings. He wishes to place himself in communion with the nature spirits, with powerful oaks, with undying evergreens, with potent bulls, with cascading rivers, and with high mountains and to mingle his blood with the blood of his life-giving totems. The votary of Isis, Ishtar, Demeter, or Cybele is a power seeker; fertility is but a means to an end, the goal being control over nature and the acquisition of her gifts in large quantities. The nearer the ritualist draws to his totemic object, the more he separates himself from other humans, who are powerless to help him because they are merely mortal. If others stretch out their hands to him, he can neither see nor hear them; his eyes are glazed with the sight of the spilled blood of the Archigallus and of the other priests and novices whirling in a furious dance, and his ears are deafened by torrents of wild music. It is of little importance that the worshipper of Cybele and others like him participate in a communal enterprise; in his enthusiasm all sense of ego boundaries is lost. Ask him for help while he is beside himself, and he will answer you, "I am busy offering my blood to Attis, who needs to be brought back to life if I am to prosper this year."

It is not only a question of helping other people. For the very reason that he is fixated at the acquisitive level of motivation, the fertility seeker is only capable of appreciating the world around him in its quantitative aspects. He implores mother earth to give him more, and he uses other people, animals, plants, and fetishes as if they were mere instruments for extracting a large bonus from nature. That the animate and inanimate objects of his awareness have an existence of their own, apart from his instrumental designs, he cannot understand. Thus, other people take on a thing-like identity for the fertility-seeker; they never come to life in their own right, but exist only insofar as they are stimulants or depressing agents. In short, the ritualist whose religious outlook is fertility-centered cannot respond to the intrinsic qualities of other people and is therefore incapable of love.

It is now possible to return to the theme of anti-sex in ritual and, to a lesser degree, in myth, and to see it for what it really is. The motif of anti-sex has little to do with the rise of ethical religion or even the advent of life-denying asceticism. In fact, there is no necessary contradiction between ethical affirmation and sexual love. Nor is asceticism an honest expression of the motif of anti-sex. In the very act of mortifying the flesh, the ascetic is already caught in Aphrodite's magic girdle, as his mind fastens compulsively on that which is denied to his senses. The motif of anti-sex is an integral part of the fertility complex and opposes the demands of the gods to the demands of human love. It is the characteristic error of the fertility-seeker that, because of his devotion to dead and dying gods who fertilize nature with their bodies and their spirits, he makes the false claim that love is part of the process by which life renews itself, and that rebirth cannot take place unless someone gives up his life.

This way of looking at love transforms it into a form of surrender in which two beings give up their separate personalities; they give up their very lives for the sake of the future, for the sake of the generation that will be brought into being. The sacrificial meaning that is given to love in this context is not to be interpreted along the lines of an ethical principle. On the contrary, the cult of fertility demands the sacrifice of all that is human, personal, social, and unique, in order to bring about the perpetuation of a type. Such love is narcissistic at worst and impersonal at best. It makes every act of creation beholden to an antecedent death, to an act of destruction. Although this sequence occurs in nature at the lowest planes of life, human love is an entirely different matter. Love on the human plane transcends the pleasure principle as well as the fertility principle and is social in its essence. Its style is idiosyncratic, and its outcome is indeterminate.

But, the quality in human love that is most disconcerting to the fertility seekers is that it is an individualistic expression of the human will; as such, it is profoundly irresponsible. Lovers do not ask permission of the gods to fall in love. Lovers sometimes invoke the blessings of the gods and ask them to strengthen the ties of love; but this is after the fact, for love bestows its own blessings and creates its own state of grace. No wonder the gods were often jealous of mortals. Human love attests to human self-sufficiency and to the fact that mortals are capable of creating relationships on the personal plane, without reference to the magical order of society with its orderings into clans, castes, tribes, and other totemically derived or religiously sanctioned groupings. Human love celebrates the magic inherent in individuals. Since it manifests itself without benefit of clergy, love is altogether taboo. It is even more taboo than sex. The cult of fertility, even in its most refined and sexless expression, is always a matter of flesh and blood, sublimate it how you will. Its social nature is incidental; its primary aim is the union of the human and the divine or the coupling of the gods themselves. In attempting to perpetuate the

finite through sacred marriage with some symbol of the infinite,
the rites of fertility succeed only in making the human plane of
existence insignificant, without necessarily bringing man into
more meaningful communion with the unconditioned Others.
On the other hand, love affirms the significance of life on the
human plane and works its magic even when the gods are asleep
or weak from too much blood letting.

I have spoken of the opposition between the demands of the
gods and the demands of human love. The gods demand much
more than the repression of sex as a condition for bestowing their
love on man; the gods require human sorrow to set them into
divine motion. I can only explain this assertion by calling attention to the overpowering element of mourning that is connected
with the historical fertility gods such as Osiris, Adonis, and others.
The worship of Adonis at Byblus, by the banks of the blood-red
river Adonis, provides a dramatic example of such mourning characterized by the loud wailing of ceremonially bereaved women
who carry effigies of the dead god to the sea for burial.[16] It is not
necessary to dwell on the many varieties of self-inflicted suffering,
not excluding self-immolation, which, far from being mere elaborations of the fertility cult, constitute some of its essential features. The devotees bewail themselves more than their broken
gods. The seasonal drama of death and rebirth symbolizes many
deaths besides that of the totemic god; it includes myriads of
human deaths and tragedies of every description that are remembered in their poignancy on the occasion of the annual festival.

It is significant that in the Adonis-Tammuz type of celebration,
the vegetation god and his consort are thrown into the sea after
their sacred marriage has been performed in dumb-show, as if to
remind the believers of the transiency of human happiness.
Would it not have been much more in the spirit of making a fresh
start if the vernal god was united with his consort after his resurrection, rather than on the eve of his destruction? However, such
a reasonable arrangement would be inconsistent with the true aim
of the fertility cult, which is not to promote growth but to have
a foretaste of death. The fertility cult is a lesson in mortality,
exactly like the warning conveyed in days of old when, at the

outset of a feast, a servant would show a small effigy of the mummy Osiris to each merrymaker, telling him that such was his fate when the good eating was over and life was at an end.

It is as if the masochistic component of fertility cults, together with the death of the god, were a compulsive acting out of a shared tragedy—the indivisible sorrow of all creation in the knowledge of its inescapable fate. It matters little that the believers know with confidence that the slain god will revive and that nature will thrive again. Their real sorrow is deeper than the theatrical lamentations of the ceremony would lead us to believe. It is a question of feeling sorry for themselves because they are as vulnerable as their gods and are indeed wedded to them in tragedy. As long as the gods are reassured that this is truly the case —that is, that man understands that he is committed to a sacred union with his totem and is moved to grief and terror through this fatal knowledge—they are appeased. The fertility gods want man to themselves; they want man to remain in nature, to be a part of nature, to participate in the rise and fall of nature, to pulsate with nature's beat, and to go down with nature in nothingness, where Persephone waits. If man accedes to this wish, he must needs violate the terms of his social contract and refuse to be a compassionate man among men.

By committing himself to his gods, the believer is left only with nonsocial alternatives. He can be a lord among men, translating his allegiance to the divine into an instrument of power; he can be a priest among men, or an intermediary between gods and men; or, he can be a wolf among men, doing the work of Cerberus in hell and uniting the souls of the living with the dead soul of Hecate.

The persistence of fertility cults through changing historical times reflects the persistence of the asocial element in civilization and an ingrained preference for the brutish in nature and for the animal spirit in man. The same quality that gives the fertility god his special power—the ability to flourish mightily on the quantitative plane, turning his every drop of blood into an anemone—is the quality that places itself in opposition to the humanizing tendency. Of course, not all historical trends that have followed

upon the phase of fertility worship have been movements away
from the "natural" order and toward a humane "social" order.
The rise of feudal forms of social organization in the classical
world was only another manifestation of the fertility cult in which
the warrior castes took the initiative away from the old priests and
priestesses. Instead of seeking to renew nature by the seasonal
shedding of blood, the new heroes found a way of sacrificing their
human victims in season and out. I am not speaking in metaphors;
the cult of the warrior was religious in nature and sacrificial in
purpose. To the extent that any progress at all has been made in
diminishing the influence of the cult of fertility, that progress has
consisted in abandoning the idea that human suffering serves a
sacrificial purpose and is the necessary price for spiritual renewal.

Let the believers in the cult of fertility confess that their error
lies in taking the world for an organism which lives and grows by
continually purging itself. Perhaps it is the will of all humans to
go on living by remembering the dead past, thus making the
affirmation of life dependent either on the memory of death or
its anticipation. Perhaps by learning to empathize with the death
of plants and animals, man arrives finally at the threshold of
compassion. This line of reasoning leads to the false conclusion
that the knowledge and vicarious experience of suffering give rise
to humanizing consequences. Far from it! To know that others
suffer and die serves only to confirm the fortunate ones that they
do not wish to join the ranks of nature's sacrificial victims. The
world-as-organism does not bind up the wounds of its sentient
members; it lops them off entirely, like boughs from a tree. Those
who would cleave to this organism, this undifferentiated consciousness, this world spirit of which the spirit of vegetation is but
one manifestation, must prepare to conjoin their will with the will
of the gods.

As for the gods, it can only be said that they view every separation from nature, every assertion of individual will, as an affront
to the sovereignty of their divine will, which animates the world-
as-organism. Fertility rites express the solidarity of man with the
gods conceived as nonhuman. Their successful performance
therefore requires the repression of every wish that is uniquely

human and that has as its object the enhancement of a human personality. The goal of the devotee is not to become more human, but more like a tree, or a horse, or an ear of corn. If he succeeds in making himself into a thing (preferably a thing resembling the material objects that he desires above all) nature will smile upon him. The gods will be pleased with the gratuitous sacrifice of his humanity, knowing in their hearts that if repression fails and man remembers that he is higher than the animals and plants, he will soon overshadow the gods themselves.

4

Ramakrishna

THE RAMAKRISHNA-VIVEKANANDA movement had its start in late
nineteenth century India, at a time when traditional Hinduism
had been placed on the defensive by Western power and influence. Against a background of increasing industrialization and
secularization of everyday life, especially in the large urban centers, the appearance of Ramakrishna (1836–1886) was viewed by
many Westernized Indians as a distinct anachronism. Ramakrishna early earned a reputation as a visionary and a mystic, but
his influence grew slowly because he often was identified with
regressive tendencies deeply rooted in the folk culture. At first the
object of a religious cult associated with the worship of Kali,
Ramakrishna eventually found himself the central figure in a
growing religious movement with distinctly modern overtones.
The moving force behind the expansion of the Ramakrishna
movement was the young disciple Vivekananda, who held the
movement together after Ramakrishna's death and fused his master's teachings with a social welfare ethic.[1]
Partly as a consequence of Vivekananda's energy and vision,

the Ramakrishna-Vivekananda mission spread throughout India and established centers of theosophic instruction in many other parts of the world, including North America. At the present time, the mission operates numerous hospitals, clinics, colleges, vocational training schools, libraries, publishing facilities, and monastic centers in various parts of India. No longer a loosely knit band of disciples, awe-struck in the presence of the master, the members of the Ramakrishna movement operate a complex of modern, bureaucratically organized institutions reflecting Western as well as Indian influences.[2]

What is most impressive is that the movement is a permanent, professionally administered network of agencies, with scarcely any traces of the charismatic leadership that brought it into being. It is also remarkable that a service-oriented organization could have developed out of the teachings of such a man as Ramakrishna, an eminently otherworldly mystic for whom religion was primarily a matter of intense and extraordinary subjective experience and heartfelt devotion to Kali.

Without suggesting that the history of the Ramakrishna movement is in any way representative of the growth of religious or quasi-religious institutions in general, it may be useful to examine several pertinent questions. What was the contribution of Ramakrishna's personality to the growth of the movement? What contemporary social forces shaped the essentially monastic movement, transforming it almost beyond recognition? What was the relationship between Ramakrishna's personality and the needs of his followers? We can attempt to formulate tentative answers— really hypotheses—that will serve to define the special relationship between personality and social milieu in the formation of a religiously inspired movement.

Specifically, the theses to be developed include the following:
1.   Ramakrishna's personality, shaped by powerful traditional village influences and given a highly idiosyncratic cast through a series of profound emotional crises, became the unique vehicle for expressing and satisfying the psychological needs of his disciples.
2.   The interplay of Ramakrishna's personality and teachings

with the special aspirations of influential westernized supporters provided the means for furthering "modernist" reforms bearing the imprimatur of traditional Hinduism.

3. Ramakrishna's aloofness from problems of organization and power and his specialized role as a divinely possessed teacher and father figure, permitted his disciples to develop complementary, differentiated roles.

4. The Ramakrishna movement benefited from its use of a traditional religious frame of reference, but its success was purchased at the price of secularization.

Life of Ramakrishna

The story of the Ramakrishna movement is as follows: Ramakrishna, the founder, was born in 1836 to poor but respectable Brahmin parents in the village of Kamarpukur, in Bengal. His parents are said to have experienced visions and other signs indicating that their as-yet-unborn child was no less than an *avatar*, or incarnation of Visnu. As the child—whose given name was Gadadhar—grew up, he experienced several brief, trance-like episodes. After his father's death, when Ramakrishna was seven, he was increasingly drawn to religious ceremonials and dramatic enactments. In a village play in which he played the role of Siva, Ramakrishna entered into a trance that lasted for a few days. As a child, he was addressed by pious village women as if a goddess had entered his body. During adolescence, he disguised himself as a woman in order to prove that he could visit some female friends of the family, who were in seclusion in the women's quarters of their home.

At sixteen, Ramakrishna joined his older brother, who was both a practicing Brahmin priest and a schoolmaster in Calcutta. In the course of assisting his brother, Ramakrishna was invited to serve as a priest in the newly constructed temple compound at Dakshineswar, on the banks of the Ganges, outside Calcutta. His major function was to preside over the worship of Kali, including the dressing and undressing of her basalt image.

Ramakrishna began to practice great austerities, remaining immobile for long periods of time in a deserted grove; he entreated Kali repeatedly and desperately to show herself to him, and he behaved generally in a way that caused him to be regarded by many as psychotic. At one point, he nearly stabbed himself with Kali's sword. He passed from a phase of great agitation to a period of exaltation during which he hallucinated actively and saw Kali everywhere, not as a goddess, but as a living woman. Ramakrishna would often offer food to the image of Kali, feeding her as if she were a child. At the height of his apparent psychosis, he even slapped his elderly patroness, Rani Rasmani, the very woman who had built the temple compound, saying that he had been angered by Rani's alleged lack of respect for the goddess Kali.

The pattern of Ramakrishna's behavior in the years that followed, though less blatantly "disturbed," continued to be one of alternating states of ecstasy, mute withdrawal, long periods of perfect lucidity, and, frequently moment-to-moment lapses of consciousness. His trance state was called *samhadi*, or divine superconsciousness, by those who admired him but was dismissed as morbid by his detractors. Amazingly, Ramakrishna was able to stabilize himself to the point where he was able to receive systematic instruction from a number of spiritual mentors. Despite his frequent loss of consciousness (petit mal?), Ramakrishna early developed an extraordinary style of preaching and instructing, conveying to even the most sceptical visitors to the temple his special quality of being *in* this world, yet not *of* it.

In an effort to "cure" Ramakrishna, his mother, Chandra Devi, arranged for his betrothal at the age of twenty-three to a six-year-old girl, Sarada Devi, who subsequently joined him at Dakshineswar for the first time when she was about nineteen. Sarada Devi visited Ramakrishna several times, living in the temple compound on a semipermanent basis until Ramakrishna's death. According to Ramakrishna, the marriage was never consummated because he regarded Sarada as the goddess Kali in person, and at least on one occasion offered up worship to her as the embodiment of the divine mother. Ramakrishna referred to his wife as the Holy Mother, and it was by this name that she was known to his disciples. After Ramakrishna's death in 1886, Sarada Devi continued to play an important role in the nascent religious movement.

Ramakrishna grew in fame as a holy man and as an inspired teacher. In 1875 he met the influential Keshab Chandra Sen, a publisher and leader of the Brahmo Samaj, an organization of religiously oriented social reformers.[3] Keshab Sen publicized the teachings of Ramakrishna over a period of several years and was instrumental in bringing Ramakrishna to the attention of a wide audience. Partly because of his own predilections, Keshab Sen emphasized Ramakrishna's universalism, seeking thereby to align his brand of Hinduism with other world religions. Ramakrishna continued to instruct numerous disciples, including his dynamic young successor Vivekananda, almost until the moment of his death at the age of fifty.

Ramakrishna's Personality

Perhaps by contrasting the personality of Ramakrishna with the personalities of his two closest modernist supporters, Keshab Chandra Sen and Vivekananda, some light may be cast on the interplay of experiential and organizational factors in the development of the Ramakrishna mystique. Ramakrishna was the personification of a "God-intoxicated" prophetic leader. He had no interest in organization or in humanitarianism, and he instructed his disciples in an almost incidental way. For many years, before Ramakrishna attained sufficient ego strength to preside over small informal gatherings of his devotees, he lived on a plane of utmost physical and emotional dependency. Protected and nurtured by relatives and friends, Ramakrishna was permitted to regress behaviorally while living an overpoweringly intense and dramatic fantasy life. The mother symbolism of Kali had a deeply personal significance for him; it coincided with his obsessive preoccupation with feeding and being fed and with his apparent identification with his own mother. Although detailed evidence is lacking, this identification was not without ambivalence, and it may have had a strong bearing on Ramakrishna's inability to enter upon a normal marriage relationship with his wife. In the same vein, Ramakrishna's repeated references to "woman and gold" provide a fairly clear picture of his negative attitude toward relationships between men and woman. Not the least of the indications of Ramakrishna's confused sex role identification is to be seen in his extended impersonation of a woman, rationalized as the fulfillment of the *madhura bhava,* or "sweet mood," in which a devotee of Krsna assumes the symbolic role of Radha, his consort.

Ramakrishna's special emotional needs, acted out without the least self-consciousness, probably influenced his choice of disciples from the very start of the movement. Numerous adolescent boys, including Vivekananda, were drawn to Ramakrishna as a result of their own identity crisis and seemed to have found in Ramakrishna a sympathetic friend and a culturally acceptable model. Ramakrishna appears to have shown the most interest in those youths who, like Vivekananda, did not attempt to imitate him in his role as a holy man. Instead, he selected as his favorite disciples boys whose spirituality was accompanied by nurturant attitudes, or at least potentially nurturant attitudes, implied by their evident need for a symbiotic relationship. Ramakrishna demonstrated considerable intuitive skill in recognizing sincere religious feeling and lack of selfishness and was quick to ridicule pious frauds of every variety. It is possible that his refusal to allow his disciples to behave as if they were holy men— that is, to imitate his own peculiar actions—was instrumental in screening out all but the most dedicated and affectionate followers.

Vivekananda as Modernizer

Without doubt, Vivekananda was Ramakrishna's favorite disciple. The young Vivekananda was spirited, highly intelligent, and attached to Ramakrishna by ties of respect and affection that had withstood the strain of initial skepticism. He quickly became the leader and organizer of the young disciples, imbuing them with a sense of mission and conveying to them a sense of shared commitment to Ramakrishna's teachings. Educated partly along western lines and combining a pragmatic, questioning mind with a passionate temperament, Vivekananda derived his sense of conviction from the mystical exaltation which he and many other disciples shared with Ramakrishna. Given his complex personality, Vivekananda was able, eventually, to effect a transposition of religious values to the plane of profane idealism.

He did so by acting upon the belief that Ramakrishna's teachings were of universal significance and that the altruistic content of those teachings was more important than the emphasis on suprasensuous experience.[4] During the period of Ramakrishna's terminal illness, Vivekananda and several of the older men who were looking after Ramakrishna began to alter the direction of the nascent movement in a decisive way. For example, in his characteristically forceful way, Vivekananda discouraged all signs of emotionalism among the young disciples, forbidding them to fast or to dance. Instead, he organized them to take turns nursing Ramakrishna and began to teach them the doctrine of service. In so doing, Vivekananda introduced new responsibilities and systematized existing nurturant routines centering around the master.

After Ramakrishna's death, acting in the name of Ramakrishna and addressing himself to an increasingly wider audience, Vivekananda moved a considerable distance from the preoccupations of the master. Armed with the mystique of the antimodern Ramakrishna, Vivekananda left India and found the courage to become India's apostle to the western world. But his message no longer had the connotations of antimodernism nor the homely touches of traditional village wisdom that had endeared Ramakrishna to his provincial followers. Instead, Vivekananda eloquently preached the primacy of spirit to an American clientele that was beginning to feel the first twinges of guilt over its materialism. The remarkable thing about Vivekananda was that while he was busy explaining the religious philosophy of India to audiences in search of the exotic, his mind was firmly fixed on the practical and prosaic as he strove to raise funds for future schools and hospitals.

There is a certain irony in the circumstance that to accomplish the modernization of Hinduism, as Vivekananda saw it, he had to present himself to the West as an examplar of the mysterious Orient. He shared with his listeners only a portion of his complex

nature, in which the modernist was ever at war with the tradition-
alist. Perhaps owing to his intense nature, Vivekananda correctly
sensed the mood of his Western admirers. They evidently craved
a return of feeling to religion—not the old revivalism of the
nineteenth century, with its public emotionalism, but some kind
of private feeling involving a personal relationship to the forces
of nature conceived in spiritual terms.

Keshab Sen as Publicist

Ramakrishna's life and death would have been less significant
if another partly Westernized contributor to the movement had
not fulfilled a valuable role. To speak of Keshab Sen is to speak
almost of an outsider in relation to popular Hinduism. The founder and editor of a magazine that was to give much prominence
to Ramakrishna's teachings—*The New Dispensation*—Keshab
Sen at first had no natural affinity for Ramakrishna's mysticism
and was hostile as well to much in the traditional outlook of
Hinduism. He was won over to Ramakrishna less by his teachings
than by his manner, which Keshab Sen identified with the behavior of an authentic saint.

Working through his own organization, the Brahmo Samaj, a
Western-influenced monotheistic sect of high-minded reformers,
Keshab Sen eventually injected into the Ramakrishna movement
a vital stream of young idealists, many of them well educated and
connected with influential families. *The New Dispensation* likewise reached many Indians who would normally have been indifferent to Ramakrishna's ultra-orthodoxy, especially in combination
with his trances, visions, and sharply antimodern attitudes. Keshab Sen succeeded in making Ramakrishna acceptable to elite
groups in Indian society, groups which, in effect, were laying the
foundation for future cultural developments of the greatest importance for India.

Once missions had been established in India and overseas,
numerous Westerners performed a role analogous to that of Keshab Sen. Writers such as Christopher Isherwood and Aldous
Huxley and their predecessors presented sympathetic descriptions
of Ramakrishna and other Hindu mystics, together with interpre-

tations of the meaning of their experiences. It was Vivekananda who had carried the message across the seas, but it remained for Westerners to translate the Word back into theological and existential terms which they could accept. Thus, though universalism was not a major point of emphasis in Ramakrishna's teachings, it assumed considerable prominence as the movement grew.[5] Strictly speaking, one cannot take Ramakrishna out of his context. It is hard to imagine a more particularistic religious figure than Ramakrishna; he knew little about the world outside his temple compound. It is all the more striking, therefore, that the universal elements and even references to monotheism in Ramakrishna's sayings constitute an important theme in the revised gospel of Ramakrishna. Without these Westernizing inflections and without the marked appeal to reformist Indians and Westerners alike of the mission's health and education programs, the movement might have remained limited in scope and parochial in outlook.

It is even possible that Vivekananda's missionary activities would have borne no permanent fruit without the help of Westernizers such as Keshab Sen. Keshab Sen's usefulness to the movement was the product of his remoteness from the emotionally charged, sickroom atmosphere of the temple at Dakshineswar and his immersion in the wider world of politics and journalism. Unlike Ramakrishna's day-to-day companions, for whom hero worship was almost a way of life, Keshab Sen was free to pursue goals of his own choosing. But, such a picture does not explain why Keshab Sen sought to integrate his program of reform with Ramakrishna's message. When it is recalled that Ramakrishna often stated that "the more you come to love God, the less you will be inclined to perform action," it becomes a matter for wonder that Keshab Sen could have affiliated himself with Ramakrishna.

Making allowance for the fact that Ramakrishna fascinated and, indeed, seemed to hypnotize his listeners by his extraordinary singing and inspired preaching, Keshab Sen seems to have found in Ramakrishna a means of coming to terms with his own religious doubts. Keshab Sen needed Ramakrishna—his blessings as well as his ambience—to legitimize his Christianizing tendencies. Ramakrishna seems to have understood something of Keshab Sen's motivation and was not well disposed toward his sophisticated admirer. When Keshab Sen was on his deathbed, Ramakrishna was brought into his house and insisted that the dying man get out of bed and greet him in an outer room (which Keshab Sen did); he then declined to give him his blessing, when Keshab Sen's mother requested it. Out of fairness to Ramakrishna, it should be stated that he was in a confused condition at the time and seemed to be hallucinating actively; he addressed himself, at moments, to the "divine mother."

Complementary Roles

If one thinks of Keshab Sen and Vivekananda as Ramakrishna's self-appointed interpreters to the outside world, it is possible to define several other, complementary roles performed by Ramakrishna's followers. Ramakrishna's wife, Sarada Devi, performed a unique function that was ascribed to her by Ramakrishna. In her role as the "divine mother" Sarada joined Ramakrishna in enacting a latter-day sacred myth. One of the essential components of the myth was the belief that, as he himself had more than hinted, Ramakrishna was an incarnation of Visnu, comparable in some ways to those other legendary *avatars,* Rama and Krsna, whose names he had assumed. His marriage with Sarada Devi was understood by Ramakrishna as a sacred marriage, never to be consummated on the physical plane, but filled with cosmic significance. For Ramakrishna, and later, for his devotees, Sarada was a deity in her own right, deserving of worship as if she had been the goddess Kali.

After Ramakrishna's death in 1886, Sarada Devi continued to be closely associated with the movement for more than three decades. Literally cast in a mothering role in relation to the young disciples, Sarada allowed the sacred charge to be transferred from Ramakrishna to herself. It is doubtful whether any other participant in the movement could have taken her place of symbolic leadership. Although Sarada was neither learned nor given to practicing rigorous spiritual discipline, her serene belief in

Ramakrishna's divinity was communicated effectively to those who came under her quiet and gentle influence.

Several followers of Ramakrishna played an important part in giving the movement a stable structure and a set of clearly defined goals. Following Vivekananda's untimely death, the young disciple Saradananda was a key figure in establishing the basis of a permanent organization. Described as calm, deliberate, and conscientiously devoted to administrative detail, Saradananda brought to the movement a certain solidity coupled with an exceptionally humane attitude toward the sick and the poor. A former medical student, he became the first secretary of the Ramakrishna mission, and he effectively held together the far-flung movement from its inception in the 1890s until late in the 1920s.

For Saradananda, the task of administering a service-oriented organization was not conceived exclusively in practical terms, nor even in terms of abstract altruism. It is important to note that Saradananda felt a tremendous sense of filial devotion to Sarada Devi. She represented to him not only the "holy mother," but a mother surrogate in the truest sense. The relationship between Saradananda and Sarada Devi would suggest that the transition from a loosely organized band of hero worshippers to a modest bureaucratic structure was facilitated by the existence of close affectional ties among the members of the core group. It is possible that the ongoing friendship between the motherly Sarada and the young disciple was more important than the memory of Ramakrishna in maintaining the continuity of the movement. Indeed, as Isherwood relates, Saradananda abruptly stopped working on Ramakrishna's biography, never to resume, when Sarada died. Instead, he supervised the building of a temple in her honor in her native village.[6]

It was not until the last years of his life that Ramakrishna's sayings were written down. This vital task was performed by an older man, Mahendra Nath Gupta (known as "M"), the self-appointed recorder of Ramakrishna's words and actions from 1882 to 1886. Mahendra Nath was not eligible to be a monk, being a householder and a teacher in a secular school. Neverthe-

less, he attached himself to Ramakrishna and was quick to grasp
the importance of recording the homely anecdotes and parables
related by the master. The recorded conversations became a kind
of gospel for the disciples which provided them with a highly
consistent, essentially traditional world outlook as well as with
inspiration for their common effort.[7]

Ramakrishna's Message

Though he never formulated it in a systematic way, Ramakrishna's philosophy of life is recognizable, despite his use of
religious terms and his over-determined (in the psychoanalytic
sense) denunciations of "woman and gold," as the characteristic
outlook of a person living in a traditional, folkloristic society. This
point of view emphasizes man's powerlessness, the absolute control of man's fate by the gods, the impossibility of understanding
the mysteries of the universe, the superiority of sincere feeling
over mere knowledge, the unchangeability of nature and the
social order, and the need for acquiescence to the inevitable. The
paradox is that such a passive outlook could have been incorporated into the activist program of the Ramakrishna mission.

Ramakrishna deviated from traditional religious assumptions in
one critical respect; he stated in positive terms his belief that all
forms of religious devotion are equally valid, that it makes just as
much sense to worship God as formless or as having form, and
that dogmatism is to be avoided. Such tolerance is not to be
confused with the easygoing indifference of Hindu village folk to
religions other than their own, or, more precisely, to religions that
do not violate their cherished customs. As remembered and
edited by M, Ramakrishna's formulation reflects a profound appreciation of the nature of religious experience. Moreover,
Ramakrishna actually experimented briefly, very briefly, with
Christianity and with the Moslem religion, in itself a remarkable
demonstration of open-mindedness in one so deeply grounded in
traditional folk culture. This is not to say that Ramakrishna understood what these religions were all about, much less that he was
familiar with their varieties of expression or their respective roles
in history. But, he was willing to assume that all men had legiti-

mate spiritual needs and a corresponding right to seek the fulfillment of those needs in their own special way.

The record of Ramakrishna's pronouncements, as kept by M,
reveals that the master's message was perhaps the least distinctive
element in his role as the symbolic founder of the movement. At
no time did he translate his own imperative need for union with
God into a universal injunction to practice self-submergence.
Following a well-established Hindu tradition, he wholly exempted
non-monks from the mystical quest, and he frequently reaffirmed
the principle that even dedicated holy men had to wait for God
to take possession of them. To be sure, he did not withhold his
admiration from householders who could combine "living in the
world" with dedication to divine service; but he reserved the
highest service for the enlightened few. One may conclude from
M's record that it was precisely the fact of Ramakrishna's perfec-
tionism that prevented him from breaking new ground; rather
than attempting to convert the unconverted and to renew the
unregenerate, he was content to winnow his disciples, seeking out
the most receptive and looking for ready-made saints.

Patterning of Roles

When the roles of the principal figures in the Ramakrishna
movement are examined in relation to each other and in relation
to the movement as a whole, a pattern emerges: Ramakrishna and
Sarada, neither of whom had any idea of founding a religious
movement, found themselves cast in the role of nurturant, inspi-
rational leaders of a divine or semidivine nature. Vivekananda, the
favorite disciple, assumed the role of organizer and evangelist,
functioning in a pioneering spirit with minimal institutional support. Mahendra Nath (M) was the recorder of the sacred myth;
he provided a vivid, first-hand account of the teachings of the
master which focused on Ramakrishna's role as a holy man and
served to transform him into an authentic culture hero. Keshab
Sen's role was that of theoretician, bringing the word to Westernizing Hindus and tempering their alienation from their own cultural traditions. Saradananda was the day-to-day administrator,
combining efficiency with humanitarianism and preserving his

ties to the "holy mother" even after the death of the symbolic leader. The young disciples were later to become monks, but they started for the most part as emotionally dependent adolescents. They progressed to a nurturant behavior pattern as the master approached death, and finally, held together by the force of Vivekananda's personality and aided materially by a handful of older "family men," they developed a sense of group identity.

The role patterning seems to show increased differentiation and increased autonomy of the group members.[8] The transition from hero-worship to responsible group membership occurred over a period of many years, during which the disciples grew from adolescence to manhood. The shift in emphasis from having a primary orientation toward the supernatural to a concern with religious education emphasizing ethical imperatives also took place slowly. Even at the time of Ramakrishna's death, it was by no means clear that the twelve disciples who had been given their ochre wearing-cloths and rosaries by the master that very year would be able to continue as a group. For example, following Ramakrishna's death and cremation, a quarrel developed between the young monks and the family men over possession of the master's ashes. The result was a tragicomedy in which the youthful disciples stole the ashes. The householders angrily deposited the remainder in a nearby village. Sarada Devi was completely disgusted by this quarrel; she left the group and went off on a long pilgrimage.

Fortunately for the nascent movement, a sympathetic householder named Gopal Ghosh bought a house for the boy monks to live in after Ramakrishna's death. The house was located in a desolate spot; it was frequented by cobras and jackels and had the reputation of being haunted. The boys accordingly called themselves danas, or ghost-companions of Siva. It is worth mentioning that while Vivekananda tried to instruct his companions about Jesus, the boys also worshipped Ramakrishna's ashes, his picture, his bed, and his slippers. Evidently, the early participants in the movement found it difficult to abandon practices which satisfied their need to relate themselves to Ramakrishna in a personal way. The subsequent strength of the Ramakrishna movement, viewed as a partly secularized institution, may be attributed in some measure to the preservation of emotionally toned personal symbols as a basis for identification and inspiration. At the same time, the possibility should not be overlooked that, once a network of functionally defined roles was worked out among the disciples, service and education routines may have become self-perpetuating, requiring a minimum of extrinsic motivation or justification.

The Need for Affiliation

I am inclined to think that the mortar that held the Ramakrishna movement together in its early stages was a need for affiliation on the part of the disciples combined with Ramakrishna's own search for some kind of human intimacy. As applied to the young monks, the term affiliation implies something much stronger than fellowship in the religious sense. It is not a distortion to say that most of the adolescents and young men who gravitated toward the temple compound at Dakshineswar were searching for a way out of their personal problems.

These problems were probably not primarily religious, but represented developmental crises produced by the fear of losing their dependent status as children and being compelled to marry, attend college, take a job, or otherwise assume unwelcome responsibilities. At Dakshineswar, it was possible to escape into a nurturant environment softened by the gentle personality of Ramakrishna and the maternal presence of Sarada Devi. Dakshineswar was entirely free of the sadomasochistic disciplines of a monastery, and Ramakrishna made absolutely no demands on his followers. Those who served Ramakrishna and nursed him—he was at no time free of incapacitating physical symptoms—felt under no compulsion to work or to deny their customary needs.

At least during Ramakrishna's lifetime, the youthful devotees were not subject to control by teachers and were free to come and go at Dakshineswar in the most informal manner. Insofar as many of the disciples visited the temple without parental supervision, and even in spite of parental opposition, there can be little doubt that the atmosphere was rather like that of a club and was conducive to the formation of strong voluntary ties among the disciples. Even the mature householders who supported Ramakrishna by paying his expenses, arranging for his transportation, and otherwise managing his affairs were rarely, if ever, officious; they apparently received as much emotional gratification from supporting the master as the disciples received from serving him.

As for Ramakrishna, it is paradoxical that his need for closeness was not shown directly or openly during his first few years at Dakshineswar. He centered all his attention on the goddess Kali, creating a strange mother-son—perhaps son and lover—relationship with the statue of the goddess. As mentioned earlier, he was not content to dress the idol and look after its jewels, but spent many hours daily embracing the statue, talking to it, feeding it, scolding it, and singing to it. The people around him, including his cousin Hriday, who looked after him, were unable to establish more than fleeting contact with Ramakrishna.

Nevertheless, a kind of affiliative motive actuated Ramakrishna. At first, he was like a child looking for his mother, seeking an improbable relationship with an image made of basalt, an inanimate and ferocious looking mother surrogate. It is striking that, even after Ramakrishna's real mother came to live permanently at Dakshineswar, he remained fixated on Kali. His psychotic behavior may be interpreted as indicating the depth of his affect-hunger.

Perhaps the clearest indication of Ramakrishna's recovery from his psychosis was his gradually demonstrated ability to take an interest in the real people in his environment and to curtail his ritualistic compulsions centering on Kali. If this be true, Ramakrishna's recovery, rather than his basic disturbance of affect and thought, marks the starting point of his career as a religious leader. An enigmatic figure who played an important part in Ramakrishna's remission from the most acute phase of his psychotic reaction was the holy woman known as the Bhairavi. Appearing from out of nowhere, this learned woman gave Ramakrishna his first systematic instruction in the Hindu scriptures. Of equal importance, she involved him in an intense and highly personal relationship. Ramakrishna accepted the Bhairavi as his spiritual mother, just as, in a more regressed condition, he had made of Kali's image a sort of fetishistic mother. The Bhairavi showed Ramakrishna that his quest for intimacy was not futile and helped him to build a bridge to other people.

What started as a pathetic struggle to experience or re-experience the most basic of affiliations between mother and child turned into a search for union with God. Love for his fellow man came later, after Ramakrishna came to realize that the unitive experience was more than a matter of embracing a stone goddess. Ramakrishna found his way back to God by awakening to the existence of man. It was as if he discovered the personalities of other people after having lived half a lifetime on the plane of withdrawal. As his psychotic condition improved, it was no longer necessary for him to repress his need for intimacy—and consequently to express it in a bizarre way.[9]

But Ramakrishna was already in possession of an independent frame of reference. The social motives and ambitions that dominate the lives of most people had never had a chance to develop during Ramakrishna's formative years, probably because of the severity of his disturbance. The result was that as he learned to relate himself to people, he demonstrated an ability to be involved socially and yet remain noninvolved. This residual detachment did not prevent Ramakrishna from experiencing people concretely and with the greatest poignancy, but it enabled him to develop perspectives that were not exclusively social. Of great importance for the growth of the movement, Ramakrishna's natural indifference to problems of organization gave his followers a free hand to develop their own structure and freed them from dependence on a dominant leader.

Subjective Experience and Meliorative Goals

The perspectives which Ramakrishna developed and which his disciples came in part to share with him involved no new religious doctrines. Instead, the key factor seems to have been an intensification of religious experience and an attempt to return to the source of religious insight in subjective experience. It was as if the Indians in Ramakrishna's circle and their Western adherents needed to redefine and reemphasize—perhaps rediscover—the meaning of their old religious attitudes in the light of immediate experience.[10]

Within the context of Hinduism, it remained for Ramakrishna to reactivate the *avatar* motif, boldly casting himself as the central character in the quintessential Hindu passion play, the sacred myth of the birth and rebirth of the incarnations of Visnu. Because Ramakrishna felt himself to be a god—the very embodiment of Rama and Krsna—he was able to breathe new life into a Hinduism that had come to seem archaic to many Indians. In effect, Ramakrishna restored the vital element of contemporaneousness to his religion, reestablishing the presence of a god in a seemingly desacralized world.

It is therefore ironic that, in the name of Ramakrishna, Vivekananda laid the foundations of what is essentially a modern theosophical movement in which the mystical and intuitive constituent is overshadowed by the secular goals of education and medicine. One might say that Ramakrishna was the last great godsmith, making a god out of himself in his own image while his disciples went on to fashion a religious movement in their image, or, more precisely, in the image of a young India mindful of Amos' revolutionary message that worship without deeds of justice and mercy is hateful to God.

If the leaders of the movement, with the exception of Ramakrishna, were eager to bring about meliorative social changes, they did not hesitate to make necessary innovations in the name of nonrational, anti-modern ideals, as preached by the Master. In the language of the sociology of knowledge, it would appear that the Ramakrishna movement originated in a society whose basic idiom was religious and used that idiom in the service of its ethical goals.[11] It is a measure of Vivekananda's sincerity that, despite his religious doubts, he was willing to work within a framework of traditional ideas in order to implement new ideas. Had he chosen, for the sake of logical consistency, to employ the rhetoric of a secular ideology, he might not have achieved any real measure of success.

A final question suggests itself. What is the general relationship of the Ramakrishna movement to the psychological needs of modern Indians or to modern westerners? Of course, it is impossible to generalize accurately about entire civilizations, but it is interesting to speculate whether the early, hero-worshipping phase of the movement or the later service-oriented phase is more in keeping with the psychological needs of Indians. It should not be assumed that because the meliorative aspects of the movement are a more recent development and presently characterize the movement that the need of contemporary men for charismatic leadership, in India as elsewhere, has grown weak. Nor is it clear that the original mystical Dionysian strain of the Ramakrishna movement, now diminished almost to the vanishing point, is irrelevant to man's needs. It remains to be seen on what basis religious movements can renew themselves in the modern world, and whether, like the successors to Ramakrishna, they will succeed in adapting themselves to new demands by invoking traditional, emotion-laden images.

5

The Myth of Osiris

THERE ARE striking parallels between elements of the cult of Osiris, the ancient Egyptian god of the dead, and primitive initiation rites. It is misleading to think of Osiris exclusively as a fertility god, or as a god of the underworld, or as a god who renders judgment upon the dead.[1] There is a pathetic human dimension to this deity who was mourned annually by his devotees. My thesis is that the slain Osiris, whose seasonal resurrection was ever awaited tearfully upon the banks of the Nile, was no less than a member of the family. In effect, there was a close relationship between the ordeals of this nature-god and the ordeals of adolescent initiation. I refer to initiation rites of the type still practiced in the Sudan in the context of tribal, preliterate cultures. These rites, in common with other soteriological practices, consist largely of a mimesis of death and resurrection. Just as the death of Osiris is a metaphor for variations in the seasons, so too the symbolic death of the novice undergoing initiation represents a rite of passage from one stage of life to another.

It is difficult to say which came first historically, the cult of nature gods who die annually or the practice of initiation, though initiation rites are widespread among peoples who have never developed a high civilization and must therefore represent an early stage of social and religious development. The aborigines of Australia are a case in point. The death and rebirth of nature gods seem to parallel the symbolic death and rebirth of the novice.

Osiris was neither entirely dead nor yet completely alive; he was menaced in death as in life by relentless Seth and was torn to pieces and but incompletely reassembled afterward. This story might well have been the historical descendant and lasting symbol of multitudes of youths who had been initiated into the tribal mysteries at puberty. Just as Osiris, inert and drugged with sorrow, lost the ability to "know" and altogether surrendered his old identity as primeval creator—so much so that he was constrained to cry out for his son to revive him—so too the initiate at puberty has had to forget his former self and enter tremblingly upon the symbolic death and mutilation from which he was destined to emerge a new man, spiritually reborn. Alas, like Osiris, the primitive youth dare not entertain the hope of entering into the realm of light, even in his new condition of liberation from ignorance after his ordeal is over. He too must remain content, with Osiris, to return to an earth-bound life of uncertainty and fear while he awaits the final submergence of creation in the primeval waters.

The improbability of identifying Osiris, the father of Horus, with a pubescent youth must at once be apparent. In the one case we are presumably talking about a man already married, albeit to his sister, Isis, while in the other instance, the image that comes to mind is that of an adolescent about to cross the threshold into maturity. But, what kind of husband and father is Osiris? In the first place, it may be remarked that his death, dissolution, and final deliverance took place before he begot Horus, his only child. Osiris, then, in spite of his bearded appearance, must have been a young man, and the legend of his affiliation with Isis is really a legend of love and devotion between a young brother and sister.

The relation of Osiris to his posthumously begotten son is never that of a father to a son, but that of a dead ancestor begging to be remembered by his descendant. There is no clear indication that Osiris was ever in a position to behave in a fatherly way toward his offspring. The real drama of the Osiris legends, at least in the domestic sphere, is enacted by the bereft Isis, who is far more the "mothering one" toward her lost and murdered husband than a wife in the actual sense. Moreover, in relation to her child, she is the sole effective parent. Indeed, Osiris is so far from being a father figure that his plight bears a striking resemblance to that of the infant Horus. Like the helpless newborn baby, Osiris, once enshrined in his tomb, needs to be guarded by Isis and by her sister, Nephthys, as well, lest Seth the Destroyer tear him to pieces again. Osiris cannot even bestir himself to help the tiny Horus when he is bitten by the demonic snake in the swamps of Chemmis. The news that the infant has been saved by Thoth from the effects of the serpent's venom is relayed, not to Osiris, but to Re, the supreme deity, who is told that his "son" has been cured! The absurd powerlessness of Osiris, in which there is more than a hint of childish dependency, is well illustrated in a myth related in the Book of the Dead: Osiris begs Re, the High God, to bestow upon him his own numinous crown so that people will respect him and so that even the ever-threatening and apparently indestructible adversary, Seth, will acknowledge the authority of the dead god. But no sooner does Osiris put on the heavenly panoply than the divine heat pours forth from it and gives Osiris an unbearable headache, so that he must resign himself to continuing without the supreme crown and, consequently, without the power to evoke awe.

Even the manner in which Osiris lies swaddled, his arms pinned to his sides, connotes a state of passivity, as if he were in the condition of an infant in its swaddling clothes. He is represented as being literally and symbolically enfolded in the mother-goddess Nut, whose emblem is the coffin. Significantly, Osiris represents the idea not only of death, but of reproduction into life, as shown by the figure of an infant always depicted beyond the sarcophagus of the dead inside the ancient Egyptian tomb. The essential characteristic of rebirth in primitive initiation rites means that upon his emergence from the regions of death, from the very bowels of the ancestral totem, the novice returns to life with a new identity, a new name, innocent of all knowledge of the past, as one born anew.

Further attesting to the childlike character of Osiris is the remarkable continuity between Osiris and his son Horus. In several representations, Horus is shown rising bodily out of the prostrate figure of Osiris and resembling him in every feature.[2] Added to the impression of physical identity is the obvious continuity in the sufferings of Horus—i.e., the loss of his eye in the combat with Seth—with the ravages sustained by Osiris. It is as if the ordeal of Osiris is merely a prelude to the long drawnout struggle between his would-be avenger and the forces of the satanic foe. To be sure, Horus is stronger than his father, and gives a good account of himself in the divine duel with Seth. But in the end, though the judgment of the gods is granted in his favor, he has little to show for his efforts but his scars. Seth is the real victor, alike over father and son, and remains immortal, in spite of everything. In both instances, it is apparent that Seth was the aggressor, and that his victim was weak and on the defensive. In reality, Osiris and Horus stand for a single sacrificial entity—the youth who must be slain so that he can be reborn, usually with some visible sign upon his body attesting to his submission to the ancestral demon.

Still another feature of the Osiris mystery calls attention to the initiatory element in the passion: Horus, depicted as a star in one of the Osiris myths, descends from heaven into the western underworld of endless waters, there to meet Osiris and to emerge with him in the east, purified by their joint immersion, and together heralding the return of universal prosperity. The motif of rebirth is unmistakenly apparent, and, moreover, points to a regeneration of nature as well as of man. This is the meaning, perhaps, behind the ancient pilgrimages to the ceremonial center at Abydos, where a new statue of Osiris was dedicated annually and where so many hopeful worshippers awaited eagerly the news that their god had awakened from his great sleep, symbolizing their own fervent wish for regeneration. It is precisely during the long sleep that the soul of Osiris hangs in the balance,[3] just as a man's soul was thought to be in an especially precarious condition in the interval between death and embalment. But, what if Seth should gain the upper hand at this decisive moment and utterly seize the soul of Osiris, thus preventing the transmission of the divine essence to Horus? In fact, anything at all can happen when one has entered the realm of magical duration, of that sacred time when life is aborning and when the face of life is indistinguishable from that of death itself.[4] Spiritual rebirth is full of risks because it can take place only on terms acceptable to the forces of death. These terms stipulate torture, self-abnegation, immolation, an end to all temporal or profane allegiances, and, above all, the dread possibility of spiritual death in the process of trying to transcend life. The passion of Osiris—three days and three nights of lamentation while the soul of the slain deity was in limbo— does not have to end in resurrection. All such ritual departures from the plane of temporality are departures as well from the familiar world of causality in which day must follow night. What if the magical night into which Osiris has wandered, drawing after him the yearning souls of his devotees, should turn out to be without end?

Very much like the primitive novice, the dead Osiris is in a state of double jeopardy because he is not only vulnerable to the depredations of totemic agents such as Seth, but because, having gone down into the earth in search of the creative principle, he is face-to-face with the earth-mother herself, the source of all life and death. The regressive element implied in this symbolic search for creative wholeness is important in its own right because it epitomizes man's condition at birth and at death; it is the condition of surrender to a higher power. This power can make man into nothing, or, by making him immortal, it can imbue him with essential being. What is demanded—really, what man asks of himself—is that one must first and last enact the drama of humbling one's self, becoming as a child as a precondition of becoming a real spiritual being. The earth-mother, by whatever name she is known, will have it no other way. Osiris is restored to wholeness by Isis, who is a kind of mother to him, as well as to Horus. But, on the way to wholeness, Osiris is nearly extinguished in the marshes. The fatal legendary act of passive trust, in which

Osiris allows himself to be clapped into a chest by Seth, denotes the beginning of his passion and sets the psychological tone of his subsequent masochistic experiences. Could it have been otherwise? Like all true martyrs, Osiris must have suspected what was in store for him. Not unlike the primitive novice, Osiris must have known that he was embarking voluntarily upon an odyssey in which, like Horus after him, he would have to float precariously on the life-giving waters, would have to strain to see a ray of light in the darkness of the totemic womb underground in the regions of the west, and, with luck, would finally emerge beaten, tortured, and thoroughly humiliated, but integral. I speak as if Osiris had been a real person, knowing that he was legendary. But, I repeat that the Osiris whom the pilgrims mourned upon the banks of the Nile and for whom the women wailed their piercing wail was no legend but a real son, delivered up into the hands of the mystery keepers, who, while seeming to unman and destroy him, paradoxically would reconstitute him as a man.

Corresponding in their actions to the role of Seth are the male relatives of the primitive novice; they serve as sacred tormentors, keepers of the mystery, and agents of the ancestral totem. Unlike Isis and Nephthys, the mothers and sisters of the novices are totally excluded from playing any role in the initiation rites of the boys. They are unable, therefore, to help the novices during their symbolic but nevertheless terribly real confrontation with death. At the point of "resurrection," however, the novice is brought back to the gentle ministrations of female relatives,[5] who help him to return by degrees to the world of the living, and watch over him until he has fully assimilated his new identity as one reborn and reconstituted on a higher plane. Thus, the presence of female kin during the phase of recovery from the trauma of initiation has its parallel in the search for Osiris by his sisters, their recovery of the slain god, and his physical reconstruction.

Is it plausible to infer that, in spite of the dramatic impact of the masculine-oriented ordeal of initiation, the erstwhile novice remains attached, after all, to his mother and sisters? Standing in obvious contradiction to this inference is the fact that the initiate does indeed enter upon his ordained masculine role, either by removing himself to the bachelor quarters or getting married. In a larger sense, however, primitive man does not emerge from his ordeal as a truly independent being. Nor is the symbolism of being reborn and returning to his mother's hut as a child a truly symbolic enactment. What is involved in participating in the initiation rites, suffering, learning the mystery, discovering incidentally the element of imposture, and assuming the conspiratorial guilt of secrecy, is the psychological act of surrender. In short, the prerogatives of manhood granted under the foregoing conditions do not include the freedom to return to the social order or to the bosom of the family under conditions differing in any essential way from the terms of one's former status as a fear-ridden child. It is the same way with Osiris. The great Listless One is destined to remain forever in the underworld, manifesting himself on earth as the disembodied spirit of fertility, without water in the depths of the earth, without air, without light, and enduring a fate altogether different from that of the other gods. Even in the underworld, Osiris remains unfulfilled, altogether vulnerable, and powerless to command the other spirits of the regions of darkness. Horus must needs send down a sort of celestial being fashioned in his own image and invested with his soul in order to enforce the respect of the underworld deities for the great Deserted One.[6]

Was the passion of Osiris all for naught? And what does the primitive novice gain by his self-abnegation? In both cases I believe that the sacrificial offering of the self is the precondition, par excellence, for becoming a part of the great chain of being. With Osiris this form of immortality is expressed through his continuous role as the god of regeneration, the keeper of the granaries, he who sustains the natural order of the world by becoming wheat, by becoming barley, by growing and decaying, but never dying. This is nothing less than immortality through immanence: By becoming everything else, Osiris has become nothing, has lost his individual soul, and his personality as a god. The primitive initiate has gained, likewise, the privilege of immortalizing himself through his progeny, and ensuring perpetuity for the sacred mysteries with which he has been entrusted, and which it is his duty to transmit. He, too, is now integral with the rest

of creation and has given of his very substance so that his covenant with nature and with his ancestors who have joined the
natural order will be complete. Like Osiris, however, the initiate
has lost something, too—if not the self in the psychological sense
of being able to know, to will, to act, to feel, to judge—then at
least the transcendant self; that is, the separate self.

This is another way of saying that there are no separate entities
in nature and that those who would place themselves in harmony
with nature must give up their contrariness, their uniqueness, like
those primordial divine beings who are still so undifferentiated as
to be neither male nor female, but both, expressing in their
"wholeness" the ultimate reality of nature, which knows no
polarities. It may be objected at this point, that the express purpose of puberty rites is to make a definitive separation between
male and female by making the male more "masculine" by circumcision or some allied process, and, in some cultures, by making the female more "feminine" by an analogous procedure.
There is a purpose, of course, in distinguishing between the sexes
by putting a mark upon them. The distinctive sex-roles are
affirmed, however, only to the end that procreation can proceed
under magically favorable conditions. With fertility as the aim
and object of so much primitive religious activity, the fulfilment
of the individual, whether as a man or as a woman, whether as
a person or as a thing, is of little or no importance.

So far, I have dwelled mainly on the aspect of regeneration in
the cult of Osiris and in primitive initiation rites. What about the
dying? The conception of death that is intrinsic to the outlook of
both archaic and nonliterate man makes death a sort of holiday
from life. The symbolic death of the primitive novice resembles
the passion of Osiris in nothing so much as the conviction on the
part of participants and spectators alike that the dying is only
spiritual, and that the sacrificial victim will return with his corporeal self largely intact. It was but a small loss, to their way of
thinking, for the spirit to be released, to be swallowed up in the
one case by a totemic monster, or, in the other, to be sublimated
as a *Ka*, pure spirit at liberty to enter or leave the body. Spiritual
death, then, does not entail the death of a personality, but only

an alteration in the essential form of communion with nature. To preserve the corporeal self, while putting its strength and integrity to the most punishing test, becomes the ultimate challenge to the celebrants of Osiris' mystery, as well as to the participants in puberty rites.

The cult of Osiris not only takes for granted the dying of the spirit of man, but vitiates the very idea of the Absolute—of the individual human soul as infinitely mysterious and precious. The passion of Osiris reveals an underlying confusion of the phenomenality of the flesh with the mystery of death. This confusion grows out of a kind of naive philosophical monism, in which only the embodied Osiris, dead or alive, is real. Every precaution must be taken to preserve the material substance of the god, because without the body, the spirit of Osiris is nothing. Every violation of the integrity of the finite embodied creature is likewise a diminution of the spirit, but above all, a tragedy in its own right. Osiris, as the dramatic embodiment of the sacrament of death, is the very symbol of the act of dying. How unlike the drama of *becoming* is this passion of dying, in spite of all the rhetoric about rebirth! Osiris cannot become anything, cannot become immortal, spiritual, or unconditioned, cannot become a transcendant deity or divine essence, cannot become—what is most important of all—a human personality.

As the death of Osiris is transformed historically from a personal, human loss into the death of a non-self, of a temporal, illusory deity whose body, rather than his soul, is immortal, so, too, the symbolic death of the primitive novice is merely a masque of death, a taste of death in the midst of life. The primitive novice, as much as he dreads the trials to which he will be subjected, must wish with a portion of his heart for the supreme moment, when, in the midst of pain, he will be vouchsaved an intensification and expansion of life. For him, death can be no more than a side effect of too much living; it has no sting because life itself has not assumed its human significance. He has not learned, as yet, to think of death as ennobled, or as greater than life, nor does he need to resist it heroically, since it is neither good nor bad, but, like life, an aspect of endless flux.

The idea of death that underlies both the cult of Osiris and the mystery of initiation is a simple, unitary conception. The modern view of death, by contrast, tends to dissolve it into its component elements. The old idea of death and its primitive counterpart today are based on the repression of death as an absolute fact. On this basis it becomes possible, and, indeed, necessary to go on interacting with the dead, to commune with the spirits or concrete relics of the dead as if they were still alive and enjoyed an even greater vitality than they had possessed during life. What becomes of life is that it is reduced to a case of antecedent death. Death itself, by a parallel process, is turned into a spectator sport, of which the chief joy is being a witness to life. Life and death are viewed as essentially the same; that is, as alternating phases of existence. In our time, of course, all this has changed; we call life "life" even at its deadliest, and we call death "death" even when its significance is greater than life! All of our modern attempts to follow the example of the ancients and to repress the consciousness of death are to no avail, because we know, despite our formal protestations, that there are two separate categories of reality, being and not-being. To avoid thinking about death, we try to "immerse" ourselves in practical affairs, in the immediacies of everyday life. When this solution proves inadequate there is still the alternative of trying to regain the lost perspective of immortality, thereby overcoming the terror of everyday, empirical life with the healing acceptance of transcendental values, including death itself as a transcendent value.[7]

In this connection, Osiris may be thought of as symbolizing either of two value orientations. Either the recumbent deity, his body inured against time and dissolution, betokens nostalgia for the temporal life that has ceased, or his attitude of death is a way of reminding his devotees to say goodbye to the conditioned life of the flesh, and to turn their faces toward immortality. The latter interpretation, if true, implies an element of imposture on the part of the god-as-effigy. The preservation of the body of Osiris negates death as a positive value and makes of the hereafter a cheap imitation of life. Osiris can transcend death only by shedding his corporeality and entering upon eternity as pure spirit.

But, this is exactly what his worshippers will not allow him to do. Along with their prostrate god, they remain fixated at the threshold of death or, if we are to take them at their word, at the entrance to life everlasting; they are reluctant as much to shake off the corruption of existence, as to embrace perfect being, out of fear of nothingness. Osiris is the perfect symbol of man's ambivalence toward life and afterlife. To be immobilized by inner conflict in life is bad enough; it is even worse to be in a state of permanent doubt as to when to surrender one's commitment to life and to commence dying.

By turning his back on Osiris, and rejecting the archaic mystical concept of life as flux, modern man gives us to understand that the individual's existence on earth is a serious fact. The realization of this fact is a shock and one that cannot be avoided by retreating into mysticism or even by learning to respect death as a transcendent value. As soon as we acknowledge that each individual has a unique personality, we pass from the stage of regarding life and death as two aspects of the same magical continuum, for the most part undifferentiated, and therefore, impersonal. This is not to say that we cease to need the consciousness of death as an aid to keeping our sense of proportion. We need also, perhaps, the guiltless consciousness of life as better than death, because in life, at least, one can try to do good deeds, but the dead are ethically neutral.

Osiris reminds us in still another sense that there has been a parting of the ways. His death and brief resurrection, when the dormant god turned on his side, and the waters of life were said to gush from his thigh, symbolized that man's magic nexus with the gods of nature was still unbroken. Osiris does not yet transcend nature, as later on the God of monotheism was to transvalue all "natural" values. On the contrary, Osiris personifies the human condition in its pathetic acknowledgement of its own seeming powerlessness. Like man, Osiris is nature's hostage, and reminds us that nature has a way of its own and a style of its own, which must go on eluding man. The worshippers of Osiris did not understand this on a conscious plane, and therefore could look to their redeemer as a creative innovator. The primitive initiate likewise believes that he is an equal partner with nature and that by approaching his totem in the correct spirit he can share fully its generative powers and its spontaneous force. For modern man the sources of spontaneity have dried up. Instead, it is necessary to create deliberately and consciously to preserve spontaneous-appearing modes of behavior, whether in cultural creations, such as art, or in the interpersonal sphere. In imitation of primitive man, with his stylistic sureness, modern man goes in search of "naturalness," tries to feel in himself "natural" pride or spontaneous courage. These efforts attest to the felt absence of the impulsive element in modern experience. Primitive initiation accomplishes the direct transmission of the magic in nature to one of its creatures, just as the vigil of Osiris ends in the spontaneous renewal of nature and of man's hope. Those archaic or primitive men whose feelings are in direct harmony with those of the unseen beings around them have no need to admire or cultivate spontaneity, since it is a pure given. Without any special inducement, nature expresses herself in the principle of inertness as manifested in Osiris, or in a more active sense, as in the "risen" Osiris. In an analogous way, the primitive novice sees nothing "unnatural" about spending a period of time inside the belly of his totemic ancestor, secure in the knowledge that what he is doing is good for him because it is a natural stage of growing up and becoming a twice-born man. As for modern man, it is useless to think of reviving the old Adam with his naivete and his spontaneous freedom, which was hedged about with taboos, anyway. A more worthy aim would be to discover man's true vocation, the substance of which cannot be found in nature, is unprecedented in nature, and, in a sense, is anti-nature. By seeking a mission man places himself in stubborn opposition to the fact of his mortality, refuses to share the destiny of other creatures, and ends by dreaming of humanizing nature, including his own nature.

The ancient Egyptians themselves reveal in their later, more cynical legends, their increasing psychological distance from nature as a source of wisdom, or even as the seat of the creative principle. It is no accident that Osiris, who presided over the judgment of generations of the dead and in whose name the four apes seated near his throne raised up the righteous and cast down the wicked liars, was himself accused by Seth of being an absolute fraud. It required all the exertions of the divine advocate, Thoth, to remove the horns that Seth had planted on Osiris' head and to clear him of the charge that he had falsely claimed to have begot Horus after he was dead. Needless to say, the level of sophistication implied in legends of this type sets them far apart from the unquestioning faith of primitive man. The primitive novice, even after he has been initiated and knows that the mystery is man made and that the stripes which he received were administered by mortal hands, remains incapable of acknowledging the cream of the jest.

I must return finally to the attitude toward life which, by implication, is disclosed by the obsession with death that is so basic to the cult of Osiris and the mystery of primitive initiation. I believe that we are dealing in both instances with the charisma of death, and with a corresponding devaluation of life. Professor Eliade,[8] for example, has attempted to demonstrate that myths take place in sacred time and that ritual activation of the myth enables the participant to place himself back in the stream of primordial time and to remove himself from mere duration. What is accomplished is a kind of release from the limitations of everyday life and escape into a more vivid, and in a certain sense, a more *real* plane of being, where it is possible to achieve identity with immortal gods and prototypic heroes. If this interpretation is applied to the cult of Osiris, and to the psychology of its devotees, it is evident that the worshippers compulsively approach the ceremonial gateway to death not only to wave to the shades of their departed ancestors, as it were, but also to undergo the experience of timelessness. It is paradoxical that man has had to turn toward death to live more vividly! Undoubtedly, Osiris had his being outside of secular time, and the drama of his death and reawakening was enacted under circumstances more vivid than those of ordinary duration. It is still a matter for profound wonder, however, how Osiris was able to generate his mythic aura as a mummy. Nevertheless, the specific charm of Osiris is to be found as much in the husk of Osiris as in the drama of his life—if one can be said to have lived who died so soon. I mean to say that the symbolism of Osiris, of a shrouded mummy held together by artifice, entirely hollow, brainless and gutless, inert, and unresponsive, is a perfect exteriorization of a distinct frame of mind. This outlook is a celebration of death, and involves the vicarious experience of passivity, of psychological mutilation, of impotence, of aggression turned inward, of saying "No" to everything vital. Although the awakened Osiris stands for generation the most compelling image is that of the suffering god, the Bandaged One held prisoner by a giant primordial snake in the netherworld. The effigy of Osiris is a most effective reminder of man's fate, a reminder of the mortality of everything that appears for the moment to be taking firm roots, an ominous reminder to all those who criticize life denial as being irrational and unintelligent. The so-called lasting verities to which Osiris bears witness are really primitive intuitions of fear, adumbrations of apocalypse and death.

Unfortunately, many dead souls yearn to lie down beside Osiris, believing that only death is deathless, and that self- and world-denial are the way to deliverance. Contemporary society is at the same time materialistic and ascetic, pleasure-bent and self-destructive. The spirit of Osiris is still with us, urging men on to world-renewal through suffering and death. Some would linger yet awhile in the spirit of ethical life affirmation, but the lovers of death are afraid that if man lingers on a little longer he will outgrow them, along with Osiris, and at last burst out of their intended tomb.

6

Jason and the Totem

J ASON SET out in search of his lost totemic fleece, but he returned instead with a witch and scarcely concerned himself with the fetish once it was in his possession. What is the significance of this substitution, and who was Medea really? The voyage of the Argo symbolizes an historical passage from totemism to matriarchal theology, and the Golden Fleece, though snatched with eager hands from the branches of the great oak in the sacred grove of Ares, was never again to be recovered in its full psychological meaning as a sacral object. In its place a goddess went to Greece as an incarnation of that very maiden, the earth-born Pandora, whom the tireless halting one Hephaestus, made at the behest of Zeus.

It was no mere literary device that caused Aphrodite to be the instrument for uniting Medea with Jason; both Pandora and Aphrodite are manifestations of the great earth-mother, and the legendary Medea was no less than a latter-day Pandora, a sort of tarnished mother of life. Of course, we see Medea through Olympian eyes as a mere priestess of Hecate, one who has access to

93

chthonic powers but who is nevertheless still a blushing maiden and very far indeed from being a fertility goddess. But Hecate was a threefold goddess,[1] a syncretic formation of a mother and two maidens, and so the virginal character of her priestess is in no way inconsistent with her essential function as the embodiment of the earth-mother and her priestess' vital connection with fertility. If it is recalled that Hera, Jason's champion in heaven, conspired with Aphrodite to make Medea fall in love with Jason, it is not difficult to see that in the persons of Hera, Aphrodite, and the paradoxically mortal Medea we have a triad of vegetation goddesses on the model of the Charites, or gift-bringers. The gift bestowed upon Jason and upon his Thessalian homeland was not and could not have been a totemic animal, such as Phrixus' self-sacrificing ram. Rather, it was a token, in the form of Medea, of the hegemony of Pelasgian Hera in the days before Zeus was master in his own house.

The flight of the ram carrying on his back Ino's intended victims, her stepchildren Phrixus and Helle, provides a clue as to how religious matters stood in Iolcus in the days of the presumably mythical King Pelias and his predecessor Athamas. Evidently Hera had not exhausted her wrath at the members of the royal dynasty in Iolcus, and it was the fate of Pelias to further enrage her by failing to give her the homage which she required. Ino and Pelias, though belonging to different generations, had this much in common: Both figures belong to the anti-Hera camp. In the case of Ino, a truly unpardonable offense had been committed, in comparison with which Pelias' oversight is of little significance. It had been Ino's scheme ostensibly to sacrifice her two stepchildren, but to whom? The intrusion of the ram in the sequence of events that followed, first as the savior of the children and later as a sacrificial victim, helps to link Ino's actions with the realm of the chthonioi, or earth-spirits, whom it was customary to propitiate with the ram as an offering. Ino may have come into conflict with the Queen of Heaven by attempting to perpetuate the primordial but now heretical practice of ancestor worship.

Although it seems reasonable to dismiss as extraneous and somewhat moralistic the explanation of the ram's substitution for the children as an allegory illustrating the replacement of human sacrifice by animal sacrifice, the perilous state in which the children found themselves remains a significant fact and is in need of clarification. More convincing as an explanation is Frazer's supposition that King Athamas was about to sacrifice his eldest son in his own place as a sin-offering, in keeping with the custom of the country.[2] Least plausible is the manifest context provided by the myth itself, namely, that Ino acted out of malice toward her stepchildren, and that their own mother, Nephele, provided the golden-fleeced ram to save her offspring from death.

I offer still another explanation which defines the danger faced by the boy Phrixus not as the threat of actual death but rather the imminence of symbolic death and rebirth in direct and frightful confrontation with some ancestral god of the underworld, such as the oracle of Trophonios at Lebadeia,[3] near Orchomenus. As related by Pausanias, who had personally undergone initiation into the mysteries of the underground oracle, it was the custom to sacrifice a ram into a trench on the night of the initiate's descent into the sacred grotto. After the initiate had climbed down into a pit, he was then dragged by his feet through a small opening and found himself in the presence of priests who instructed him in the mysteries.

It is plain that, like the Papuans and other primitive peoples of our time, the ancient Greeks at Lebadeia practiced initiation rites in which the novice had to submit to being swallowed by a monster, who was really the totemic representative of his ancestral ghosts, as a precondition for his spiritual renewal. Hence all the mummery about going down into a pit after having taken the precaution to placate the spirits with numerous animal sacrifices, culminating in the slaughter of a ram. It is understandable, too, why the initiate had to go back via the same route through which he had been forcibly drawn into the symbolic stomach of the totem, for by emerging from the depths of the earth by means of a small opening, the initiate was able to mimic the process of rebirth. I will not say that Phrixus—who is, after all, a make-believe character—was prevented by his mother from undergoing some specific ritual of initiation. I wish to suggest only that the

Jason legend has its beginning against a background of totemism, and, though the religious notion of the animal-as-ancestor was probably on the decline when the myth was in its formative stage, we are still a long way from the age of the Olympians.

Against the waning influences of totemism, it is necessary to posit the rise of the goddess as earth-mother, especially in her underworld aspect as the patroness of dead ancestors. The image of Medea may have been evoked by the mythmakers out of the realization that the totemic gods had taken flight or were fast fading. With her explicit links with the powers of darkness, Medea has her being partly in the world of dead souls and partly in the domain of the living as a symbol of the eternal woman. She has magical power over the sacred serpent who guards the fleece at the same time that she is a priestess of Hecate. What is the serpent but an emblem of some chthonian spirit? Symbolically enough, the serpent is overcome by the woman, not only in her aspect as a witch armed with drugs and ointments, but also in her capacity as a sweet singer, that is, in her human capacity.

Nor must we overlook the shade of Phrixus, the spirit that yearns to be laid to rest in his homeland; he reminds us that we are dealing with the familiar wrath of a dead ancestor, one who has been denied proper burial, dishonored, and forgotten. If the dead ancestors are not returned to the earth, there to work their life-giving magic as fertility spirits, the land of Iolcus cannot prosper and must suffer even the hardships of plague and famine. Phrixus is the ancestor-in-the-totem, a divine king who has had the ill fortune to die in the wrong place. It is too soon for Pelasgian Hera to take his place. As a mother-goddess in the making, she is not strong enough to promote fertility in her own right. The mythmaker senses this inadequacy and evokes a nostalgia for the lost totem. Otherwise, Jason's mission would be meaningless and would lack dramatic urgency.

I must return, however, to my central point, which is that the quest for the fleece is only a pretext for a more significant undertaking. I will not say that Jason acted in bad faith, but that unconsciously the mythical hero knew what he wanted. It is remarkable that the return of the fleece is an anticlimax, and that its restoration to Iolcus takes place without fanfare, without any noticeable enhancement of the fertility of the land, and, it need hardly be added, without ushering in a new reign of righteousness. Far from it. The fate of Pelias at the hands of Medea tells us that we are in for a new dispensation. Not only has the totem returned to its proper place, but a new force is abroad in the land. I speak now of Medea as a dissociated aspect of the early Hera, as her dark side, and as her herald approaching the twilight of totemism. Even the Queen of Heaven must first go down into the depths and be a sorceress before she can become sublime. Acting in the name of the goddess Artemis, Medea contrived to fulfill the demands of totemic ritual by sacrificing Pelias as the personification of the divine ram, the very fate that had awaited Phrixus a generation earlier. Apparently, Pelias' death was the prelude to the enactment of fertility rites, since he perished in a cauldron of regeneration.[4]

Medea's choice of the goddess Artemis as a cover for her plan of retribution against Pelias bespeaks the considerable prestige of that virgin goddess; at this point in her evolution as a divine being, Artemis may still have had her original attributes as a mother-deity. Again, it may be assumed that Artemis' charisma in Iolcus indicates how far the cult of Hera had yet to develop toward its classical apogee. Judging from Medea's Hecate-inspired improvisation of the rites of the virgin huntress, even Artemis' fame rested at this point largely on her reputation, rather than on intimate knowledge of the details of her worship. At any rate, Hera did not see fit to interfere in Medea's sanguinary deeds, and it may be conjectured by implication that Hera was still on a friendly footing with Artemis and had not yet conceived the hatred for the old fertility goddess that led her later to strike Artemis with her own bow, as described by Homer.

Artemis casts her shadow even more directly over the principals in the Jason saga at an early stage of their quest. At Pegae it was Hylas' turn to be offered up as a sacrificial victim. Upon seeing Hylas about to fill his pitcher at a spring, Dryope, one of the nymphs of Artemis, affectionately drew him down into the water and he disappeared from sight. Apparently, Hylas had been served

after the manner of Orpheus, whom the Maenads slew as a divine
priest-king whose immolation was a ritual prerequisite for the
purpose of communion with the local totemic god. As in the case
of Orpheus, the stream is intrinsic to the legend and doubtlessly
provided a means of purification for the priestesses, alias nymphs,
who had sacrificed the noble Dryopian youth. Idmon, too, though
the legend says that he was gored by a wild boar during a brief
stopover by the Argo at Mariandyne, may have perished at the
hands of the meadow spirits. Again, a reed filled stream lay close
at hand to receive the ceremonial slayers, their boar disguise
tossed aside, as they sought absolution, if not from sin, then from
blood pollution. In a sense, the gratuitous deaths of these companions of Jason indicate the need on the part of the wanderers to
offer up hostages to the complex of pre-Olympian fertility goddesses whose worship they affirm by their quest for the fleece.

The return of Medea to Iolcus is already a consolidation of the
victory of the earth-mother over the purely animalistic conception
of the totem. At that moment when the many-coiled serpent
closed his eyes, overcome by the guiles of the all-conquering
Medea, the magic powers of the earth, of the sea, of vegetation,
and of wild things passed from beasts to human deities. These
powers were naturally redolent of the dark places and the savage
animal hearts from which they had been received. No wonder
that Medea was possessed of demonic powers and encompassed
the death of her own brother Apsyrtus. Later on in her mythical
career, and finally in her depiction by Euripides on the stage, she
is transformed into the symbol of inhumanity. Medea's transformation at the hands of the mythographers is especially instructive
in throwing light on the psychological meaning of the transition
from outright totemism to worship of deities in the form of
humans disguised as animals. As goddesses of fertility displaced
the purely animal embodiments of the creative principle, they
followed in the footsteps of Medea, preserving and enlarging in
a terrifying way the animalistic nonhuman essence of their brute
predecessors. Their male equivalents (who were not their equals
at all), the divine priest-kings who served as their consorts and
who were united with them in the ceremony of the sacred mar-

riage, were frequently slain in order to insure a more perfect union. Whereas the slaying of the animal totem, however cruel and bloody, cannot be regarded as a tragic enactment, it is another matter entirely when a person dressed as the totemic animal is dealt with in an identical manner. Paradoxically, then, the humanization of religion through the introduction of anthropomorphic deities represents a regression from the standpoint of compassion.

The early fertility goddesses, like Medea herself, have need of human love, but, since they possess solely the creative and destructive passions of their prototypes in nature, they are incapable of communion in the human sense. In the long run, of course, the fertility goddesses triumphed over their own animal instincts, and the animal-in-the-deity was externalized and made a thing apart, such as the owl and the goat that are associated with Athene, or Artemis and her stag, or Hecate and her hell-hounds. In the process of evolving into frankly anthropomorphic gods, the male consorts did not succeed at first in removing the blood-stained hide of the slain totem and remained for a long time half-human and half-animal—centaurs, satyrs, and the like. With regard to such Egyptian compound deities as Hathor, Anubis, Horus, Seth, and others, representing an early stage in the progression away from totemism, both male and female deities retain prominent traces of their infrahuman origin. It needs only to be added that with the ascendancy of the patriarchal form of social organization in Greece, the fully humanized male deities appear as having outgrown their animal origins. From time to time, Zeus takes the form of some animal or other, such as a cuckoo or a quail or a ram, but only as a temporary expedient and on the same basis that Zeus disguised himself as a mortal in order to achieve worldly aims.

In maintaining that the early fertility goddesses show an affinity for the animal totems that they have replaced in their savage, death-demanding aspect, it is necessary to recognize the claims of a conflicting interpretation to the effect that the fertility goddesses came by their malevolent traits at a late stage in their evolution, after they had been dethroned and symbolically ravaged by the conquering male deities of Olympus. Starting with the latter premise, it is easy to see in the degradation of Hecate or in the dehumanization of a Medea the inevitable penalty suffered by gods and goddesses whose votaries have been defeated in political or theological wars. But, we need to understand why certain defeated deities such as Hermes in the days when he was still a manifestly phallic deity, or the revered Hestia when she was mother earth, or Aphrodite when she was a queen bee, did not degenerate into malevolent gods. The inference could be drawn, of course, that a selective factor was at work and that it determined which of the gods would turn into devils upon their demise. We know that certain gods, such as Proteus or Thetis, possess great powers of transformation and that Zeus himself, for all his glory, does not disdain to change his shape. Is it not possible that the cults of some gods retained their essential character upon being challenged by alien cults and that others were debased, to the detriment of the gods involved? I think that without in the least contradicting this line of reasoning, it may be concluded that witch goddesses such as I presume Medea to have been may have retained the animalistic traits of the animal totems whom *they* had displaced, whereas other gods and goddesses, once they began to undergo the process of humanization, never again looked back to their sinister origins, but progressed steadily toward a higher spirituality. Thus Medea, viewed as a transitional religious symbol, was bad from beginning to end and not just in the days of her decline. For this reason, it is difficult to see how a theory of the transformation of the gods that finds the dynamic basis for change in the vicissitudes of political history can provide an adequate explanation for the god making—and god unmaking—process.

By adding a psychological dimension to the study of syncretic phenomena in the history of religion, it becomes possible not only to explain the persistence of divine or demonic traits, or their transformation, but also to understand the social roles projected onto gods and goddesses. The phenomenal quality of Medea or of her foil Jason, which we cannot experience directly, is nevertheless more accessible to our modern consciousness than the phenomenal meaning of the full-blown deities, cults, priestly traditions, or oracles to which they are related as almost human godlings. How to interpret the phenomenal, as distinguished from the numinous, essence of these totemically derived but recognizably human creatures becomes an important problem and one that is no less challenging than the more familiar problem of tracing the process of god making against the panorama of historical events.

The death of Apsyrtus provides certain insights concerning the attitudes that archaic man directed toward his gods; their nature was an extension of his own nature, and their deeds represented the fulfillment of his own wishes or the consequences of his fears. It is not necessary to dwell on the fact that Apsyrtus was murdered or, more likely, sacrificed at a temple of Artemis, the fact that Medea was herself sprinkled with his blood, or the fact that Jason dismembered him, thus confirming the fertility function of the ritual slaying. It is likely that Apsyrtus, whose name means "swept down," was cast into the waters and that his body was carried downstream in the tradition of Osiris, Orpheus, and Adonis, whose images were thrown annually into the sea. Subsequently, Jason and Medea received absolution from Medea's aunt, the magnificent witch Circe, who purified them with the blood of a pig. The manner in which the murderers were released from their state of pollution seems to have a close connection with the nature of their crime. If we think of Apsyrtus as a sacrificial victim on the model of Adonis (as has been suggested), and if we relate the pig-goddess Demeter to her kindred fertility goddess Astarte-Aphrodite, it can be seen that the ritual purification of the guilty slayers by the killing of a pig is a reenactment of the sacrifice of Apsyrtus to Demeter, viewed as a personification of her ancestral totem, the prolific pig. When it is recalled that Adonis himself was probably once a pig in the old totemic days, the original slaying of Apsyrtus reveals itself as the sacrifice of a pig-substitute to a goddess with the attributes of a sow. What is the meaning of the substitution of a human victim for an animal, and why do the mythographers describe the act as one of murder? After all, it was the custom in those days periodically to slay the consort of the vegetation goddess and to call the slaughter a sacramental act.

By transposing ourselves into the phenomenal world of Jason

and Medea, we find ourselves surprisingly removed to a time and place only partly mythological, when the deliberate slaying of a human being is about to be called or is in fact already called an act of murder. Indeed, that two such ruthless characters as Jason and Medea should feel sufficient guilt over an everyday act of assassination to go in search of absolution is surprising in itself. To be sure, Medea has brought about the murder of her brother and not a stranger, yet we are not told that Medea was conscience-stricken after precipitating the death of her seven sons and seven daughters, who were stoned to death by the Corinthians. On the contrary, her next step was to marry King Aegeus of Athens, after first helping Hercules, himself the murderer of his own children, to regain the sanity which he had abandoned in the ritual of sacrificing the king's son.

The designation of a once sacramental act—in this case the killing of a human being in connection with fertility rites—as a heinous crime indicates a reversal of the planes of sacred and profane. What was once holy is now taboo, *although the same essential action continues to be carried out.* There is even a sequel of feeling guilty roughly analogous to the need for ritual purification by immersion. Have we entered a world filled with compassion, so that at last, at the dawn of classical civilization, even religiously motivated deeds that bring suffering are judged to be wrong? I do not think so, but I suspect that we have indeed set foot in the modern world defined as a place in which profane actions still deeply rooted in their sacred origins are performed with religious intensity.

Here is a reversal of the usual sequence that we associate with hypocrisy, in which pious actions flow from profane motives. It is as if Medea, thinking that she had caused Apsyrtus' death out of malice, that is, for a profane reason, had caused him to perish for sacramental motives. Logically, then, Medea should feel free of guilt and should not stand in need of Circe's ministrations. But, what an infernal priestess she has chosen for the remission of her sin. We know that Medea acts in bad faith, but we must be willing to consider the possibility that acts performed by men throughout history and understood to take place on the secular plane, out of seemingly practical considerations, have been conceived in bad faith and executed under the watchful gaze of the totem, who has blood in his eye. I am not referring to the Freudian distinction between conscious and unconscious motives, nor even to the possible influence of archetypes, as described by Jung. Neither motives arising out of the personal unconscious nor those coming from the collective unconscious have as their aim the preservation of sacred ritual in an existential world. It is precisely because the world has long been conceived in existential terms, even in the days of the Olympians, that the sacred must perforce appear in the guise of the profane, accompanied by invocations of necessity on the one hand or free will on the other.

What are those profane actions in which, to an inordinate degree, one can discern the old sacrificial butchery? I believe that the more an act or a sequence of acts shocks us as a profanation, the more likely it is that its motivational source derives from an archaic magical stratum of history. Although I agree with Professor Eliade[5] that profane man imagines himself to be a participant in human, as distinct from sacred, history, I would add that profane man is self-deceived and that he is more religious than he consciously knows himself to be. A world conceived in existential terms is one in which man can offer up neither himself nor others as a gift to the gods. Unlike the true existential hero, the ordinary profane man lacks the heroic qualities that would allow him to act as if the gods were still alive while knowing that they are dead and *is forced to act as if the gods were dead,* while knowing in his heart that he is still a man possessed by something other than himself.

We live in sacred time more than we realize, but men are ashamed to admit that they are still looking for the Golden Fleece or for the sources of magical power and fertility. Much of what we call secular life consists of sacrificial holocausts—the gift of ourselves or others—to no god in particular. On the surface, the sacrifices that men make in work, in struggle, in discovery, in loving, and in hating are all made in the name of human necessity and human ideals. To be sure, modern religion stakes out for itself certain highlights of man's existence—birth, initiation, marriage, death—and tries to imbue them with sacramental significance. Formal prayers and devotions are obviously also part of the claim of religion. It is ironic that as the shrinking domain of formal religion reveals the tell-tale signs of secularization, the expanding empire of the profane discloses the old totem in its heart. In this connection, I cannot agree with the widely held view that the ideologies of our time are the modern, secularized myths that men live by. It is not on the ideational plane that the archaic imperatives work their magic; it is on the plane of action where the old physical Adam, the Adam of the senses, is still very much at home. The modern ideologies may be viewed as systems of ideas, or as rationalizations of one sort or another, or as collections of emotionally toned slogans, or even as explicit programs of construction or destruction, but they do not provide any real clues to their significance on the plane of action. Like Jason, modern man starts by looking for the fleece and does not know that he will end by becoming a murderer and a thief. Could Aphrodite have known, when she sent Eros on his errand of invisible matchmaking, that the love for Jason that was to be engendered in Medea's breast would end in the murder of Apsyrtus?

In spite of rational ideologies and quite apart from the influence of unconscious irrational motives, man is ever prepared to respond to his environment, especially his human environment, by performing actions that have been preordained and dictated by that environment, which is where the something-other-than-the-self resides. In a certain distorted sense, there is something transcendent about the demands of the environment, as if gods and demons still invested it, demanding homage from man. But what is really demanded—by tradition, by the presumed expectations of other people, by the apparent vulnerabilities of others, by unexpected situations, by opportunities that present themselves, by the finalities that cannot be reversed, by the very seasons—is that man show the outward signs of his demonic possession, not in proof that the gods are alive, but rather that they are dead, and that their spirit has entered into his being. Regardless of his ideational starting point, man is led on by the something-other-than-the-self until he ends in profanation. The more completely modern man has identified himself with his ancestral totem, the more terrible the sacrifice of himself and others that must result. This is why the more radical oriental philosophies make so much of non-action. Their adherents have intuitively understood that action leads to pollution. No doubt, their explanations are prelogical, but I believe their philosophy is not without an empirical foundation.

Now, in speaking of the profane world as centered around the totem, it is also necessary to mention the role of ritual outside the sphere of formal religion. Apart from a few residual rites—graduation, the beginning of the New Year, housewarmings, the launching of ships—now thoroughly secularized but once sacred,[6] one must search out the ritualistic component in the most obvious areas of profane existence. For example, the interpersonal sphere provides many proofs of the ceremonial character of even the most intimate human associations, in which communication often takes place on the basis of mutual expectations flowing from prescribed social roles. Even where such roles are in a process of transition and have begun to yield to more spontaneous forms of behavior, communication continues to be confined within traditional channels of expression. Above all, interpersonal relationships continue to be deeply influenced by ceremonially derived expressive traits, stylistic poses related to social roles, patterns of deference rooted in tradition, and, increasingly, forms of social manipulation in which the impersonal aims of the mandarin are concealed by the appearance of ingenuousness. Conversely, the substantive element in human relationships—the element of genuine involvement and concern; the exchange of feelings, opinions, and beliefs; the recognition of other people in their uniqueness —are all obscured by the masque of manners, including informal manners.

Institutional arrangements reflect the transposition of ritualistic forms of behavior from the sacred to the profane plane even more strongly than relationships between individuals. It has become a truism that mass society, which had its beginning in the fragmentation of the old order with its sacred constancies, has developed its own hierarchical forms of social organization, its own commercially inspired litanies, its own spurious communion of the mass media, its own periodic rituals of blood-letting together with their facile purifications and token penances, and its own forms of hero worship. Imitating the succession of the seasons and in the same spirit of compulsion found in archaic religion, mass society produces its vernal floods of activity, production, and forced enthusiasm and its slack seasons of demoralization and insecurity. I say that society produces these changes in the consciousness of its members because man has not broken his magical links with nature, which is not visibly progressive, and so feels compelled to seek, through his collective life, the dual elements of growth and decay. Eschatological psychology exerts a potent influence in the profane life of mass society with its portents of ecological disaster, nuclear war, and economic collapse. As for the task of averting disaster, it is often pursued in a ritualistic spirit, with symbolic actions and sanctimonious prayers, rather than by more direct or effective means.

The great failing of Jason and Medea is that, even using ritual for their profane purposes, they are still unable to rediscover the old totem as a sacral object external to themselves. The return of the Golden Fleece to Iolcus is all for naught; the legend is not even clear as to whether Jason won or lost the kingdom that was to be his reward after enduring so many hardships. The historical rise of mother goddesses of the type of Demeter or Artemis, or the coming of their virginal successors, such as Athene, points clearly to the eclipse of the animal totem. It is Medea's mission to bear witness to the mere thing-like quality of the Fleece, which retains but a shadow of its former magical power and can perform no wonders comparable to Medea's feats. If we think of Medea as a personification of the old totem and if we regard the serpent which she overcame as having been assimilated to her human form, it becomes possible to understand why Jason's quest was bound to fail. Every profanation of Medea's is a ritualistic effort to exorcise the animal-in-the-goddess. Neither can the totem be recovered as an external object, in the old sense of an animal ancestor, nor is he yet ready to relinquish his hold. This is why Medea is a witch. Her one virtuous quality—that she resists Zeus' advances—is emblematic of her vice; she chooses to remain profane and eschews union with the divine.

Unlike the other gods and goddesses who wear their shaggy aegis on the outside to announce to believers and unbelievers alike that they have indeed slain the totemic animal whose hide they have appropriated, Medea is the very vessel of the totem. Like Medea, profane man wears his totem on the inside and unknowingly carries the sacred charge into every morass, every pit, every charnel house of his existence on the plane of temporality. I am not talking about a devil-in-the-flesh that compels man to perform deeds which the doer himself knows to be evil. My reference is rather to the pagan god trapped in the human skin, the special devil who leads man to do evil deeds which the doer half-suspects to be sacramental. Hence, profane man does not need to know the meaning of remorse; that which others call evil and which profane man himself agrees is evil, he understands with another part of his being to be a religious necessity and not a sin.

The religion of everyman is to lead a profane life, not because he despairs of attaining to spirituality, but because he senses that every act of desecration is pleasing to the gods and that every holocaust carries the smell of sanctity straight up to Olympus. Profane man, then, has a divine model of his own, and being faithful to it—that is, abasing himself before the totem and listening to his own voice—he is barred from transcending the limits posed by temporal existence. Thus profane man lives and dies by the grace of his totemic gods; being earth-born and immanent in nature, his gods cannot lead him toward the spiritual plane and cannot imbue him with a transcendent ethic. Such an ethic aims at the replacement of the hedonistic imperatives of nature by the ethical imperatives of man's condition. Those who cherish such a humanized ethic, having lived all along without the blessing of the totemic gods, are prepared to die without the grace of these gods.

7

The Ramayana
and Ram Lila

W HETHER THE Ramayana of Valmiki[1] is regarded as a pure fable, as an embellished historical chronicle, as an edifying moral discourse, or, as Aubrey Menen has suggested in his satirical version of that epic,[2] as a corruption of a genuine expression of early skepticism, it is still necessary to account for its enormous religious appeal. I do not wish to imply that the Ramayana contains any hidden religious symbols nor that it is a self-conscious allegory. Nor would I insist that the religious ambience of the Ramayana, whether viewed as a sacred text, or, in its Ram Lila[3] aspect, as a devotional performance, justifies the modern interpretation of the epic as a struggle between good and evil.

My view is simply that the Ramayana is a religious myth and, as such, contains a considerable ritual substructure, some of which is apparent in the thematic content of the traditional story, and some of which survives, though partially secularized, in "Hari's play," the Ram Lila. The psychological meaning of the Ramayana —that is to say, its significance for those who allow themselves to be touched by its human triumphs or tragic defeats—is to be found, accordingly, neither in its artistic or literary merits nor in its spectacular appeal as a sort of morality play, but in its functional relationship to Hinduism as a whole and to the orientation of the Vaisnavite sects in particular.

I refer to the devotees of Visnu because the hero of the Ramayana, Ramcandra, was an avatar or incarnation of Visnu. As the legend relates, Rama was commissioned by the gods to save the universe from the power of the evil demon Ravana, who, by dint of great austerities and penances, had extorted from Brahma, the creator, not only the power to destroy the world, but also the boon of invulnerability to the gods themselves. Since only a mortal man could vanquish Ravana, it was necessary for Visnu to assume the form of the earthly prince Rama. The epic then goes on to tell how Rama performed various prodigies—how he won the hand of the furrow-born princess Sita; how he endured many years of exile with the faithful Sita as well as his brother Laksman at his side; how Sita was carried off by Ravana; and how, at last, Ravana was destroyed. Taken by themselves, the legendary or partly historical events that make up the Ramayana fail to reveal the essentially religious nature of the myth. As I will try to demonstrate, the dynamic tension in the myth is between the forces of creation and destruction—between the cosmic principle, Sakti,[4] and the life-denying principle whose epiphany, paradoxically enough, is the phallic god Siva. This struggle did not take place in the past nor was it resolved once and for all when Rama triumphed over the many-headed Ravana, thus ushering in the Golden Age, or Ramraj; the contest between Visnu, the preserver, and Siva, the destroyer, takes place every season. Each autumn Rama is fated to lose Sita to Ravana; Ravana, all in black, enfolds her in his deadly embrace, thereby forestalling that divine union which alone can renew the chain of being. Does it really matter that I choose to associate the Sakti principle of female fecundity with Sita, the consort of Rama/Visnu, rather than with Parvati, who must be the real consort of Ravana/Siva, the weeping Mandedari notwithstanding? One could as easily speak of the fertility goddess Durga-Sakti in her fearful aspect of Kali and place her in opposition to the world-maintaining Visnu and his

benevolent consort Laksmi. Either way, the polarity of nature
aborning on the one hand and nature dying on the other needs
to be recognized.

The gods and devils of the Ramayana are manifestations of a
single divine spirit; that spirit makes no distinction between good
and evil, between the old and the new, or between the slayer and
the slain. It is the seasonal nature of the Ram Lila enactments,
as a prominent part of the harvest festival of Dasahra,[5] that links
the Ramayana to nature and the sacralities that attach themselves
to the rhythms of nature. Just as the sugarcane is harvested during
the Dasahra season, so is the barley seed committed to the earth.

Of course, the Ramayana is too sophisticated a work to concern
itself with nature in its generative aspect, and its rich descriptions
of nature are framed in esthetic terms. The business of an epic,
after all, is to portray heroic characters performing great deeds.
But, transposed to the Ram Lila setting, which is in every way
devotional, those same figures assume their proper sacral character as living representatives of the gods within the framework of
folk religion. In these roles, the leading actors are adolescent
Brahman boys;[6] they are worshiped by the spectators, who give
gifts to Rama upon the occasion of his wedding to Sita and his
consecration as king. Their connection with nature is less obvious
than their role as objects of ritual veneration. The cosmogenic
element in the Ramayana (as well as in the Ram Lila) is easier
to discern by viewing the major and minor characters and the
elaboration of the plot against the background of the many seemingly irrational deviations from the main story line—the intru-
sions, as it were, of irrelevant gods, demons, men, and animals.
These intrusive figures are supplemented in the Ram Lila by
various pageants, processions, ceremonials, benedictions and
other forms of spectator participation that seem to broaden the
scope of the performance enormously. It is precisely these apparently extraneous components that provide the cosmogonic perspective that has been all but obscured in the progressive refine-
ment of the Ramayana along literary lines by Tulsi Das and
others.

What is the significance, at the very outset of the Ram Lila

performance, of the dramatized wedding of Siva with Parvati?[7]
How does this event tie in with Siva's slaying of Kamadeva,[8] who
had tried to make him fall in love with Parvati? Rather than to
dismiss these episodes as interpolations, it may be useful to consider the ways in which Siva hovers like a shadow over the
Ramayana and, from the very beginning, imposes his presence, in
spite of the fact that we are ever within the sphere of Vaisnava
piety. Why, for example, is it necessary to commence a Ram Lila
performance with a marriage ceremony—and with Siva's wedding, at that? I believe that answers to the above questions and
other related inquiries must be formulated in terms of a single
unorthodox assumption, namely, that the story of Rama and Sita
is really a Vaisnava re-creation of certain legends that pertain to
Siva and Parvati. To begin with, I will describe a number of
more-than-incidental parallels between the legendary lives of Sita
and Parvati, and of Rama and Siva. I will then return to the
question of the ritual substructure of the Ramayana myth and
consider the thesis, hinted at earlier, that the ritualistic core of
the Ramayana is a sacred marriage. The various untoward events
which constitute much of the dramatic content of the epic will
be reinterpreted as mythological analogues of the dreaded perils
attendant upon the performance of sacred rites. In essence, the
Ramayana will be approached as a story of star-crossed lovers
whose hardships may be viewed as a literary treatment of the
impediments encountered in insuring the efficacy of fertility rites.

First of all, the goddess Parvati bears a striking resemblance in
point of origin to the quasi-divine Sita; both figures are daughters
of the earth. In the case of Parvati, in her earliest incarnation as
Uma,[9] she is plainly a daughter of the king of the mountains,
Himavat. Not only is Parvati a mountain goddess, but she is also
worshiped as a symbol of motherhood. In relation to Siva, she is
the active or creative principle and, as such, the emblem of
fertility. For her part, Sita may be taken as a representative of the
ubiquitous earth-mother who at last received her with open arms,
taking her back into the ground from which she had so mysteri-
ously appeared while her father was ploughing. The account of
Sita's birth, though replete with sexual symbolism, is strangely

similar to a description left by a European observer in which he
describes certain tribal customs that are alleged to have existed a
few hundred years ago in the forests of the Malabar region.[10]
Among the aboriginal inhabitants of this district, it was the general practice for the mother of a newborn baby to dig a shallow
trench in the earth and to leave her infant there daily, unguarded,
while she went off to look for food. Whether the description of
Sita's birth derives from the dim memory of such an archaic
practice or whether we are dealing with a reference to her character as an earth-goddess—or even if the manner of her birth is a
reminder of the widespread primitive belief that infants are born
out of the earth and that their spirit enters the mother's body
directly from their natural abode in the ground, in the trees, or
in the water—it is clear that Sita's connection with the earth-
mother is basic to her identity.

Uma, the first incarnation of Parvati, and Sita have in common
their commitment to the principle of asceticism. Uma not only
gave herself up to a life of contemplation, but performed various
austerities, such as fasting. As a result of her self-mortification,
Uma achieved divine wisdom. Sita also enters upon a life of
self-denial in the jungle, wandering from hermitage to hermitage
with Rama and dressed, like him, in the rough bark clothes of an
anchorite. Her qualities of character, like those of Uma, attest to
her excellence and, above all, to her wholehearted devotion to
spiritual ideals. Sita's renunciation of a life of ease was dictated
by her love for the banished Rama and by her deep wish to share
his hardships. Parvati, too, had courted many hardships as primordial Uma in order to be worthy of Siva. Although Parvati's austerities were performed during two separate incarnations, Sita was
destined to undergo the privations of an ascetic life at the beginning and again at the end of her married life, since in the Uttara-
Kanda or Supplement to the Ramayana proper we are told that
Rama sent her off to an hermitage in the forest in order to appease
his subjects, who claimed that Sita had been compromised by her
stay under Ravana's roof.

Still another legend related in the Adhyatma version[11] of the
Ramayana explicitly identifies Sati with the Kali incarnation of

Parvati. In this version of the story, Sati transforms herself into the formidable Kali and, under that aspect, defeats Ravana after Rama, overcome by weeping, admits that Ravana has proven more than a match for him. Curiously enough, Kali does not revert directly to her mortal form as Sati; instead, intoxicated by the blood of the slain giant which she had imbibed, she dances furiously, threatening to destroy the whole universe with her pounding feet. Not until Siva prostrated himself on the ground and got in the way of Kali's whirling movements did she halt her gyrations, thereby sparing the world. Only then did Kali once again become the sweet and harmless Sita. Since, in her excitement, Kali scattered the remains of the lifeless Ravana in every direction—that is, all over the fields—it is possible that this episode represents a mythical transformation of a fertility rite not unlike the Khond sacrifice of Meriahs[12] and similar practices in many other societies in the past.

As difficult as it is to imagine that Sita and Kali are even remotely related, the connection between them is consistent with the syncretic principle which underlies the formation of gods with dual and even multiple personalities. In a sense, Sita's goodness is no farther removed from Kali's awfulness than is the wise and beneficent nature of Parvati; Parvati *is* Kali or at least represents an important psychological side of the syncretic complex, Uma-Sati-Parvati-Kali-Durga. Sita seems to stand in the same relation to the Great Goddess of fertility as to the Kula Yoginis[13] or fairies who live in trees and who are described in some texts as gentle and full of grace. These beautiful spirits of vegetation are local representations of Durga-Sakti and are worshiped in the extremely ancient cult of the tree. The apposition of woman and sacred tree is depicted in what seems to be an incidental picturesque way in the Ramayana in the scene in which Hanuman, Rama's emissary to the imprisoned Sita in Ravana's palace, proceeds to tear up the Asoka grove outside the demon's palace. Hanuman destroys everything in the garden except the Asoka tree under which Sita is resting, leaving us with a tableau which is surely more religious than literary in its underlying motif. But, a moment before Hanuman's discovery of himself to Sita, the scene

in the Asoka garden had contained a third iconographic element
—the presence of the demonic tempter, Ravana, urging Sita to
yield to him and threatening her with death. How reminiscent of
Eve, standing beside the Tree of Knowledge and listening to still
another tempter. The analogy must not be overdrawn, however.
Although both Sita and Eve stand for life, Sita clings to her
innocence and is not ready to experience Eve's fatal illumination.
In the Ramayana, we are still at the threshold of the Kali-Yuga,[14]
the corrupt age of iron, and the spirit is everywhere triumphant
over the phantoms and illusions that grow out of man's immersion
in the mundane condition.

If Sita is truly linked with the forces of vegetation and with the
spirits of the trees and of the earth, why is she defended by the
vulture Jatayus who, like his winged father Garuda,[15] is the vehicle of Visnu in his special aspect as a sky-god? If, as I have
suggested, Sita's real affinity is for Parvati and Siva, her champion
ought to be a serpent, the proper emblem for Siva and the symbol
of the life-giving properties of the moist earth that snakes inhabit.
Assuming for the moment that the fierce contest between Jatayus
and Ravana that took place when Jatayus tried to stop the giant
from abducting Sita in his flying car was a restatement of the real
as well as of the mythopoeic enmity between serpent and bird,[16]
it is hard to see why the victory is given in a Vaisnavite narrative
at least temporarily, to the king of the giants in the earth. Moreover, this demonic king has the essential snake-like quality of
self-rejuvenation; as soon as Rama shoots off one of his many
heads or numerous arms, another member takes its place. Ravana
even looks like the many-headed snakes that are still inscribed on
nagalkals, or stone votive tablets that are erected under holy trees
by women who desire offspring. It must be noted that Jatayus'
destruction by Ravana is totally inconsistent with the Indian
tradition that views Garuda, the snake-destroying bird, as the
conquering principle.

Zimmer[17] provides a possible clue to this unusual situation in
his analysis of the mediating, as distinguished from conquering
role of Visnu, the Preserver of the Universe. It is no part of
Visnu's function, as Zimmer points out, to resolve once and for

all the necessary tension between the various forces of nature, but to see to it rather that life on earth is sustained and that the powers of destruction are restrained without being eliminated. Illustrating this point, Zimmer recounts the legend in which Visnu in his Krsna incarnation overcomes the serpent-king Kaliya, but spares his life and banishes him from the inland waterways to the ocean.[18]

At any rate, far from being the end of the struggle between Rama and the king of the raksasas, or demonic host, Ravana's victory over Jatayus was but a preliminary event or stage-setting for subsequent encounters, the outcome of which was a foregone conclusion. Just as Rama's ultimate victory is preordained, so is Ravana's transgression a part of his destiny which neither Jatayus nor any other creature can alter. This is why the mythographer makes Brahma the Creator cry out, upon seeing Ravana make off with Sita, "Sin is consummated!" By this exclamation Brahma gives us to know that the machinery of retribution—or redemption—has been set in motion. To make matters worse, Ravana's sin goes beyond the limits of immorality and has cosmological implications. The act of flying through the air with Sita—a feat that presents no great problem to a magician of Ravana's stature —is at the same time an abduction, a magical flight, and an expression of mystical liberation. It must be remembered that Ravana is in his own way a great yogin, one who has proved his powers and overawed the gods themselves by standing on his head for many years in the midst of raging fires. Now the presumptuous demon ascends to the heavens.

It is not clear whether Ravana has acquired the ability to fly— to "soar" as it were—because he has achieved liberation by means of meditation and austerities or whether his flying car is a clever illusion. The gods, of course, have nothing to fear from the great necromancer in his capacity as trickster, but they stand to lose everything if, as I have indicated, Ravana's power to fly is due to his mastery of yoga, and constitutes a mystical breakthrough from the realm of maya, or illusion—wherein even the most powerful magicians must languish—into the realm of spiritual liberation and the home of the gods.[19] It is significant that Rama, who is presumably no less than the almighty Visnu himself, cannot pursue his antagonist through the air, but remains earth-bound, wandering forlornly through the jungle in search of Sita and pathetically asking the trees—the jasmine, the rose apple, the mango, and the bell tree—if they have seen his Sita. That he should address himself to the trees is consistent with the idea that Sita is a manifestation of the fertility goddess and that her epiphany takes place in connection with the tree cult.

Ravana's flight with Sita suggests an obvious psychoanalytic interpretation in keeping with the cosmological significance of Ravana's ravishment of Sita. The sexual symbolism of flying is fairly obvious, or has become obvious as a result of the work of Freud and others on the relationship between personal and mythical symbols and the unconscious. It is equally apparent that Sita's ravishment by the Hydra-like Ravana constitutes an affirmation of the fertility principle. According to a Bengali account,[20] Ravana was a devotee of Durga, the Great Mother, whom he worshiped in the spring. Seeing that Durga had taken up Ravana's cause, and wishing to enlist her formidable powers in his own behalf, Rama began to worship her in the autumn. The fertility goddess thereupon came to Ramcandra's assistance.

To this day, Durga's great festival occurs most often in the autumn. Ravana's connection with the cult of Durga, to say nothing of his designs upon Sita, attest to his carnality and stand in strong contrast with the chaste Rama, whose union with Sita throughout their long banishment is a barren one. Sita's abduction, viewed against the background of her sterile marriage to Rama, can no longer be regarded in purely moralistic terms. It is not "sin" that has been consummated; it is rather the Sakti principle that has been reaffirmed, although in an irregular manner. The snake-like Ravana, libidinous, self-regenerating, and devoted to Durga-Sakti, is assisted in the early phase of his struggle with Rama by no less than Siva himself and wears a mask that scarcely conceals his true identity as the blue-necked god Siva. Siva is to this day adored in the form of the lingam, or phallic symbol. Siva speaks through Ravana and promises to fulfill the destiny of the fertility goddess in mortal form, Sita. We are told

in the Bala-Kanda, or first book of the Ramayana, that Rama had
won Sita by not only bending the enormously powerful bow of
Siva, but by actually breaking it, thereby blocking the energies of
creation and regeneration, of which Siva's arrow, like the lingam,
is the vehicle. Rama was not put on earth to usurp the vitalizing
function of the divine bowman, but merely to confine the destructiveness of the yogi-god in his evil Ravana aspect.

It is true that Ramcandra, like Siva, is presented as an intrepid
archer as well as a forest-dwelling anchorite, but he lacks the
essential life-giving powers which Siva possesses and which alone
can make his marriage with Sita a fruitful one. It is no accident
that Ravana appears to Sita in the jungle in the guise of a hermit
who practices austerities in the wilderness. Siva's natural milieu
is in the forest among the animals, of which he is the patron. He
is also the god of ascetics, and so it is natural for Ravana to present
himself to Sita as a wandering holy man. The ascetic side of Siva,
as of Ravana, is but a single aspect of that complex character. Just
as, in his capacity as a fertility god, Siva delights in singing,
ecstatic dancing, intoxication, and sex—in short, in the unre-
strained release of energy—so Ravana, too, is quick to cast off his
hermit's weeds and to stand revealed in the presence of Sita as
a magnificent Prince of Darkness who is done with penances and
ready for the kind of self-assertion which will call for new penances in the future. In Rama's case, the role of ascetic which he
assumes has a different significance and seems to symbolize in a
fitting way the barrenness of his union with Sita.

The meaning of the ascetic orientation to nature is to be found
in the psychological attitude of ambivalent surrender to the forces
of death, destruction, and barrenness. The anchorite in his tomb-
like cave in the forest or in the lifeless desert celebrates the
principle of death, or not-living, while seeming to be alive. His
ambivalence toward death and toward nature in her wintry aspect
shows itself in his quest for magical life-giving powers through
meditation, intense absorption, yogic self-discipline, auto-intoxi-
cation, and, finally, self-inflicted cruelties that are designed to take
him outside of himself so that he can achieve fusion with his god.
Unfortunately, Rama is caught in this death spell of asceticism,

and, though he does not carry his austerities to great lengths, he remains throughout the greater portion of the Ramayana an unproductive and resourceless hero.

Rama's commitment to a life of asceticism was not a self-determined act, but was an externally imposed condition of his banishment. However, his initial impulse was to go into exile without Sita. It is Sita who pleads to be allowed to share his banishment. There is, then, some element of ambivalence on Rama's part toward his loving wife. Rama's uncertain feelings are more clearly expressed toward the end of the story when he treats Sita with unmistakable coldness, after having gone through great dangers to rescue her from her captor. Finally, he asks her to undergo the dreaded ordeal by fire in order to prove that she was faithful to him while she was in Ravana's power.

In the seventh book, or Uttara-Kanda, Sita is again asked to prove her innocence after a lapse of many years, but she declines this time and returns to mother earth at her own request. Only once does Rama allow himself to be truly moved, to be more human than divine, to be more like Siva than Visnu, and to show his love for Sita by his desperate, despairing search for his missing wife. Siva, too, had once acted in the same manner, when his wife, in the form of Sati, had sacrificed herself in the fire for the sake of her husband's honor. Siva, grief-stricken and fainting with pain at his loss, rushed at length like a wild man through the jungle until the gods took pity and, mingling their tears with his, promised him that Sati would be reborn soon in the form of Parvati.[21]

If Rama became a hermit half-unwillingly, it must be remarked that Ravana set about his mission wholeheartedly, so that not even Siva could restrain him. At first, Siva appeared to Ravana in the form of a dwarf resembling a monkey and warned him that he would be overcome by swarms of monkeys if he provoked Rama. Ravana, certain of his own strength, tried to pick up a mountain to convince Siva of his might, but Mahadeva forced the mountain down with an effortless pressure of his toe. Angered that the demon should have questioned his judgment in the first place, Siva crushed Ravana in his arms for a thousand years before he released him.[22] It is not easy to say whether this is a case of enforced intimacy bordering on identity or whether the antagonism is real and originates in a true polarity between god and devil.

Notwithstanding the warning he had received, Ravana overcomes the scruples of the forest-dwelling fiend Maricha and sends him forth as a counterfeit golden-tinted deer to distract Rama so that Sita will be left unguarded. The choice of a deer disguise is interesting in the light of Siva's long-standing connection with the beasts of the forest—he is known as Siva-Pasupati, Lord of Beasts—and is reminiscent of a carving discovered at Mohenjo-daro which shows an unmistakable prototype of Siva seated on a throne with two deer at his feet.[23]

What is the explanation for Ravana's steadfastness of purpose? To say simply that he is a mythological demon whose base nature leads him to carry off a beautiful princess is tantamount to forcibly abstracting the Ramayana from its historical and cultural contexts. It is important to see both Ravana and Sita, superficially so different in that one is a beauty and the other a beast, as literary embodiments of the historic resistance of the popular, pre-Vedic fertility cults to the process of Hinduization. Ramcandra, the incarnation of the essentially Apollonian Visnu, has a customary serenity—though he is far from resembling the rude Vedic gods—and is nevertheless representative of the virtues of a sublimated Brahmanism. The real contest of the Ramayana is between Visnu, the successor in his moral qualities and in his stability to the Vedic Varuna, and Siva, who is more patently the successor and no doubt the predecessor as well of the violent Rudra of the Vedic period. The object of their contest is to gain possession of the life force, call her Sita, Laksmi, Sakti, or by any other name. The defeat of Ravana might lead one to conclude that the aboriginal gods were successfully assimilated to Brahmanism. If we think of Visnu in his Ramcandra aspect as typifying the sublimated qualities of the Vedic pantheon—the gods of the conquerors—and if we recall Sita's tragic end in the Uttara-Kanda, it is clear that the Ramayana does not end with a clear-cut victory for the spirit of Brahmanism.

Sita's descent back into the earth tells us that the popular fertility cults, the worship of the Sakti principle, and the whole complex of vegetation religion—all of which predated the religious innovations of the Vedic and post-Vedic cults—held their own in the face of priestly Brahmanic influences. The persistence of the cult of Siva and Parvati and the great popularity of the mother goddess Kali-Durga, attest to the power of the primordial pair to hold the imagination of the masses of India. What about Visnu and Laksmi and their viability? After all, they are the nominal winners in the Ramayana, and they are supposedly the divine sources of Rama and Sita. What they lack, however, and what Siva and Kali possess to an almost unbelievable degree, is the monstrous aspect, which is their psychological link with Ravana. Siva and Kali have a marvelous affinity for everything that is grotesque, degraded, ghoulish, and "unnatural." Their haunts are in the outskirts of towns, in the cemeteries, on remote mountaintops, and in the midst of tangled jungles. Their powers of fascination reside in no small part in their hideousness; they are personifications of the Id, of the unconscious, of the irrational, and of the criminal. Was not Siva guilty of the sin of Brahmanicide when he cut off the fifth head of Brahma? For this crime he was banished from civilization and doomed to carry in his hand forever the severed head of Brahma. Luckily, he received absolution in the holy city of Benares, though he had to adopt the life of a homeless mendicant. In all probability, Siva, in some aboriginal form or other, had been a god of the wild places from the beginning and a symbol of the lawless, untamed, and nonhuman aspects of the environment. His son Kartikeya is in fact the mythological god of thieves, as well as being a war god.

The absolute badness of Ravana, like the heedless, gratuitous destructiveness of Siva and the blood-thirstiness of Kali, is psychologically more convincing than the absolute goodness of Rama. In this respect, the villains of Indian mythology are interchangeable with the heroes of Greek and Roman epics. In a sense, they are superior to those heroes because the mythographer, to the limited extent that he develops their character, does not endow them with the slightest heroic pretensions, so that we know all along that they are exponents of evil. In the case of such Greek heroes as Odysseus, Achilles, Jason and many others whose representative acts are destructive and contain as well an unmistakable sadistic component, psychological realism is approximated but never fully attained, because the story is told mainly from the self-justifying point of view of mythological figures who become heroes because they happen to be the victors and not the vanquished.

Possibly, neither ethical nor psychological yardsticks should be applied to the heroes and villains of mythology. Their struggles, particularly as portrayed in the Ramayana, pertain to crises in the natural order rather than in the social order. It would be an error, for example, to ascribe the motive of moral indignation to the boys who, toward the end of the Ram Lila performances and associated spectacles, rush upon the improvised stage or field and tear to pieces the paper and bamboo fort of Ravana. Similarly, it would be a distortion to label as expressions of righteous joy the cries of "Victory to Ramcandra!" that enthusiastic audiences address to the actors in the Ram Lila. It is all ritual—religious point and counterpoint—and every battle is a dance.

The protagonists of the Ramayana do not represent good and evil so much as the polarities of the life process; creation and destruction, separation and sacred reunion, and the ebb and flow of life are typified in the events of the Ramayana. When Rama's brother Laksman is seriously wounded by the demon Meghnad, he is not brought low by any ordinary weapon, but by a magic device, the sakti. Sakti is nothing less than the vital principle of Durga—the great mother, the patroness of Ravana, the dark lady who can awaken the energies of the cosmos with the touch of her foot or sever the thread of life with her scissors. Kali shows her death dealing powers in the heart of the Ram Lila wedding procession of Rama and Sita when she jumps down from her float and menaces the spectators with a sword.[24] Siva and Parvati are also represented in the wedding procession—strange guests indeed, at a Vaisnava festival!

Less strange in view of the fact that Sita is referred to over and over again in the Ram Lila as mother, for who is "mother" but

Parvati, Kali, Durga, etc.? The hordes of monkeys led by Hanuman are the children of mother nature, engendered by the wind
and by the rain and dwelling in the forests. Hanuman's knowledge
of nature enables him to bring back medicinal herbs from the
far-off Himalayas in order to save the lives of the stricken Rama
and his brother and to bring back to life countless fallen Vanars,
Rama's loyal warriors. The armies of monkeys and bears that
appear magically and place themselves at the disposal of Ramcandra are not poetic substitutes for aboriginal tribes that helped the
Vedic invaders conquer India; they are the sylvan creatures, the
satyrs, the genii that represent the beneficient and fruitful aspects
of nature; they are the gift of mother, of Durga-Sakti, to Rama,
now that it is his turn to revitalize the energies of the cosmos, just
as Ravana's demons and giants, when the planting season was
young, and it was seed time, were nature's boon to him. In
relation to Rama and Sita, the animal hosts symbolize the forces
of generation, ready for a new season and a fresh start now that
the harvest has been safely gathered.

The marriage of Siva and Parvati at the start of the Ram Lila
series is part of this same grand commencement. The flame worship associated with the Ram Lila performances reminds us that
we are in the presence of a fertility rite and that, according to the
ancient Brahmanical usage, fire is the product of the union of the
male and female principles. The slain Ravana and his vanquished
hosts are emblematic of Siva and Kali in their destructive phase;
once benign, they are now, at season's end, burnt-out spirits,
menacing devils who must be put to rout lest they invade the
granaries and spoil the harvest. Perhaps Siva was in this deadly
state when Kamadeva shot him with his arrow of love so that he
would respond to Parvati's charms. The great yogi-god became
angered while mourning for his lost Sati and reduced the Indian
Cupid to ashes with one glance of his frightful third eye. How the
ascetic Siva thrashed about, wounded by love, trying vainly to
contain his feelings! It was no use; as the stricken Siva fled
through the forest, the very wives of the holy men who lived there
deserted their saintly husbands to be with the awakened god.

Is it unreasonable to suppose that Siva's awakening, like Rama's victory, can take place only by a casting out of devils who, at the start of the planting season, were themselves on the side of the angels? Let the quickened Siva be Visnu or let him be Rama; let Parvati take off her ugly Kali mask and turn into wealth-giving Laksmi or into gentle Sita. It is all the same; angelic hosts and monstrous devils, gods and anti-gods are all part of the eternal flux, and all are a part of each other in an undifferentiated cosmos. For this reason there is no suffering in the Ramayana. Even noble Sita, a martyr to the end, leaves this world in the knowledge that she has fulfilled her role in the cosmological scheme by producing the twins Kusa and Lava during her second banishment. What one might be tempted to call suffering in the Ramayana is really pathos. The modern age, Kali-Yuga, the age of dissention and of unreconciled opposites, has not yet begun. Day still follows night with certainty; the seasons flow into each other without hindrance; and the Tree of Knowledge, whose fruit consist of understanding the difference between good and evil, between suffering and nonsuffering, remains untouched.

8

Female Initiation Rites

THE CONTEMPORARY study of folktales is marred by nothing so much as the absence of conceptual frames of reference. Instead, we are provided with endless classifications of motifs taken out of their story contexts and treated in the most superficial manner. All attempts at etiological explanations are dismissed as either farfetched or irrelevant. Psychological interpretations of folktales are similarly out of fashion. I have the impression that folklorists wish to preserve their numerous variants of stories from the profaning consequences of analysis and that they are pleased to contemplate the disorder of their field as if sheer multiplicity were an end in itself.

The contention that the folklorist must be guided primarily by his data conceals a certain timidity, despite its apparent reasonableness. Data have no meaning of their own, and if the folklorist comes to his task intellectually unprepared and piously smug because he has never committed the sin of deductive reasoning, his mania for collecting will not lead him toward understanding. This is precisely the condition of folkloristic inquiry today; it stands in sore need of broad theory and of painstaking efforts to relate the many-layered content of folktales to the serious preoccupations of real people, both past and present, living in a variety of cultures. The fact that the ambitious theories of the past—such as the solar interpretations that were in vogue nearly one hundred years ago, or the more recent psychoanalytic theories—have suffered from overgeneralization does not mean that the only alternative is a suspension of the imagination. In a real sense, past monomythic interpretations of folkloristic materials represent the first systematic attempts to make order out of chaos; moreover, these attempts have quickened empirical research at the same time that they have generated searching hypotheses. But, where the monomyths tried to encompass too many facts in too restricted a schema, the present situation in folklore leads to the neglect of all abstract formulations and precludes the possibility of partial synthesis. Limited theories are badly needed if the study of folklore is to be saved from sinking into antiquarianism and from the overvaluation of the parts of the discipline in relation to the rational whole.

The entire domain of magical thinking has been neglected too long as a source of insights into folktales, especially as found in archaic religious rites. Although Saintyves[1] has made a promising start in this direction in his highly original analysis of Perrault's tales, his contribution has been ignored as speculative. I propose to continue Saintyves' line of inquiry, speculative or not, and, to make matters worse, I will use psychoanalytic concepts wherever I think they can be helpful. The present chapter deals mainly with a collection of old French fairy tales compiled by the Comtesse de Segur.[2] I have selected these tales because in each instance a consistent theme is developed from beginning to end, accompanied by a rich elaboration of seemingly incidental—almost decorative—details. Admittedly, we are dealing here with a highly polished literary treatment of ancient stories. In addition, patently "primitive" or "savage" details are not present to a conspicuous degree. No effort has been made to pick stories simply because they contain visible survivals of barbaric customs. In fact, the present collection is distinguished by its freedom from the violence and cruelty that abound in folktales generally. It is this quality of restraint that provides the first clue as to the general drift of the five stories in question.

In their modern form, the stories—"Blondine," "Good Little Henry," "Princess Rosette," "The Little Gray Mouse," and "Ourson"—have been given an unmistakable cautionary, moralistic flavor. This quality explains in part the relatively "civilized" tone of these stories, but it is not the complete explanation. Discounting the fact that the protagonist of "Good Little Henry" is obviously a boy, the stories seem to be about girls, and even Henry is cast in the role of a girl; he keeps house for his mother and does sweeping, cooking, and sewing. The absence of blood and thunder, among other things, suggests that the narratives in question are stories designed for the edification of girls and may have something to say about the psychology of women.

My thesis is that the present collection provides a series of allegories of female initiation. As I will try to make clear, a story may emphasize one or another phase of the initiation process, so that a complete cycle of initiation crises—spiritual death, exile, esoteric instruction by the dead ancestors in totemic form or in some other guise, rebirth, and finally marriage—is not evident in each story. The stories nevertheless seem to be made up of psychologically similar motifs at the same time that they defy classification into a single type, along the lines laid down by Aarne, Thompson,[3] et al. The inadequacies of the conventional index of tale types are well known and need not concern us here. The motif index is likewise unsatisfactory, depending as it does on purely logical resemblances that fail to take into account the functional role of the motif in its story context. In this collection, different motifs appear in psychologically related stories and derive their common significance from their functional and symbolic affinities, rather than from surface similarities.

I do not venture to say anything with certainty about the historical connection between initiation rites and the thematic content of folktales. It is possible to speculate, for example, that the crises of the folktale are all that remain of what were once real crises as exemplified by the rites of passage, and that as the latter ceased to be acted out ritualistically, they were preserved in verbal form as a means of maintaining influence over the young. Another possibility is that with the desacrilization of initiation rites it became permissible for storytellers to transmute ritualistic sequences into secular narratives, thereby bringing into the profane sphere of life numerous ineffable mysteries whose disclosure had previously been forbidden. A third hypothesis would be along the lines of suggesting that certain folktales are a direct outgrowth of sacred narratives—really recitations of sacred myths—that originally accompanied the performance of religious rites. The structure of the folktales under consideration, and perhaps of folktales in general, adds some weight to this supposition. In many instances the problem situation consists primarily of overcoming various obstacles which have been created by magical means expressly for the purpose of being overcome. It is not important that the obstacles take many outward forms that do not resemble the elements of initiation ceremonies. For example, the main obstacle to be overcome is frequently another person, usually malevolent. In other instances, obstacles take the form of geographic barriers such as mountains and rivers. We often encounter a cruel taskmaster in one form or another. Nor is it unusual to find obstacles in the form of prohibitions that are hard to uphold.

Again and again, we see that the protagonist is someone who is "put upon," be it by an enchantment, ill will, unfavorable circumstances, or as a consequence of his own weakness. By eliminating the obstacles that are placed before him, the protagonist not only achieves a moral victory but enters upon a new status in life. The forces arrayed in opposition to the hero do not enact a personal vendetta with him but seem to resist his progress in a ceremonial manner, as if it were their office to test him and others like him. Giants, ogres, witches, and animals appear out of nowhere, make demands on the protagonist, impose handicaps on him, or threaten to punish him, despite his innocence. Their opposition comes close to being personal only in those cases where the mother or father of the protagonist has offended the spirit world by an error of omission or some other slight. But this is a mere pretext, and usually the punishment visited upon the protagonist is out of all proportion to the fancied slight.

The structure of initiation rites and the structure of the stories under consideration have still another element in common—the taskmasters are not generally the parents themselves in recognizable form, but rather agents of the spirit world who are older and cannier than the protagonist; and the demons are not of the generation of the child-hero or heroine nor do they compete with them in a contest between equals. In the beginning, the adversary is invincible, armed with magic weapons and tricks, and fear-inspiring. Even when the protagonist has accumulated enough mana to offset the unnatural advantage of his adversary, the final victory is a triumph of weakness over strength. Highlighting the relative helplessness of the young protagonist is a feature often found in folktales, namely, that the hero endures his ordeal in the company of another young person or persons. Sometimes, as in the tale of "Blondine," to be described below, a group of young maidens clothed in white share the heroine's ordeal, emerging from their enchanted condition as gazelles only when the heroine has surmounted her numerous trials. This sort of shared ordeal is not unlike the primitive initiation process, in which many children participate at the same time. A closer examination of "Blondine" will clarify the relationship between the components of the tale and the initiation process.

The plot is as follows. The Princess Blondine was born shortly before her mother died. Her father, the king, remarried after three years, and Blondine's stepmother immediately manifested a violent dislike for the child. Blondine was subsequently mistreated by her new half-sister, Brunette, as well as by the cruel queen. When Blondine was seven years old, the queen contrived for her to wander off into the dreaded magic woods, called the forest of lilacs. It was a peculiar characteristic of this enchanted forest that every time the king tried to build a wall between the royal garden and the forest the wall would disappear. Once Blondine had violated the rule about entering the forest, she found herself surrounded by lilacs, which she at first rejoiced to gather. Needless to say, she was soon hopelessly lost and fell asleep, tearful and exhausted.

Upon awakening, she was befriended by a beneficent white cat, who fed her and led her to a beautiful castle with a white marble vestibule. The mistress of the castle was a white hind who, unlike the cat, had the power of speech. The hind reassured Blondine of her good intentions, adding that she was a friend of the king. She revealed, moreover, that Blondine was now in the power of the magician of the forest of lilacs but would be reunited with her father eventually. Blondine was provided with luxurious living quarters amidst furniture and hangings embroidered with pictures of animals, birds, and butterflies. Her attendants were gazelles who watched over her even in her sleep. Most remarkable of all, after Blondine had awakened from what seemed like a night's sleep in the palace, she discovered that she had slept for seven years and was now a beautiful, full-grown girl of fourteen. During her long sleep, her hosts had instructed her in the arts and in literature, with the result that she found herself a polished young lady. By means of a magic mirror, she learned of her father's overpowering grief at her disappearance, his banishment of the guilty stepmother, and the marriage of her cruel stepsister to a certain Prince Violent, who was determined to reform her by punitive measures. Blondine passed six months with her new friends.

The hind, whose name was Bonne-Biche, gave Blondine to understand that at the age of fifteen she would return home. In spite of the hind's reassurances, Blondine allowed herself to be deceived by a wicked parrot, who tempted her into picking a certain rose, which, he declared, would secure her safe return to her father. No sooner had Blondine entered the forest and picked the rose than the parrot and the rose revealed themselves as evil spirits who had tricked her into magically destroying her erstwhile benefactors by her act of disobedience. In her grief and remorse, she was consoled by a crow, a frog, and, later, by a beautiful cow called Blanchette, who sustained her with her milk.

Meanwhile, mysterious voices urged Blondine to repent. For

six months, Blondine survived in the forest in a shelter of branches and leaves, nourished by the unfailing cow and filled with deep sadness over the fate of her devoted friends, the hind and the cat. A giant tortoise appeared at last, informed Blondine that her friends were still alive, and then transported her for six months on her back in absolute silence. Although the tortoise's progress was extremely slow, Blondine restrained herself from saying anything and was brought eventually to a castle where she was received by young girls dressed in white—the former gazelles, as it turned out.

Conducted into the presence of her good fairy, Bienveillante, she was instructed to open a chest in which she found the skins of her old friends, the hind and the cat. Upon making this terrible discovery, Blondine was informed that she had no cause for alarm and that the fairy Bienveillante was no other than her friend, the hind. The cat, too, now appeared in his pristine form, which was that of a handsome prince, the son of Bienveillante. The fairy explained to Blondine that by plucking the rose she had released her and her son from an evil spell, while bringing upon herself the hardships of her long vigil in the forest. Blondine's restoration had been the work of no less a personage than the queen of the fairies, who was satisfied of Blondine's genuine repentance for her sins of disobedience: straying into the forest of lilacs and, later, listening to the false promises of the evil parrot. Blondine was finally carried to her father in a chariot drawn by four white swans. After eight days of celebration, the king married the fairy Bienveillante, and Blondine was wedded to the prince.

The story of Blondine contains two related motifs. First is the motif of the novice who must practice asceticism and then receives enlightenment in the forest; second is the psychological theme of regeneration through repentance. The process of spiritual rebirth takes place in the sacred precincts of the forest, literally, in the spirit world. The central agent who stage-manages the regenerative and punitive process is Blondine's conveniently absent mother. Her death following her daughter's birth is no more than a pretext for removing all blame from her for the many privations that are visited upon the girl. The marriage of the king to a cruel woman who becomes the instrument of Blondine's banishment is similarly a device for displacing hostility from the true mother to someone else. By the same process, the final marriage of the king to the fairy Bienveillante is the means for bringing the real mother back into the picture upon the conclusion of Blondine's long ordeal.

The white hind represents the totemic mask of the mother-intercessor, who, as the agent of the parental generation, has the dual task of making the rites of passage as dramatic and as convincing as possible without surrendering entirely her protective, nurturant role. The latter function is performed by the white cow, Blanchette, in the strikingly symbolic form of practically nursing the young girl with her own milk. Blondine's prolonged abstention from all foods except milk together with the circumstance of her dwelling in a sort of natural lean-to point to an ascetic motif with overtones of purification. Her drinking of milk is reminiscent of the symbolic references to milk that are associated with Orphic mysticism and the ritual of spiritual rebirth.[4] Here the taking of milk is both an act of communion with the deity and an affirmation of purity.

In Blondine's case, the theme of purification appears to be linked with the mimesis of rebirth. The tiny shelter of twigs within which Blondine passively exists for many months corresponds to a kind of intrauterine environment from which she emerges as one reborn and obliged to imitate the speechless state of an infant. The recurrence of the color white—the white cat, the white hind, the white cow, the white marble castle entrance, the girls dressed in white, the white swans, the milk, and Blondine herself, who is fair in contrast to her dark half-sister Brunette—is consistent with the apparent emphasis on purification.[5]

The episode with the cow and, later, the appearance of the tortoise who returns Blondine to her father seem to represent the culmination of her initiation ordeal. The first stage of her journey into the spirit world consists of her entry into the sacred enclosure of the lilac forest. By entering this magic ring,[6] Blondine passes from her previous status as a child to her new status as a novice. Now she is "dead" to her old self, and her father goes through the motions of mourning her death, although he is soon informed by the white hind that his daughter is safe and will be restored to him. Blondine knows that her ties with her father have not been severed, and, by means of a magic mirror, she is permitted to see what has been happening in the king's castle. These reassuring touches heighten the feeling of make-believe and add to the impression that "Blondine" is a dramatic enactment no less than the process of initiation itself.

From the forest of lilacs to the enchanted castle of the hind is but another stop for Blondine in the direction of the secret shrine wherein her enlightenment is to take place.

The hind's castle is a place of instruction or initiation into certain mysteries. Such instruction can be transmitted only while the novice is in a special state of receptivity—literally, in a dormant condition. During her hibernation, Blondine matures physically, awakening to find herself a grown woman, and in possession of such skills as pertain to the status of an educated woman in the old-fashioned sense—reading, writing, drawing, singing, and playing on the piano and harp. But what is the reason for her enlightenment during sleep, that is, with her *eyes closed?* I think if we consider the esoteric character of the initiation process, and the taboo that attaches to sacred objects involved in religious ceremonies, it becomes clear that Blondine's sleep is an equivalent for the Dionysiac custom of veiling[7] in the presence of the mystery. The use of the veil is, in all probability, emblematic of passage from a prior condition to a new status in life, as van Gennep[8] has suggested. Also, it would appear to indicate that the veiled person has been consecrated.[9] If such explanations sound farfetched in the present instance, it is only because Blondine's long sleep cannot be explained in commonsense terms. We are dealing with an irrational and "unnecessary" feature of the story, which, along with other strange happenings—talking animals, enchanted castles, etc.—indicates that in "Blondine," as in other fairy tales, the manifest contents of the narrative are no longer self-explanatory.

Blondine's attitude toward Bonne-Biche, the hind, is curiously ambivalent. She cannot accept the hind's interdiction about entering the forest—that "fatal" spot—and is unable fully to believe that she will see her father in a year's time. Her suspicions that she is being held a prisoner are reinforced by her meeting with the brightly colored parrot, who urges her to free herself. It is curious that the parrot succeeds so well in picturing the gentle hind as one who would cut his throat if she knew of his presence. He adds, convincingly, that he has previously rescued victims from the hind. In a sense, Blondine's situation is not without its terrifying aspects, and her own helplessness is highlighted by the hind's seeming omniscience and her occult powers generally. What is the true character of the hind?

In a story called "La Biche Blanche" described by Saintyves, we find a forest setting in which a seemingly benign hind leads a young hero into a trap presided over by her mother, who happens to be an ogress. The ogress gives the youth difficult tasks to perform, on pain of being eaten by a dragon. With the help of the hind, the hero overcomes the various obstacles placed in his path and wins the hand of the white hind—obviously an enchanted girl—in marriage. Fearing treachery, the couple flee during the night and escape destruction.

I will not comment on the hostile role of the ogress in relation to the young couple nor on her effort to prevent the consummation of their marriage. It is more pertinent to consider the hind and the ogress as two aspects of a syncretic entity—that is, as a woodland deity with a benign as well as a monstrous epiphany. Indeed, the ogress is referred to at times as a fairy. Of course, Blondine's hind does not threaten her young charge, nor does she show any traces of wickedness. Nevertheless, the link between Bonne-Biche and the evil genius of the forest is never revealed, so that in some measure she remains his deputy as well as his prisoner. The white hind stands in the same relation to the evil genius as the other white hind, specifically called, "La Biche Blanche," maintains to her ogress mother. In both stories, the human protagonist is in turn helped and menaced by enchanted woodland creatures as a precondition for returning to "this world" fully prepared for the sacrament of marriage. The principle distinction between Blondine's ordeal and that of the youth in "La Biche Blanche" is a distinction between feminine and masculine requirements—Blondine's trial is one of impulse-control, to avoid picking the Rose; the hero of "La Biche Blanche" must prove himself by the performance of great feats.

When Blondine at last allows herself to be influenced by the parrot, we know that she has entered the critical stage of her initiation. Her symbolic sin of self-assertion is a necessary preliminary so that she can pass on to the inevitable ascetic stage of her initiation, of which atonement and purification are the central features. Whether the Rose has a sexual meaning[10] or not, it is safe to say that it is something taboo and that the violation of the taboo brings to a close the stage of esoteric instruction. Why are we led to believe that the hind and the cat together with their beautiful castle have been destroyed as a consequence of Blondine's transgression? It is a matter of specifying the prerequisites for spiritual rebirth; for Blondine to be reborn, her past associations must be erased. The psychology of regeneration presupposes a "dying-to-the-past," and, indeed, Blondine's subsequent half-life in the forest lean-to is exactly such a symbolic death. In this connection, the role of the white cow suggests that her function, symbolically speaking, extends beyond nurturance. Her presence may serve as a reminder of the archaic custom in which a novice is made to pass through the body of a cow, or some other totemic agent, in a mimetic birth process. As Saintyves[11] points out, in ancient Egypt the dead were wrapped in a shroud of steerhide and treated like initiates, with the understanding that they would be reborn.

Blondine's coming-of-age is signaled by her successful journey on the tortoise's back. For the first time, Blondine displays the necessary degree of self-control by resisting hunger and thirst, remaining immobilized on the back of the tortoise, and, above all, maintaining complete silence for six months. Brought into the presence of her good fairy, she is not spared one final ordeal, that of being shown the skins of her erstwhile benefactors, the hind and the cat. The fairy explains that "this last punishment was indispensable to deliver her [Blondine] forever from the yoke of the cruel genius of the forest of lilacs." Blondine faints on this occasion and is restored to consciousness with the fairy's magic wand.

I wish to comment first on the requirement of prolonged silence. It seems to me that this injunction is not arbitrary, but may be related etiologically to one of the stipulations of initiation— namely, to take the vow of secrecy with regard to the revealed mysteries. Again, Blondine's enforced abstention from all food during her voyage on the tortoise's back appears to repeat the motif of purification noted earlier. But now, the act of purification must be viewed as a sanctification or as a preparation for confront- ment with the *sacra*, which I take to be the skins of the hind and the cat. The custom of preserving the skin of the sacrificed totem has been described at length by Frazer.[12]

It is noteworthy that the fairy Bienveillante keeps the animal skins fastened with diamond nails inside a beautiful wardrobe made of gold and ivory. Even before she is given the key to the wardrobe and asked to open it, Blondine finds herself drawn toward it. There is no mistaking the centrality of Blondine's confrontation with the sacred relics, both as a dramatic climax and as an overpowering confirmation of her guilt feelings over having caused the destruction of her friends. It is not improbable that the episode of the Rose is a screen for the violation of a more fundamental taboo—the taboo against killing the totem. In effect, Blondine has brought about the ritual death of her totemic protectors in the venerable tradition of slaying-the-god in order to facilitate the process of regeneration. Now she is at the thresh- old of receiving the mana that flows from the slain totem. Like the participant in the Eleusinian Mysteries, she might well have said "I fasted, I drank the Kykeon, I took from the chest, I put back into the basket and from the basket into the chest."[13]

Blondine has viewed the *sacra* and is ready to assume the role of a mature adult. As a consequence, she marries the Prince Parfait and lives out the rest of her life in perfect happiness, undaunted by the memory that she has extinguished her totemic gods as the price of her own regeneration.

Turning to the second story, "Good Little Henry," we find ourselves far removed from the trappings of the court. Now the setting is entirely wild and almost surrealistic. Henry lives in a remote, lonesome place with only his poor, sick mother. The woman is dying of some mysterious malady, and the fairy Bienfaisante, upon being summoned by little Henry, informs him that he must obtain the "plant of life" in order to cure his mother. He is given to understand that his mission is difficult and will require great persistence as well as bravery. The plant of life grows atop a mountain that has never been scaled, and it is in the possession of a certain little "doctor" who presides over a garden of medicinal herbs. To summarize the plot, Henry starts out by rescuing a crow, a cock, and a frog, and earns from each of these creatures the promise that they will meet again. Subsequently, the cock carries him across a formidable river. Upon approaching the mountain, he is stopped by one of the malicious genii of the mountain, a little old man who challenges him to harvest his vast fields of wheat, to make the wheat into flour, and then to make the flour into bread. This task occupies Henry for over a year but is accomplished successfully. His only reward is a small box containing some tobacco.

Henry climbs further up the mountain, only to be blocked by a high wall. This time a giant appears and demands that Henry harvest his grapes and put them up in wine casks. This task takes no less than ninety days. The reward, once more, is an apparently useless object—a thistle. Henry is challenged a third time by a huge wolf who demands that the boy catch all the game in the surrounding forests and cook it. At first, Henry tries in vain to shoot the numerous animals of the forest, but he is finally assisted by the crow whom he had saved at the outset of his journey. It remains for Henry to perform the womanish task of cooking the game. The task is completed after one hundred fifty days, and after the crow has slain almost two million animals and birds. Henry is rewarded with a magic stick and is also transported on the wolf's back across a bottomless pit, seemingly the last remaining barrier before reaching the mountaintop.

But one final test awaits Henry, and this time his taskmaster is a giant cat who demands that Henry catch for him an infinite number of fish and that he salt and cook them as well. Henry proves to be a complete failure at catching fish, but he is rescued from his hopeless situation by the timely arrival of the frog that he had helped earlier. The frog catches all the available fish over a period of two months, and it takes Henry another two weeks to salt and cook the enormous catch. The cat rewards Henry by tearing off one of his own claws and giving it to the boy with the assurance that the claw is a talisman against sickness and old age.

As a final gesture, the cat extends his tail across a wide ditch, thus permitting Henry to cross over to the other side, where is to be seen the garden containing the plant of life. Once inside the garden, Henry is greeted by the little doctor, who gives him a branch from a special bush, apparently the tree of life. Henry is warned that if he lays down the branch it will disappear. No sooner is the plant in his possession than Henry jumps on his magic flying stick, and is transported instantly to his mother's side. His mother awakens to find that her son has grown a head taller, and is indeed considerably older than when he left her. The fairy Bienfaisante now appears and gives Henry's mother a detailed account of his feats and hardships. Henry opens the box given to him by his first taskmaster, and at once a marvelous house is constructed for him. Using the giant's thistle he is able to obtain food, clothing, linen, and, in fact, everything that he will require for the rest of his life. Of course, thanks to the cat's claw, neither Henry nor his mother ever grow old, and they live on together in a state of perpetual bliss.

For all its simplicity, the story of little Henry is more complex than that of Blondine because it contains important elements from the *mise en scène* of initiation as well as from the drama of seasonal renewal. The connection between initiation rites and the cult of fertility is brought out clearly, showing the unity of prelogical thought. Puberty rites signalize the renewal of the generations and of a human community through a reaffirmation of the covenant with the totemic ancestors. Of course, fertility rites insure the renewal of nature, the seasons, the crops, and the livestock. One form of rebirth cannot occur without the other, consistent with the principle that primitive thinking makes little distinction between the human and nonhuman planes of life and consequently sees them as interdependent.

In the case of little Henry, the initiation ordeals so completely overshadow the fertility motif that it is easy to miss the significance of the latter. The many tasks assigned to Henry—harvesting wheat, gathering grapes, catching game and fish—are the familiar tests of fitness to determine if an adolescent is ready to perform the functions of an adult. What is less obvious is the meaning of his mother's sickness and the fact of her recovery upon the successful completion of his trials. For an insight into the nature of the mother's malady, it is instructive to turn to Jessie L. Weston's book, *From Ritual to Romance*, [14] and to consider certain parallels between the symbolism of the stricken fisher king of the Grail legend and the mother's illness. In both instances, the task of the hero appears to go beyond the restoration of the health of an ailing individual and in fact involves the revival of the generative powers of nature as embodied in the dying person. Weston has characterized the fisher king as the type of priest-king whose life is magically tied up with the forces of nature. In a similar vein, perhaps Henry's mother is a symbol of mother earth —dormant, wasted by sickness, and waiting for the healing juices of the plant of life.[15] At the moment of her recovery, life burgeons out; when Henry opens the little box given to him by the old man of the mountain, a beautiful house is at once built for him and a pretty garden as well as "a thick wood on one side and a beautiful meadow on the other" are made to appear.

To be sure, Henry, unlike Gawain or Perceval, does not carry a sword or lance with the power to restore life to a wasteland. However, his branch from the plant of life appears to serve the same purpose, though its phallic character is less pronounced than the instrument carried by the doughty knight of the Grail. As for his other talismans, Henry has only to smell the thistle—the gift, it will be recalled, of a giant—in order to secure clothes, furniture, food, and anything else that he desires. His magic staff is likewise a useful acquisition, permitting him to travel at will. The cat's claw prevents sickness or old age and is therefore no less useful than the plant of life. All in all, Henry's fetishes are as efficacious as the lance-and-cup fertility symbols of the Grail accounts. That they are the gift of totemic agents is no less certain.

The various taskmasters who make such outrageous demands of the hero may be thought of as representing the generation of the fathers. Their several disguises—the old man, the giant, the wolf, the huge cat—reveal them in their initiatory role as tempters and would-be destroyers. Since the novice is not expected to measure up perfectly to adult standards of performance, he is aided by another group of masters, represented in the present instance by the cock, the crow, and the frog. These creatures help Henry in the critical trials of hunting and fishing, where he is at a complete loss and can do little more than cook the game, again suggesting that we are dealing with an initiation ceremony for girls. Even the taskmasters preserve much of their benevolence as totemic guardians, imparting to Henry the highest rewards for obedience—the gifts of health, prosperity, and immortality.

Henry's extraordinary accomplishments in harvesting wheat and baking over four hundred thousand loaves of bread taken together with his production of a whole cellar full of wine made from grapes which he had gathered point to activities in which women have historically played a prominent role. It may be noted that Henry requires no help in these agricultural pursuits, once more indicating the possibility that the tasks imposed on the protagonist are familiar ones of the sort that might be connected with female initiation rites.

A word needs to be added concerning the physical barriers that continually interpose themselves between Henry and his goal, the plant of life on a remote mountaintop. First of all, the mountain itself is not an accidental destination, but a sacred place where heaven and earth meet and where it is most likely that the cosmic energy—the life-force, as it were—would be concentrated.[16] Henry's quest is therefore in the nature of an ascent to a consecrated region, the spirit world itself. The ancient Graeco-Roman tradition that during initiation into the mysteries the candidate's soul is released and ascends to the upper regions to return touched by divinity, has its echo in Henry's ascension. We know, too, in what garden the legendary plant or tree of life is situated—Eden itself, the source of all life and the fountainhead of the four great rivers. Of course, the tree of life is the secret hiding place of the gift of immortality and is not to be shared with mortals. Henry has a special dispensation which enables him to acquire the talis-

man of immortality, and one may suspect that he owes his gift
to the grace of his totemic ancestors. As if to confirm the centrality of the immortality quest, the story ends with the statement
that "It is supposed that the queen of the fairies made them
[Henry and his mother] immortal and transported them to her
palace. . . ."

The relationship between initiation rites—whether of the adolescent variety or in connection with the mystery religions—and
the idea of immortality is an intimate one. Initiation confirms the
continuity of the human community, as well as the unity of the
individual candidate with all creaturely things, with creation itself, and with the life principle, that is, with deathlessness. What
are all the trials that the hero must endure but opportunities to
demonstrate that life is stronger than death? The hero's wander-
ings amidst dark forests surrounded, as in Henry's case, by deep
pits, impassable rivers, and high walls, represent no more than a
side trip to hell on the way to paradise.

The barriers themselves partake of holiness. The mountain that
Henry must climb is both an obstacle and a magic destination.
Similarly, the river that surrounds the mountain and which Henry
is able to cross only with the help of his friend, the cock, is both
an impediment and an important positive element in a larger
iconographic and mythological motif. This motif is made up of
the following components—mountain, sacred tree, goddess, and
life-giving waters.[17] In effect, the act of bringing the plant of life
to the stricken mother serves to complete the iconographic motif
in which the association of plants, water, and a woman symbolize
life.

It remains only to mention the enigmatic person of the little
doctor, who presides over the botanical fairy garden atop the
mountain. He is similiar to the doctor who revives the dying vegetation spirit or King of the May in modern survivals of archaic
nature rituals that take the form of folk dramas, mumming plays,
etc.[18] The doctor in our story, like the mummer's doctor, is
literally a medicine man, and the medicinal plant that he gives
to Henry has much in common with the legendary herb that was
reputed to have the power to bring the dead back to life.[19] By

reviving his unconscious mother, Henry resuscitated all of nature, and, by bringing back a sprig from the plant of life, Henry procured his own admission to a higher status. Now he was no longer a child, the passive recipient of the boon of life; now he had the power to bestow life, like an adult.

Our third story, "The Princess Rosette," resembles the familiar tales of the Cinderella type and seems to lend itself to the obvious interpretation that a child who has been rejected by her parents has a fantasy in which she is a great social success, marries a prince, and overcomes her jealous sisters. On a similar level of analysis, the story can be viewed as a wish fulfillment involving a fantasy mother, who is benign, and the real parents, who are perceived as malevolent and punished for their misdeeds. However, the story contains a number of features that are not strictly necessary for the development of the manifest theme and which suggest a remote ritual source.

Briefly, Rosette is a good and beautiful princess who is banished by her unloving parents shortly after her birth. Her two older sisters are the favorites and have been destined by their parents to make brilliant matches and to live a life of luxury; this is in contrast to Rosette, who is brought up on a farm and deliberately kept out of polite society. At the age of fifteen, Rosette is asked to appear at the palace for the first time in order to attend the festivities associated with her sisters' prospective marriages. In the meantime, under the tutelage of her godmother, the fairy Puissante, Rosette has become a well-educated person and an accomplished musician. As Rosette prepares to depart, all dressed in white, the fairy transforms her clothing so that it becomes coarse and outlandish. In addition, she adorns Rosette with a necklace of nuts, a hair-band of burrs, and bracelets of dried beans. Rosette accepts this substitution with good cheer after overcoming her initial stupefaction.

At the palace, Rosette is housed in the servants' quarters and waited upon by a coarse servant who serves her only bread and milk. Although the princess faithfully dresses herself each morning in her rude clothes, she finds that her costume is changed at once into resplendent, jewel-bedecked robes. Thus attired, she wins the admiration of the entire court, the intensified hatred of her parents and sisters, and the love of the Prince Charmant, whom her fairy godmother has chosen for her future husband. When the wicked queen threatens to return Rosette to the farm, her godmother intervenes and in turn threatens to turn the king and queen into toads and the two sisters into vipers. Similarly, when the queen tries to arrange to have Rosette thrown by an unruly horse, her efforts are foiled. A third attempt to eliminate the princess by crashing into her magic chariot during a race results in the humiliation of her sisters, who are thrown from their chariots and severely disfigured.

These hostile acts follow hard upon a series of overwhelming social triumphs by Rosette, who displays on numerous occasions her great personal charm as well as her remarkable dancing and singing skills. Fearing that her ability to protect the princess and her lover is about to be diminished, the godmother spirits the couple away to the prince's kingdom, and preparations are made for their marriage. Afterwards, Puissante provides the prince with an explanation of the preceding train of events. The gist of this explanation is that Rosette had shown herself to be obedient and deserving of her good fortune, that the godmother had been responsible for her miraculous escapes, and, finally, that Rosette's parents and sisters had been suitably punished—the former by being turned into beasts of burden and the latter by being married off to brutal husbands. The fairy prevails upon the prince not to reveal these punishments to the tenderhearted Rosette. Immediately thereafter, Rosette and her prince are married and spend the rest of their lives in contentment. The farm on which Rosette had been raised is transported at once to her new palace grounds, together with her faithful old nurse and a few trunk-fulls of the extraordinary gowns that Rosette had worn during the three-day festival at her father's palace. The fairy godmother disappears after the marriage ceremony, stating that she must give herself up to the queen of the fairies and lose her power for eight days.

Although the didactic aspects of the story are prominent and we are told why Rosette is such a good girl—because she obeys her godmother, no matter what—it is much less clear why her parents banish her from their sight when she is only an infant. Like many other heroes and heroines of folklore and myth, Rosette is evidently perceived as a threat by her parents and sisters. The only explanation that is provided is that her sisters are jealous of her because she is under the protection of the fairy Puissante. I believe that the connection between Rosette and Puissante is fundamental to the story and that the ascribed motive of jealousy is a modern touch. The relationship between the godmother and the princess is in the pattern of "declining mother" and "ascending maiden," vaguely suggesting Demeter and Kore.[20] The following series of events seems to point, at any rate, toward a sacred rite incorporating nature symbolism with elements of an initiation process: Rosette is banished to the countryside and grows up in a sort of social limbo; she is brought back into the light by her godmother at the age of fifteen; she wears a series of sensational costumes, alternating with coarse clothes decorated with a hen's egg, nuts, burrs, beans, and a pullet's wing with feathers; she undergoes certain perils or trials, including her participation in an incongruous chariot race; she is saved repeatedly by the intervention of her godmother; and she enters upon marriage just as the godmother's magic powers begin to wane.

Consider first the matter of Rosette's costumes, alternately civilized—indeed luxurious—and "barbaric." What is the meaning of the hen's egg which she wears in her hair? Is this a reference to the primeval egg of Orphic tradition, once an important element in the instruction of initiates into the mysteries?[21] The cosmic egg is easily recognizable as a symbol of life and of birth and rebirth; its role in an initiation ceremony is perfectly natural. The egg is also an emblem of spring, of the New Year, and of the resurrection of the dead. These meanings are consistent with its use in the old mystery religions, with their strong interest in spiritual regeneration. The wearing of nuts in the form of a necklace reinforces the seed symbolism of the egg. Similarly, the hair-band of burrs and the bracelets of dried beans would seem to be symbolic features of a vegetation ceremony. The beans in particular have been associated since earliest times with the idea of fertility. The costume bestowed upon Rosette, then, must have had something to do with the creative aspects of nature and may be thought of as consisting of a number of specific fertility charms. Why her simple white dress, so well suited for purification rites, was replaced by a rough garment is hard to say. Perhaps the coarseness of her clothes is consistent with her stay in the servants' quarters and with her subsistence on bread and milk— all details referable to the ascetic phase of initiation.

Although it is not customary to think of graceful ballroom dancing in the same context as horse racing or chariot racing, these activities are not entirely unrelated. In the world of archaic man, dancing frequently served the purpose of magically stimulating the forces of nature to grow and to multiply. In this category probably belong the martial dances of the Kouretes[22] in the extremely ancient ritual of the mother and the son, the leapings of the Arval priests in Roman times to promote the growth of crops,[23] Pueblo snake dances, etc. In modern times as well, peasants in various parts of the world resort to leaping dances in order to encourage their crops to grow tall. Of course, Rosette's dancing is refined and bears not the slightest resemblance to these wild cavortings. It is a singular fact, however, that for Rosette dancing is a trial ordered by no less a person than the queen for the ostensible purpose of embarrassing her.

A more dangerous set of trials, though answering to the same purpose as the enforced dancing, is seen in the episode involving, first, an unruly horse provided for Rosette by the queen and, later, a chariot race against her hostile sisters. It might be noted that the chariot episode involves a dual threat—the menace emanating from the enraged sisters as well as the menace of uncontrollable horses. The horse motif and the chariot crash tell us that we have arrived at the termination of a sacred king's reign.[24] The two spiteful sisters who are all but dashed to pieces when their chariots collide with Rosette's magic vehicle are surrogates for the king himself. It was the latter who, like Hippolytus, was fated to be dragged to death by horses or, like Glaucus, entangled in the reins of his overthrown chariot and devoured alive by his mares. In our story, the king is not eaten outright but is turned into a beast of burden, thus being assimilated to an animal form. The symbolism

of the horse is familiar as the spirit of vegetation, sometimes
embodied as Virbius,[25] the divine woodland king, sometimes as
Poseidon, with the epithet Hippios.[26] Legend has it that Poseidon (in his equine form) coupled with Demeter, who had turned
herself into a mare to elude him. Although there is no hint of a
horse cult in "Rosette," there is the faintest suggestion of a
mare-headed costume in the description of the riding clothes
worn by the heroine; she wore a suit of sky-blue velvet with *a long
white plume* attached to her blue cap and hanging down to her
waist (her white horse is also caparisoned in blue velvet). Be that
as it may, the demise of the king is a fitting prelude to the
enactment of a sacred marriage between the prince and Rosette.
The queen, too, is displaced, of course, but I believe that the
disappearance of the fairy godmother is the more significant
event, heralding the advent of Rosette to her new status as queen
and her initiation as an autonomous woman.

"The Little Gray Mouse" appears to be a variant of the familiar
Bluebeard motif, though without Bluebeard. The story is simple:
For the first fifteen years of her life, Rosalie, a princess, is reared
in complete isolation by her father, Prudent, a sort of wizard who
is under the protection of the queen of the fairies. Prudent warns
Rosalie to guard against her principal fault, curiosity. Disregarding his advice, she opens the door of a forbidden little house at
the end of her garden and finds herself in the power of the fairy
Detestable, in the form of a mouse. Rosalie tries to destroy the
mouse with fire and with water, but she fails. Her father returns
and discovers that she has disobeyed him. He then relates that he
deliberately left the key to the forbidden house within easy reach
in order to test Rosalie's self-control and that he acted upon the
instructions of the queen of the fairies. He further reveals to
Rosalie for the first time that he is a genie and that her mother
had been a mortal princess. He adds that the fairy Detestable is
their common adversary and is determined to avenge herself upon
him for not having married her daughter. Apparently, Detestable
had also caused the death of Rosalie's mother out of spite. As
punishment for this crime, Detestable had been turned into a
mouse by the queen of the fairies and shut up in the little house.

It was understood that Detestable would be restored to her original form as a fairy if Rosalie could be induced to yield to her curiosity three times.

The immediate consequence of Rosalie's disobedience is that her home is destroyed by fire. Separated from her father, Rosalie wanders far and wide, ever accompanied by the cruel mouse and spurned by all good people because of her apparent association with this evil-appearing creature. Rosalie's ordeal lasts for about two weeks, terminating just before her fifteenth birthday. On the eve of her birthday she is discovered sleeping in the forest by Prince Gracious, who had been hunting by torchlight in pursuit of a deer. The prince is unable to awaken Rosalie and removes her to his palace. The following morning, the prince, once more dressed in hunting clothes, discloses to Rosalie that he is her cousin and that the queen of the fairies had arranged for him to go hunting by torchlight expressly to find Rosalie and to marry her. Rosalie is delighted at this news and prepares for her imminent marriage.

In the meantime, the prince warns Rosalie not to look at a certain tree that is entirely covered with a cloth. This tree is to be the prince's gift to Rosalie, but cannot be viewed by her until after she becomes his wife. At the first opportunity, Rosalie inserts her fingers into a seam of the cloth covering the tree, tears off the cover, and gazes with admiration at the shining tree, with its coral trunk and its leaves of emeralds. The tree bears fruit in the form of diamonds and pearls. Almost at once, the palace burns down and the prince, after barely escaping from the flames, abandons Rosalie after reproaching her for yielding to her curiosity. The wicked mouse reappears and taunts Rosalie, stating that it was she who made Rosalie look at the forbidden tree.

Overcome with anguish, Rosalie sinks to the ground and resolves to spend the entire day without food or water in expiation for her misdeeds. An old woman appears and entrusts Rosalie with a shining casket, cautioning her not to look in it. Overcoming her compulsion to look and disregarding the artful but treacherous promptings of the ubiquitous mouse, Rosalie remains steadfast, awaiting the dawn of her fifteenth birthday. Finally, after the clock has struck twelve, an owl appears overhead and drops a stone which shatters the casket. In an instant, the queen of the fairies materializes and congratulates Rosalie upon her triumph over Detestable. She presents Rosalie with a rare fruit "of which a single mouthful satisfied both hunger and thirst." A chariot drawn by two dragons brings Rosalie back to the prince's palace, which, the queen of the fairies explains, was not really destroyed by fire; it was only an illusion designed to evoke remorse in Rosalie. Rosalie is united with her father and marries the prince on her fifteenth birthday, as the queen of the fairies had ordained. We are told in the closing sentence of the story that Rosalie and the prince chose powerful fairy godmothers to protect their children from wicked fairies and genii.

I suggested earlier that there is a touch of Bluebeard in the story of Rosalie. I was referring, of course, to the injunction to refrain from opening a secret room. There is also a degree of similarity to the story of Psyche and Eros,[27] based on the taboo that stipulated that Rosalie could not view the hidden tree until she was married. The phallic symbolism of the tree is fairly transparent in this instance. I suspect, however, that the story of Rosalie and the gray mouse has much more in common with the Bluebeard account than with the much more sophisticated legend of Eros and Psyche. Both fairy tales seem to deal symbolically with precocious sexuality and its perils for girls. Whatever its ritual origins, Apuleius' charming tale has something modern to say about the nature of the love relationship. By contrast, our present story centers almost exclusively on Rosalie and relegates her lover to a secondary role.

What is the true nature of Rosalie's temptation? I would say without hesitation that the trials designed for the heroine have as their main purpose to determine whether she can abandon the presexual onanistic level of functioning while at the same time remaining chaste until she is properly married. Her secluded life with her wizard-father is nothing less than a phase of esoteric instruction in the mysteries, with particular emphasis on the maintenance of sacramental purity and on practicing patience until such time as the ultimate *sacra* are revealed to her eyes. The fairy Detestable plays a role that is similar to that of the father —that is, the role of the tempter—with the difference that the evil mouse serves as a convenient object for Rosalie's displaced hostility toward the elders who are responsible for her ordeal.

Why Detestable is represented as having the form of a mouse is uncertain. Perhaps the mouse represents the malignant spirit of a dead ancestor, thereby symbolizing the harshness of the initiation demands made by the generation of elders. Such an interpretation would be consistent with the primitive belief in an external soul and the related peasant superstition that the soul may leave the body in the form of a mouse.[28, 29] The little garden house, mysterious and windowless, has much about it to suggest an initiation lodge tucked away among the trees. Its symbolism in the present context would seem to be twofold: first, it is a sacred shrine and, as such, taboo; second, it is also, in psychoanalytic terms, an unconscious way of symbolizing the human body—in this case, Rosalie herself. These two levels of interpretation, the one etiological and the other motivational, are applicable to fairy tales in general. On the one hand, it becomes possible to "explain" apparently fantastic or illogical happenings by searching out their origins in ancient ritual and myth; at the same time, an insight may be gained into the reasons for the lasting appeal of fairy tales to grown-ups and children alike. In effect, certain motifs and certain objects—such as the little house—are recognizable as belonging to the symbolic language of the unconscious. This language is understood intuitively by children and adults who are not entirely removed from their own feelings. If we think of the little house as a paradigm of Rosalie's physical self, it is evident that in this aspect, too, the house is inviolable.

The struggle between Prudent and Detestable provides some clues to the strategy of initiation rites at puberty. Two opposing forces contend for the novice's soul. Arrayed on one side are benevolent beings who impart by magic the gifts and graces that come with initiation. A host of evil spirits, misanthropic fairies, cruel stepmothers, or even—as in the case of Psyche—jealous sisters strive either to ensnare the novice or to poison his mind against his benefactors. Presumably, the practice of dissociating the "bad" parents from the "good" parents facilitates the process by which the initiate identifies himself with the members of the older generation and learns to repress his resentment of their demands. Sometimes, as in the case of the Oglala Dakota Indians and the Sun Dance they perform as part of tribal initiation ceremonies, the conflict between the benign spirits who instruct and the malevolent deities who torture is dramatized in the form of a sham battle.[30] Strictly speaking, the novice rarely saves himself, but relies faithfully on the magical intercession of his sponsors. To be sure, there are periods of apparent isolation and abandonment which try the faith of the novice. Rosalie endures such a trial during the period that she wanders from house to house in the company of the evil mouse, only to be turned away and denied even a place to rest. This period of deprivation may be regarded also as punishment for her transgression.

It would probably be a mistake to view the destruction of her home in the light of a similar punishment. It is more likely that the simultaneous loss of home and father denote a definite transition from one status to another—that is, a change from dependency to autonomy. The story of Blondine contains a similar motif in the destruction by fire of the white hind's palace after Blondine had picked the forbidden rose. In both instances, it may be suspected that the heroine is about to be "reborn" and that the destruction of her home denotes a dramatic and final break with her past. In Rosalie's case, as in that of Blondine, the spiritual death that ensues takes the form of a protracted sleep in the forest during which the novice is sustained by the "natural" foods—fruits, nuts, and water—that she had eaten before falling asleep.

The arrival of the prince, dressed for the hunt and carrying a torch in hand, introduces still another note of sacred ritual. Once again, we are back in Diana's grove in the wilderness, where burning torches are unmistakenly linked with the quest for fertility.[31] In modern times as well, European peasants have been observed to go through their orchards and fields carrying torches and urging the plants and trees to be fruitful. The prince arranges for the sleeping girl to be carried to his palace on a litter, like a veritable lady of the May carried on a makeshift bed of green boughs and personifying the spirit of vegetation.[32] Rosalie is decked out in silks and finery and is not a little reminiscent of the Little May Rose.[33] Moreover, her name, Rosalie, like that of Rosette in "The Princess Rosette" and like that of Violette in our last story, "Ourson," is distinctly a vegetation name. There is a curious similarity as well between Rosalie's going from door to door and begging for food and the May Day practice of children going from house to house and asking for presents.[34] Evidently, the prince is destined to be Rosalie's gift.

Having completed her rites of separation, Rosalie is ready to enter upon a sacred marriage affirming her solidarity with the gods whose priestess is the queen of the fairies. She is now ritually marriageable,[35] providing she can pass her remaining tests. First, there is the vexing matter of the tree concealed under a cloth. The taboo against seeing the tree seems to be a precaution against premature consummation of the projected marriage. Rosalie yields to her curiosity and is again visited by all sorts of supernatural dangers; this time she brings about the destruction of the prince's palace and almost causes the death of her lover.

Why is it that Rosalie, having failed twice before, is able to restrain herself from opening the casket that has been entrusted to her by an old woman? In like circumstances, Psyche had shown herself to be far less resolute, and, as a result of her indiscretion, she had been thrown into a deadly sleep due to the machinations of the unrelenting Aphrodite.[36] It may be that Rosalie has grasped the significance of the casket—it belongs to an old woman and can hold nothing of value for a young bride-to-be. As if to confirm the asexual character of the casket, an owl, the vehicle of the sexless Athene,[37] flies overhead and shatters the casket with a stone. The casket belongs to Rosalie's past as a maiden. The arrival of the queen of the fairies, her provision of a chariot drawn by two dragons, and her presentation to Rosalie of a fruit to satisfy her hunger and thirst all indicate that Rosalie is about to cross the threshold into a new domain in which the guiding principle is that of fecundity, as symbolized by the earthbound serpents and the magic fruit.

Rosalie's marriage and the birth of her children are noted in a summary manner. Her choice of powerful fairy godmothers to protect her offspring against wicked fairies is only natural in view of her own experience and throws some light on the process by which essentially adolescent themes are eventually adapted to the emotional needs of much younger children. The threat posed by the fairy Detestable is easily recognized on the strictly fairy tale level as the threat of abduction or the fearful prospect of being left to the tender mercies of a stepmother (Detestable has daughters of her own and belongs to the category of the bad mother). The substitution of motifs in this instance implies a tendency toward downgrading of numinous themes (such as those deriving from sacred rites), with the result that practices and beliefs that were originally at the heart of archaic religion and taken seriously by adults become bedtime stories for children.

"Ourson" is a long and involved tale that involves a prince who has been cursed with the hairy appearance of a bear and a young princess, Violette, who ultimately takes his curse upon herself to free him from his enchantment. This story is of special interest not only because of its fairly transparent links with key elements of the initiation process, but also because it contains a number of striking references to the historical process by which matriarchal religious, social, and political arrangements came to be superseded by patriarchal forms of organization.

The narrative is as follows. King Ferocious has banished his queen, Aimee, after first attempting to kill her. Under an assumed name, Agnella, the queen lives with her young maidservant Passerose on a little farm called the woodland farm. One day, Agnella angrily kicks a huge toad that she detects in the act of devouring some cherries. The toad reveals herself as the fairy Furious and curses Agnella saying, "You shall have a son covered with coarse hair like a bear's cub." The good fairy Drolette appears in the form of a lark and palliates the curse, giving the unborn child the power to exchange his skin with anyone who is willing to make the exchange out of "gratitude and affection." The toad then departs, spitting venom which destroys plant life wherever it falls.

Within a few months, a son is born to Agnella, and his appear-

ance is indeed that of a bear. Although the boy, Ourson, is loved
by his mother and her servant, he is shunned by everyone else.
At the age of eight, he finds a little lost girl named Violette who
turns out to be his cousin. We learn that her parents were slain
by the king and that Violette was saved by the good fairy Drolette. Violette grows up with Ourson in his mother's house. Unknown to Violette, her good fairy has left a casket of precious
stones to be held in trust for her "until she shall have been lost
and found." The little girl is raised under the tutelage of Ourson,
who is five years older. He teaches his cousin to read, write, and
keep accounts. By some mysterious process, books and clothing
materialize in Violette's room.

One day, when Ourson is fifteen and Violette ten, the fur-
covered boy rescues Violette from the clutches of the evil toad
Furious, who nearly succeeds in drowning the little girl. Unfortunately, Ourson is mortally wounded by the toad's venom. The
price for his recovery, exacted from the grateful Violette by her
good fairy Drolette, is the promise that she would gladly sacrifice
her own happiness to save the life of her adopted brother. On a
subsequent occasion, two years later, Ourson saves Violette from
a wild boar after the girl has been driven to take refuge in a tree.
The lark Drolette openly urges Ourson to propose a change of
skins to Violette, but the boy refuses to take advantage of Violette's gratitude. The young couple spend the night in the forest.

A third crisis occurs when Violette is fifteen. This time, the
house burns down, and Ourson rescues Violette as well as his
mother and Passerose. In addition, he returns to the burning
structure, finds Violette's casket of jewels containing her "happiness," and remains two days in a dry well until he is discovered
by Violette. Violette incidentally joins him at the bottom of the
well for a short while, until a ladder can be lowered to them.
Ourson relates that he was sustained magically by food and wine
in the dry well and that he was visited by the fairy Drolette in
the form of Violette during his confinement. The fairy had informed him that he would descend once more into the well—or
"tomb," as she calls it—before he finds his "happiness." Having
learned the nature of the "sacrifice" that she was expected to

make in order to prove her gratitude to Ourson, Violette eagerly
awaits the next visit of the fairy Drolette.

There follows an interlude during which the entire family is
compelled to live in a stable, since they have lost their house. As
if to add to their troubles, Agnella discovers that she has lost the
magic ring given to her by Drolette, the ring that had provided
them with all their necessities through the years. It now becomes
necessary for Ourson to find employment in order to support the
menage. His efforts are uniformly unsuccessful; he is turned away
first by a farmer, then by the superintendent of a castle, and finally
by the master of a forge. In each instance, Ourson is mistaken for
a bear and threatened with death. Following this series of humilia-
tions, Violette determines that the time has come for her to make
her "sacrifice," which she accomplishes with the help of Drolette.
Now Ourson is revealed in his true nature as Prince Marvellous,
and Violette assumes the bearskin. This climactic scene is followed by still another climax in which the fairy Drolette does
battle with her hideous sister, the red-haired toad Furious. The
two fairies fight in chariots, the one drawn by toads, the other by
larks. Victory is gained by Drolette when Furious, her toads
blinded and worsted, curses the queen of the fairies and is at once
reduced to impotence.

With Furious out of the way, Drolette informs the prince that
his father, the king, has been killed by his subjects and that he
is to reign in his stead. The prince begs the disfigured Violette
to be his queen, but the girl, mindful of her ugly appearance,
declines his offer and he, in turn decides to give up the throne.
As a reward for his devotion, Drolette orders Marvellous to descend once again into the well and to bring up the casket containing Violette's "happiness." It turns out that the casket contains
two bracelets and a vial of perfume. Drolette explains that the
bracelets are talismans for procuring health, riches, beauty, intelli-
gence, and happiness. As for the perfume, no sooner are a few
drops sprinkled on Violette than she is restored to her original
beauty. The next day, Violette and the prince are transported to
the prince's kingdom in a chariot drawn by larks. Violette is
wedded to the prince; she is dressed in a gown adorned with
diamond larks and wearing a crown of jeweled larks.

For eight days preceding the wedding, the fairy Drolette is absent. Shortly after the wedding, Agnella—now Queen Aimee —is spirited off by the genie Bienveillant, who has fallen in love with her. Once married to him, she shares fully his great powers, which include immortality, eternal youth, and the ability to travel instantly from place to place. We are informed, finally, that the persons who menaced Ourson when he was looking for work are suitably punished. The farmer is eaten by a bear; the superintendent of the castle is slain by a serpent; and the master of the forge is burned to death by his own workers.

Viewed as an initiation drama, "Ourson" is primarily the story of Violette's initiation at the age of fifteen. The central feature of her initiation is the act by which she undergoes symbolic incorporation by the bear totem, putting on his hide as a token of her kinship with her ancestors and then ceremonially removing it to signify her rebirth as a mature young woman. In his hairy incarnation, Ourson stands for the ascendant patriarchal totem with its magical saving powers and its requirement of repayment for favors rendered. Violette, whose name suggests her primordial fealty to the spirits of vegetation and the matriarchal fertility goddess, is required to sacrifice herself—i. e., to give up her previous identity—and to accept a new protector. Thus, her puberty rites, as reflected in the fairy tale, represent the historically important process of transition from the hegemony of the fertility goddess—in this case Aimee, probably a love goddess, and her handmaiden Passerose—to the domination of masculine deities.

The prominence given to two major "lunar" animals—the bear and the toad[38]—is in line with the supposition that "Ourson" deals above all with death and rebirth as symbolized by the submergence and the reappearance of these animals with the seasons. It is not surprising that the toad, an animal with strong affinities to the chthonic serpent, is cast in the role of antagonist and is defeated. The fairy Furious is clearly the negative image of the earth mother, Aimee, and, though her destruction is presented in the most dramatic terms, it is equally certain that at the end Aimee has been vanquished—indeed, ravished by a powerful genie—and subjected to his benevolent domination.

All in all, the victory belongs to the masculine sky-gods, for not only is Aimee carried off in a whirlwind, but the defeat of the toad is accomplished by larks. We know that the bird is a symbol of the conquering Zeus in the early stages of the consolidation of the mother cult and the religion of the sky-gods. The serpent and the toad are appropriate offspring of mother earth, and their historical subjection is reflected in their downfall in the fairy tale. The crowning of Violette with a tiara of larks signifies the transfer of her allegiance from the matriarch Aimee to the prince. The long period of Ourson's imprisonment in his bearskin would seem to refer to a period of subjection of the masculine bear totem during its nascent stage. In this sense, Ourson was indeed under a curse originating with the chthonic powers. The queen's banishment by her husband, King Furious, may similarly be seen as part of the larger theme of tension between two opposing forces, the one masculine and the other feminine.

Ourson's role in relation to his young charge Violette is that of a priestly instructor to a novice. He teaches the girl everything she has to know. Although Aimee/Agnella would have been better suited for preparing a young girl for her initiation, it must be recalled that the heroine is not fated to participate in a feminine mystery, but rather to submit to a masculine totem. Only after she has been "lost and found" under conditions acceptable to the bear totem will she be eligible for marriage. The *sacra* that belong to the bear totem are buried deep in a well and cannot bring her happiness until Violette herself descends into the well. Ourson, who has spent two days at the bottom of the well, is cast in the role of the ancestral bear spirit, hibernating underground and nourished by bread and wine. Violette also partakes of these magic foods, thereby effecting her communion with the totem.

The slaying of the totem is symbolically represented by the transfer of the bearskin from Ourson to Violette, the novice. This is a rather refined version of the ancient religious practice of putting on the skin of the dead totem animal.[39] When I speak of the "slaying" of the totem—in this case, the beloved Ourson —it may seem hard to believe that such a hostile act toward a sympathetic character can have a legitimate place in this narrative. Nevertheless, it has been the custom until modern times among various primitive Siberian tribes, as well as among the Ainu of Japan, for a bear cub to be affectionately reared by a woman—even nursed in some cases—and then killed as a totemic god and eaten in a communion feast.[40] Such a cub may even be called "son" and "brother," the names applied to Ourson. Strangely enough, the Gilyaks of Siberia place the slain bear totem on a trough on which is carved in relief a bear on one side, and a toad on the other.[41] Both the Gilyaks and the Ainu have been observed to lower the bear's carcass into the ceremonial hut either through a window or a smoke-hole, rather than carrying him in through the door.[42] In a similar fashion, Ourson rescues Violette and the others from their burning house by entering the structure through an open window. There is some reason to believe that the burning of the house is connected with the ritual death of Ourson, since the house collapses while he is in it looking for Violette's casket. On this occasion, Ourson is given up for lost and is mourned for two days. He is figuratively resurrected when Violette discovers him in the well under the charred remains of the house. It is not unlikely that Ourson's prototype in real life was less fortunate.

As far as Violette is concerned, the burning of her home marks the end of her childhood. Her remaining trials are experienced vicariously. It is Ourson who goes out into the world to look for work, *really to beg for food or to try to survive in some other way,* satisfying one of the key requirements for admission to adult status. His failure is consistent with a trend that runs through all the stories in the present collection—namely, that the ordeals of initiation cannot be overcome through independent action but require supernatural assistance. Twice previously, when Violette had been exposed to danger, her rescue had been mediated by her totemic protector Ourson with the help of the good fairy Drolette. The defeat of the fierce boar, no less than the escape from the fairy Furious who tried to drown Violette in a stream, are symbolic statements of victory over supernatural forces aligned with the cult of the earth mother, the boar being a blatant fertility symbol of the type associated with Demeter and the toad an emblem of the generative power of the primeval waters, the source of all life. Finally, Drolette's disappearance just prior to Violette's marriage signifies that the maiden is ready to replace her supernatural mother—that is, to become a mother in her own right. In like manner did Demeter give way to her daughter Persephone upon her annual release from the underworld.[43] In fairy tales, of course, Kore never turns into Hecate, so that, even though Violette turned into a mature woman, she never grew old.

9

A Medieval Love Story

MEDIEVAL *FABLIAUX*, or short tales in verse, have received little attention from scholars concerned with ethnography and related disciplines. At best, they have served as texts for linguistic analysis or have been viewed merely as precursors of later narratives. On the whole, critics have had little to say about the origins of such tales as "Aucassin and Nicolette," "Floire and Blanchefloire," or the numerous other tales and ballads of the troubadours, and the result has been to reduce these works to the status of literary curiosities and to take them out of their proper context. Paradoxically, many of our best insights into medieval literature have been provided by historians such as Hallam,[1] Luchaire,[2] and others, who have succeeded in placing the writings of the Middle Ages within their framework of feudal usages and role relationships. However, much work remains to be done using the conceptual tools of modern psychology, anthropology, and folklore study to conduct a systematic and comprehensive analysis of the considerable literary remains of the Middle Ages. The present chapter represents a small step in this direction. I have chosen the story

of Aucassin and Nicolette because it is deeply rooted in the
courtly psychology of the Middle Ages and because it brings
together important themes from folklore, anthropology, and developmental psychology.

"Aucassin and Nicolette" is by no means a typical product of
the literary imagination of the twelfth century, though it is believed to have been composed by an unknown troubadour during
that period. The single surviving manuscript was written in the
medieval dialect of Picardy, but the setting of the story is clearly
that of southern France, and it is necessary to view this *cant-fable*
as indigenous to the culture of Provence. It is not improbable that
the composition was transmitted orally by *jongleurs* over an unknown period of time—perhaps a generation or two, perhaps
longer—before it was recorded in its present form. It is unusual
in that, unlike most troubadour productions, it was composed in
alternating prose and verse, and, perhaps even more important,
it departs from the usual formula for troubadour poetry.

Instead of celebrating illicit, unrequited love for a noble married woman, "Aucassin and Nicolette" is a story of innocent
young love; instead of dwelling on conventional romantic con-
ceits, it moves rapidly from one dramatic tableau to the next;
instead of depicting its heroine as a passive love object, it portrays
a young woman who is active and resourceful; instead of project-
ing a stylized image of a brave and seasoned warrior, it deals with
a tearful princeling who does not wish to be a knight; instead of
refraining from satire, it counterposes to the spirit of romance a
strikingly modern sense of irreverence; instead of dealing in trite
nature imagery, it provides a number of concrete descriptive
images of great originality and artistic power. Above all, "Aucassin and Nicolette" is unique in its blending of folklore motifs with
more sophisticated themes. These motifs include references to
local religious customs, iconographic tableaux, the use of unconscious symbolism grounded in folk experience, and other nonliterary components, as I will try to demonstrate.

"Aucassin and Nicolette" must be approached at several levels
of interpretation. The most familiar level is, of course, that of
sheer literary appreciation. Suffice it to say that we are dealing

with a real work of art, skillfully constructed and polished, and reflecting a high degree of literary consciousness. I will not concern myself with the esthetic side of the tale at this time, but I hope the reader will not conclude that my analysis of its many layers of meaning denotes a lack of respect for the integrity of the work. At the same time, I do not wish to go beyond the esthetic assumptions that are implicit in the composition or to read into it a multiplicity of meanings that would have been beyond the conceptual grasp of its medieval author. I do not pretend that my interpretations—chiefly along folkloristic and psychoanalytic lines—have anything in common with the troubadour's intentions. I affirm instead that if the tale is to be understood in all its richness, it must first be dissolved into its imagistic and thematic components, and these components, in turn, must be resynthesized in the light of pertinent contextual factors relating to individual and group psychology.

Leaving esthetic considerations to one side, then, I propose to proceed on three levels of interpretation:

1. The tale as a recitation of the rites of passage of an adolescent boy and girl, not unlike the type of running narrative that sometimes accompanied the actual performance of initiation rites connected with the ancient Greco-Roman mysteries.[3]

2. The tale as a vehicle for incorporating pre-Christian and Christian local customs associated with seasonal holidays and festivals. It should be emphasized that these quasi-religious practices, as well as the literary devices to which they have given rise, are closely related to the drama of initiation, but reflect a shift of emphasis away from the individual and his rites of passage and toward affirming and strengthening the renewal of the natural and social orders on a seasonal basis.

3. The tale as a projection of unconscious sexual and aggressive motives associated with Oedipal rivalry and other psychological conflicts.

The following is a summary of "Aucassin and Nicolette," based mainly on Bourdillon's English translation,[4] along with his type-transliteration of the Old French derived from Suchier's redaction of the text[5] and on an examination by the author of a photofacsimile of the manuscript.[6]

The Count Garin was old and feeble and had outlived his day. He had only one son, Aucassin. Although the Count was besieged by his enemy, Count Bougars, Aucassin would not help his father in the defense of the castle nor would he assume any of the duties of knighthood. Instead, the youth pined for his love, Nicolette. This beautiful maiden was the ward of Count Garin's vassal, the Viscount, who had bought her from the Saracens as a child and had arranged for her baptism.

Aucassin's father wanted him to make a favorable marriage, so he prevailed upon the Viscount to confine Nicolette in a tower, hoping that Aucassin would forget her. He then promised Aucassin that he would permit him to see his love briefly if only he would put on his armor and ride out to do battle against the enemy. Aucassin believed his father and fought bravely, capturing his father's archenemy, Count Bougars. The father, however, did not keep his word, so Aucassin released his prisoner, making him swear to continue his opposition to his father. Subsequently, Aucassin was imprisoned in a dungeon by his father.

During his imprisonment, Aucassin composed a song which he addressed to the absent Nicolette. It told of a stricken pilgrim who was cured forthwith when Nicolette raised up her dress before him and revealed her limbs. The song ended with references to the amorous pleasures that Aucassin and Nicolette had shared in the past.

In the meantime, Nicolette had escaped from her room by lowering herself to the ground. She left behind an old woman who had been assigned to watch her, but had fallen asleep. Since it was a bright, moonlit night in May, Nicolette made her way furtively to Aucassin's prison. On her way, she had to tuck up her skirts to avoid wetting them in the dewy grass. She approached Aucassin's dungeon and spoke with him. The two lovers vied with each other in declaring their steadfastness, Aucassin swearing that if Nicolette ever slept with another man he would kill himself. As they were talking, the nightwatchmen appeared, but Nicolette was warned in time by the sympathetic warden and hid from view. After the nightwatchmen had passed, she slipped Aucassin a lock of her hair through a crack in the wall. She then told her lover that she was leaving to cross the sea to a distant land.

Nicolette proceeded to the moat surrounding the castle. She was frightened, but crossed herself and slid into the moat. After great effort, she climbed out on the other side, bruised and bleeding in twelve places. She had used a sharpened stick to cut a foothold for herself in the side of the moat. Impelled by the fear of being captured and burned at the stake, Nicolette preferred to face the dangers of the forest. She did not go deep into the woods, but spent the night at the edge of the forest, concealed behind some bushes.

In the morning Nicolette emerged from the forest and saw some shepherd boys eating their breakfast near a spring. She begged the boys to give Aucassin a message, the gist of which was that if he would go hunting in the forest, he would find a quarry that would cure him of his ills. At first, the shepherds were reluctant, thinking she might be a fairy, but they consented when she paid them five sous. Taking leave of the shepherds, Nicolette plunged into the forest. She made her way deep into the woodland, stopping when she came to the intersection of seven paths. There she built a leafy bower of lilies and other flowers and, hiding nearby, awaited Aucassin.

Following Nicolette's disappearance, Count Garin released Aucassin from his prison and sought to comfort him by preparing a feast in his honor. A knight who was present at the feast suggested to the woeful Aucassin that he might find solace if he rode into the forest. Aucassin rode toward the woods and found the shepherds at lunch. They grudgingly gave him news of Nicolette in return for ten sous, telling him that if he found his quest in three days, he would be cured of his wound. At once, Aucassin rode into the forest, and so headlong was his passage that his body was badly torn by briars, leaving a trail of blood.

Searching for Nicolette, the weeping Aucassin met a tall stranger with a big black head, wide-set eyes, large cheeks, and a flat nose. The stranger was dressed in clothes of bull's hide, and he carried a huge club. Aucassin lied and told the stranger he was looking for a lost white greyhound. In turn, the stranger said he was searching for a lost ox, one of four belonging to a rich farmer who had hired him. He told of having gone without food for three days and of his fear of returning empty-handed. The stranger added that his poor mother had been compelled to give up her only possession—a straw mattress—in default of the lost ox. He then rebuked Aucassin for being distraught over the loss of a mere dog. Aucassin did not seek to defend himself but paid the man twenty sous to compensate the owner of the lost ox, and the two parted.

Riding into the night, Aucassin discovered Nicolette's lodge in the forest, but, as he attempted to dismount from his horse, he fell and dislocated his shoulder. He crawled into the lodge and, looking up at the sky through an opening among the branches, sang a song to the brightest star in the sky, calling it Nicolette's abode. Nicolette entered the bower and the two lovers embraced. She then attended to his injury by putting his shoulder back into place and binding it up with flowers and grass and a strip of her dress. They climbed on his horse and rode off together. Aucassin kissed his love as they rode, stopping only when they came to the edge of the sea.

The young lovers at once boarded a merchant ship that was sailing nearby. Before long, a tempest arose and drove the ship to a strange land called Torelore. Disembarking, Aucassin and Nicolette rode up to the castle of the king of Torelore, only to make the surprising discovery that the king was in childbed while the queen was off doing battle. Aucassin angrily upbraided the king for his unmanly conduct, beating him with a cudgel until he promised to end this strange practice.

Leaving Nicolette behind, Aucassin and the king joined the queen at the battlefront. Noting that the warriors were merely pelting each other with apples, eggs, and cheeses, Aucassin dashed forward and began to slay the king's adversaries with his sword. The king restrained him, and they returned to the castle.

Aucassin and Nicolette lived together in great happiness at Torelore, even though at one point the king tried to persuade Nicolette to marry his own son. Three years went by until, at last,

Aucassin and Nicolette were carried off by Saracens who had captured the castle of Torelore. The lovers were parted—Aucassin making his way back to his home in Beaucaire while Nicolette was borne to Carthage. As it turned out, Aucassin's parents had died during his absence, so Aucassin was made Count of Beaucaire upon his return. Nicolette, finding herself in Carthage, remembered that she was the daughter of the king of Carthage and that fifteen years earlier she had been carried off from her father's castle. Restored to her former status, Nicolette still thought only of Aucassin, refusing all offers of marriage.

Shortly before she was to be married off to a neighboring king, Nicolette escaped and stayed with a poor woman at the edge of the sea. There she stained her face brown, disguised herself as a minstrel, and took ship to Provence. Arriving at Beaucaire, she presented herself before Aucassin and his nobles and related in song the story of Aucassin and Nicolette. She reassured Aucassin, who did not recognize her, that his love was safe in Carthage and remained loyal to him, turning away all suitors. At Aucassin's urging, Nicolette promised to reunite the two lovers. She then departed and went to the house of her godmother, the viscountess (the viscount having died). There, she related the story of her adventures and rested for eight days. At the conclusion of this period she removed the brown stain from her skin by means of an herb, dressed herself in fine clothes, and asked the viscountess to summon Aucassin. Aucassin came at once and the two lovers, overjoyed at finding each other, remained together all night. They were married the following day and lived happily for the rest of their lives.

Let us proceed to look at the tale from the standpoint of the drama of initiation. It is clear that significant elements of both male and female initiation rites have been incorporated into the romance. To understand the centrality of these rites, it is necessary to begin by examining the identities of the two central characters. How old are they? What is their status in relation to their elders? It is easy to think of the protagonists as a young man and a young woman because of the romantic superstructure with its unmistakable motifs of self-assertion and eroticism. However, there are occasional references that suggest that the substructure of the tale involves individuals who are not yet full adults. For example, the opening lines of the story refer to the protagonists as two fair little children *(deus biax enfans petis)*. Aucassin is described as a boy *(vallet)* in one place and as a Squire, or aspirant for knighthood *(damoisiax)*, in another. At no point is he called a man, although the author depicts him as tall and strong. As for Nicolette, we know that she was abducted from Carthage as a small child and was absent from her ancestral home for twelve years. It is not unrealistic to suppose that she was about sixteen or seventeen years of age at the commencement of the story. At the end of the story, after three years at Torelore, she had been absent from Carthage a total of fifteen years, being then about nineteen or twenty years old. She is referred to as a young girl, using the Arabic word, *meschinete,* [7] and is also called the viscount's god-daughter *(fillole)*. At the same time, there can be no doubt that Nicolette is more than a mere girl in those modern parts of the story that contain the motif of eroticism.

Although speculation about the meaning of the names of the protagonists may seem farfetched, a few observations may be made relative to their presumed age and status in life as suggested by their names. The name Aucassin may be of Semitic origin, bearing a close relationship to the Hebrew word for bridegroom *(chassin)*, just as the name Nicolette has some resemblance to the Hebrew word for bride *(kala)*. [8] Although it is not feasible at present to trace the process by which these Semitic words might have found their way into southern France, there can be no doubt that the Near Eastern literature of courtly love had a profound influence on the compositions of the troubadors. [9] The evidence for such influence is considerable and need not occupy us further in the present context. As I will try to demonstrate, Aucassin and Nicolette are more than romantic lovers; they belong also to the category of novices undergoing ritual preparation for marriage. Thus, it is appropriate that their names should be derived from words signifying bride and groom.

In addition to the possible Semitic sources for the names of the protagonists, there may be a basis in local usage—the dialect of

Limousine, a district of Provence; the name Aucassin has a strong resemblance to the local word signifying married *(casado)*. [10] It also suggests another term that defines rather precisely Aucassin's relationship to his father; I refer to the Limousin word denoting a son who absents himself from his father's house in order to devote himself to amorous activities—the term is *caseur*, [11] a word that would seem to have a more-than-accidental affinity with Aucassin.

Nicolette's name also seems to have some links with a Limousin word meaning married, namely *nicha*. [12] Closely related to *nicha* is the Limousin term *nicho*, which means a nest or a lodge,[13] words that have a special meaning within the context of Nicolette's adventures in the forest. One may state the hypothesis, then, that the names Aucassin and Nicolette seem to be multi-determined and that they point possibly to rites of passage associated with marriage or preparation for marriage.

It is not necessary, however, to place much emphasis on word derivations, since they are often ambiguous. A content analysis of the story indicates that each protagonist is made to pass through a series of stages culminating in marriage. For Aucassin, the process involves a clearly defined passage from youthful rebellion to a demonstration of manhood in the spheres of aggression and sexuality, ending in the achievement of full knightly status as lord of the manor.[14] Nicolette's progression is equally systematic and involves her transformation from a status of passivity to the position of a resourceful, self-directed young woman who is sexually experienced and qualified to be the lady of the manor. To be sure, the protagonists do not mature in the manner prescribed by their elders; they consummate their relationship on their own terms. But, the persistent note of defiance is consistent with the psychological demands of their situation, which requires independence, daring, and a willingness to endure the condition of spiritual loneliness as a prerequisite to confronting a sacred mystery.

If we examine Aucassin's development, it is relatively easy to identify the principal crises in his life and to see their relationship to his long-range goal. His destiny is clear from the start: to replace his declining father, who is described as old and feeble and as having outlived his time. The first step in his growth is to learn to put first things first—that is, simply to agree to discharge the duties of a warrior as a precondition for earning the right to see his sweetheart. Aucassin's initial reluctance to engage in combat, rationalized as romantic preoccupation, would seem to illustrate his fear of entering upon a dangerous rite of passage. His father's breach of faith serves as a kind of object lesson to boys who may seek to evade their obligation to prove themselves on the field of battle, and it may be seen as a not unmerited punishment. Count Garin's disapproval of his son's love affair with Nicolette, a girl of uncertain antecedents, is in keeping with the feudal practice of strategic matchmaking. The fact that, in the end, Aucassin has his way does not invalidate his father's demands, nor do the claims of love entirely mitigate the seriousness of Aucassin's act of disobedience. In effect, Aucassin's waywardness is ambiguously instructive to all future novices—it is clearly wrong to decline to be a warrior, and it is no less wrong to disobey one's father, but it is permissible to commit such transgressions vicariously through the medium of fantasy.

Having survived the ordeal of combat, Aucassin is subjected to a second trial, in which he is imprisoned in a cell because of his continued defiance of his father. There is an unreal, ritualistic quality about his endless, stylized lamentations during his imprisonment, just as there was a distinct element of mimesis about his participation in armed combat, in which it was made clear to him that he was under no compulsion to harm his adversaries, but was expected merely to set an example of valor by his presence. Aucassin's imprisonment by his father, though fully consistent with the heavyhanded customs of feudal lords, is strikingly reminiscent of a common feature of ancient initiation rites. Imprisonment, deprivation, torture, mutilation, confrontation with terrifying monsters—all these elements, ending in some kind of illumination, are fairly constant features of initiation rites. Aucassin's imprisonment does not include any of the special features listed above, but his experiences in the forest after his release constitute a logical continuation of his ordeal.

Before turning to the forest episode, it is worth mentioning the libidinous song which Aucassin composed in his marble cell. Certain features of this song combine eroticism with ritual in an intriguing way. First of all, the song anticipates the motif of Nicolette-in-the-woods by associating the heroine with the symbolism of the lily. More important, the tale of the pilgrim who was cured by a glimpse of Nicolette's naked limbs is more than a sexual allusion. It is a kind of revelation, the act of showing a mystery to the novice.

The mystery, of course, is of a sexual nature, but it is a mystery having to do with sexual identity; that is, it is a rite of passage in which the novice is confirmed in his sex role. The closest parallel is a ceremony that has been reported among a tribal group in the South Seas.[15] In this initiation rite, at one point, the masked initiator undresses completely in the presence of the novice, revealing his sex in the most unambiguous way. The fact that the *Tubuan*, or masked initiator, is of the same sex as the novice is of the greatest importance insofar as it represents a bond of solidarity between the novice and the other members of the secret society. By contrast, the bond that unites Aucassin with Nicolette is libidinous. In both cases, however, we are witness to a ceremony of regeneration. The pilgrim (Aucassin) is cured of sickness *(tant que ta ganbete vit / garis fu li pelerins)*, while the primitive novice is freed of his pregenital status, incorporated into the secret brotherhood of warriors, and confirmed as a reborn man. Aucassin, it will be recalled, earlier proved his eligibility for the status of a warrior by a trial of arms. It should be added that Aucassin's song does not say the pilgrim was sick of love or some other poetic conceit, but speaks of sickness in literal terms *(malades de l'esvertin*, "dizzy, epileptic").

Aucassin's forest episode carries his initiation several steps further, unfolding according to a ritualistic scenario. The forest itself represents a boundary, and to cross this boundary is to enter a sacred domain. At first, Aucassin is obliged to pay a sum of money to the shepherd boys, in return for which fee he is told in enigmatic terms to pursue a quarry with curative powers. In this case, the payment of a fee is distinctly ritualistic, corresponding to Nicolette's payment of a small sum to the same shepherds. In effect, the novice is given permission to undertake his magical quest. As to the nature of the quarry, we have seen what curative powers Nicolette possesses. It remains only for Aucassin to acquire his symbolic wounds so that he can be made whole again and invested with new powers.

Aucassin's first wound consists of being pierced by briars and thorns so that he bleeds in thirty or forty places and leaves a trail of blood. These injuries constitute a kind of mutilation belonging to the category of rites of separation and incorporation, according to Van Gennep.[16] By means of a visible sign together with the direct experience of pain, exhaustion, and great desperation, the loud-lamenting Aucassin enters upon a new status. The ordeal of the thorns closely resembles a ritual flagellation or beating of the type often encountered in primitive initiation rites, where it serves the purpose of insuring the submission of the novice to his elders. In addition, Aucassin's spilt blood is symbolic of sacrifice, expressing not only the idea of appeasement of the divine powers and their mortal surrogates, but also renunciation for the sake of a higher goal.

Having been properly scourged by the impersonal thorns, Aucassin comes face-to-face with the individual who might very well have been his ritual tormentor in a primitive initiation ceremony. The tall, ugly man whom Aucassin meets in the forest is no mere spirit-of-the-woods. All in all, his description suggests an initiator wearing a bull mask and clothed in a bull's hide. The narrator leaves no doubt about Aucassin's fear in the presence of this monstrous being, whom he addresses politely as "fair brother" (biax frere). It is a mistake to assume that the stranger's grotesque appearance corresponds to the aristocratic conception of a peasant during the Middle Ages, although his appearance is clearly stereotyped.[17] He seems to belong to the same genre as Holland's modern Black Peter, with his menacing cudgel—the frightening masker who accompanies Saint Nicholas on his rounds. Like the katchina of the American Southwest, the stranger's essential function seems to be to overawe and to instruct. By condemning Aucassin for bemoaning the loss of a mere greyhound and contrasting his own situation with Aucassin's more fortunate condition, he gives the hero to understand that a man must have a sense of proportion. The stranger makes a special point of the circumstance that his mother has been deprived of her only possession, a straw mattress, in retaliation for his failure to recover his master's lost ox. Surely an important truth is revealed in this account, a lesson in filial responsibility and, in a broader sense, a commentary on the hard facts of life. As if to underline the seriousness of his accusation against Aucassin, the stranger, seemingly a mere peasant, ends with the following malediction: "A foul curse upon he who shall ever esteem you again!" Aucassin's response is very soft indeed, in the light of his princely status: "Certes, thou art of good comfort, fair brother! A blessing on thee!" I see no satirical intention behind this encounter but view it rather as a lesson taught to a frivolous youth by an authoritative representative of the elders, complete with the totemic mask of the bull, the ancient divinity of Provence.

Aucassin undergoes a second ordeal in the forest when, discovering Nicolette's bower, he falls from his horse and dislocates his shoulder. This wound is more grave than the scratches caused by the thorns and seems to represent the culmination of Aucassin's forest trial. Perhaps it is a punishment for invading the sacred grove within which Nicolette is performing her vigil, a mystery that is taboo for men, but I think it is more likely that Aucassin's injury is an essential part of his initiation. He is spared the full term of solitude and suffering that is normally demanded by the initiatory scenario by the prompt appearance of Nicolette, who cures him.

Nicolette's therapy seems to constitute an initiation through love, as in the secret practices of the *Fideli d'Amore,* a thirteenth century cult dedicated to the mystery of spiritual love.[18] That there is a physical element, as well, in Nicolette's ministrations is stated explicitly. The sexual symbolism of Nicolette's action is striking: "She felt him about, and found that he had his shoulder out of place. She plied it so deftly with her white hands, and pulled it [as God willed, who loveth lovers], so it came again into place."

Apart from the sexual symbolism of Aucassin's injury the whole machinery of the lovers' encounter in the forest appears to be soteriological. The forest itself, with its invisible wild beasts, its demonic, bull-faced stranger, and its all-but-inpenetrable briars, is a kind of hell. Aucassin descends into this hell and is symbolically maimed, undergoes a ritual death, and is revived after a brief sojourn in Nicolette's womb-like bower in the wilderness. Nicolette appears in the role of a protective nature spirit, no less than as a mortal, because her healing gifts depend upon her use of flowers, leaves, and grass. The restorative powers of her torn skirt, as a symbol of sexuality, should not be underestimated in relation to Aucassin's disjointed condition.

If the episode in the forest is Aucassin's moment in hell, his ride to the sea with Nicolette before him in the saddle is a kind of prelude to heaven. Having spiritually died from his old life as an immature youth and having been revived by the wonder-working Nicolette, Aucassin is ready for purification in the waters of the sea. No longer the green knight or squire, Aucassin has also passed through the phase of the black knight of tribulation-in-obscurity and is about to become the white knight—the illuminated one. All that remains is to cross the primordial waters and to be miraculously washed up on the shores of far-off Torelore, there to enjoy three years of perfect love.

Perhaps Torelore is based on the half-legendary North African *Turlande*, where Raimond, a knightly pilgrim from Bousquet, near Toulouse, is reported to have been carried by Arab pirates in the tenth or eleventh centuries.[19] We have this on the testimony of one, Bernard, a priest of Angers who has left an account of the Odysseus-like adventures of Raimond; Raimond may have been a real personage or simply a fictional copy of his Homeric prototype. I prefer to believe that Torelore—where kings underwent the couvade,[20] where warriors battled with roasted crab-apples, eggs, and fresh cheeses,[21] and where all barriers to the consummation of love vanished—is that heavenly destination for which Aucassin's trials had prepared him. Once illuminated and purified by his passage over the waters, Aucassin is qualified to rebuke unmanly kings and to slay men in combat *as a matter of principle* and not impulsively, as in his earlier combat before the walls of his father's castle. Also, he has a license to make love to Nicolette without having to bother with a formal marriage ceremony. The interlude in Torelore is not extraneous to the initiatory drama but seems to represent a modern desacralization of what originally may have represented a mystical union. Of course, the comic element predominates in our present version of the episode, but the didactic—and climactic—elements are not entirely obscured. Once again, we cannot overlook the Oedipal motif suggested by the beating administered to the king of Torelore by Aucassin.

As far as Aucassin is concerned, Torelore is the end of his initiation. His return to his native land and his assumption of his father's title is merely the formal goal of initiation, confirming Aucassin in his manly status. It is curious that the mythographer separates Nicolette from Aucassin at this crucial junction in the young man's life. Strictly speaking, however, Nicolette has fulfilled her role in Aucassin's initiation, having helped him to attain sexual maturity. The rest of the narrative, in which Aucassin waits upon Nicolette's initiative to bring her to his side, is no longer Aucassin's story, but belongs to the drama of Nicolette's spiritual rebirth.

It is time to return to Nicolette and to trace her adventures. Her initiation is in some ways closer to the heart of the story than that of Aucassin. I say this because Nicolette is a more active agent than Aucassin and because her imprisonment at the start and her triumphant return at the end round out a complete course of initiation. Aucassin's adventures are compressed into a shorter time-span and are rather specialized, revolving mainly around his painful ordeals. In Nicolette's case, we see a wide range of initiatory experiences, embracing not only severe trials, but including also puberty rites of isolation and purification, tests of ingenuity, and the assumption of interim roles and identities.

It is best to start with Nicolette's curious status as the ward and god-daughter *(fillole)* of the Viscount. We are given to understand that she is of non-Christian origin, was purchased from Saracens, and was baptized by the Viscount. The motif of the captive prince or princess is not unusual in tales of the Middle

Ages. No doubt, this preoccupation reflected practices associated with the endless wars between Christians and Moslems and gave rise to the literary convention illustrated here. It is not so important that Nicolette was of foreign origin, but rather that her status as a full-fledged member of the community is uncertain up to the very end of the story. Nicolette resembles a novice who is sponsored by her god-parents but cannot receive the recognition of her community as an adult woman until she has undergone ritual purification. Her status as an outsider is symbolic of her estranged condition as a would-be adult. Only when she has prepared herself for her adult role can she be exhibited to the community, thereby announcing, as Eliade suggests, that the mystery has been accomplished.[22]

Nicolette's imprisonment in a tower standing in a garden is not to be confused with those frequent acts of cruelty by which medieval nobles distinguished themselves. This is not merely a case of punishing a recalcitrant daughter by locking her in a cell. The circumstances of Nicolette's confinement are altogether fantastic. Not only is she imprisoned with an old woman to keep her company, but the two of them are *sealed* into their chamber with a supply of bread, meat, and wine![23] The vaulted room *(canbre vautie)*, with its strange wall paintings, suggests a secret initiation cave more than a prison. The rumor of Nicolette's disappearance is tantamount to an announcement of her ritual isolation, that is, of her state of being taboo. We have no way of knowing what sort of esoteric instruction she was to receive. We are told only that she is forbidden to Aucassin. The Viscount twice repeats the formula that Aucassin's father had enunciated earlier, namely, that Nicolette is not suitable for Aucassin. The basis of her ineligibility is not, however, her "unwholesome blood" defined in terms of lineage, but, more likely, her ritual impurity until such time as her puberty rites shall have been completed.

As long as Nicolette remains in the sacred precincts of the enclosed garden, she is inaccessible. No wonder she puts on her best silk dress in order to climb out of her prison tower and to escape from the garden, completing the first phase of her enforced isolation. The text does not give the color of her dress, but it would not be surprising if it were white, a color that is symbolically appropriate for girls undergoing initiation and that is especially appropriate for Nicolette, whose name is frequently linked in the text with the lily *(flors de lis)*.

Nicolette's successful attempt to communicate with the imprisoned Aucassin is instructive on two counts. First, it is a forbidden action, punishible by public burning. Second, the substance of the lovers' conversation deals with the issue of fidelity. On the first count, Nicolette's approach to Aucassin's dungeon violates the taboo against female encroachment upon the sacred ground where the male novice has been segregated. This is the only way to explain the severe penalty facing Nicolette, whose act of disobedience is not in the category of capital offenses, even if judged by medieval standards. The menacing approach of the nightwatch, with their "naked" swords and their harsh orders to slay Nicolette on sight adds not only a note of melodrama, but underscores as well the mortal risks attendant upon Nicolette's interruption of her own rites of passage.

The lovers' quarrel as to who is the more devoted and Aucassin's threat to dash out his brains if Nicolette were to become another man's mistress seem to represent a departure from the initiation scenario. This exchange, with its romantic exaggerations, has a modern ring at the same time that it suggests the *Fedeli d'Amore,* with their cult of the "one woman." Although Nicolette leaves a lock of her hair for Aucassin, it cannot be said that she has engaged in an exchange of vows with him, because she insists that their relationship cannot continue in the face of opposition and relates her plan to sail to a far land. For Nicolette, the interlude outside Aucassin's prison is a departure from her prescribed plan of action, which must at least temporarily lead her away from Aucassin. Her destiny for the time being is in the forest, where she must undergo isolation and purification in a natural setting. Only then can she receive Aucassin.

Nicolette's descent into the moat is the first step toward ritual purification. To be sure, it is a dry moat, and there is nothing to indicate that a ritual bath has taken place. Yet one's suspicions are aroused by the circumstance that Nicolette is reported to have bled in twelve places while lowering herself into the moat. Why twelve places? Can this be a symbolic reference to the twelve menstrual periods of the year, and their associated rites of isolation and purification? Even if this possibility is ruled out, it is evident that the moat represents a highly significant boundary, crossed at great peril. It serves the purpose of placing Nicolette beyond the reach of the cloistered, presexual world she has left behind, and enables her to set foot in the wild, liberating precincts of the forest, with its magical healing powers and its dangerous beasts representing the perils of a life of unbridled impulse.

Nicolette's encounter with the shepherd boys seems to be quasi-ceremonial, paralleling Aucassin's transaction with them at a later point, when he seeks news of his beloved. First of all, Nicolette describes herself as a quarry for Aucassin's hunting, to be overtaken in three days if the latter is to be cured of his wounds.[24] The use of the quarry metaphor not only indicates a sort of ritual circumlocution, but is a reminder that Nicolette has a special role to play in Aucassin's initiation. She enables him to realize his striving to become a complete man in the sexual sense, and she is also the instrument of his matriculation as a huntsman. Aucassin's evasive answer to the monstrous stranger in the wood, in which he tells of searching for a lost hound, is in keeping with Nicolette's introduction of the huntsman motif.

Nicolette's self-description as an animal of the forest is reminiscent of the theme of the French tale "Bonne Biche,"[25] in which an adolescent girl lives with an enchanted deer, who serves as her godmother and instructor in the mysteries. In this tale, the initiation theme is very clear and reveals the affinity between esoteric instruction and the use of totemic maskers impersonating deer. Perhaps Nicolette is such an animal momentarily, on the symbolic level, until she has fulfilled the requirements of her initiation. In fact, we begin to see at this point her new connection with nature. Nicolette's entry into the forest places her in contact with the magical, life-giving powers of the wilderness. If she is to make the transition from girlhood to womanhood, it is necessary for her to receive the mana that flows from trees and flowers and which, in primitive lore, is the great storehouse of fertility and abundance.

This is the basis for her quarry metaphor, in which she partakes imaginatively of the wild nature of a forest animal, perhaps making her obeisance to the totemic ancestor who may have figured prominently in archaic initiation rites.

When we turn to Nicolette's sojourn near the leafy bower in the forest, we discover the most important element in her initiation. This secluded shelter, covered with flowers and located at the intersection of seven pathways in the forest, is essentially an initiation hut, that is, a place where a neophyte undergoes symbolic death and rebirth. In Nicolette's case, nothing of consequence happens in the hut until Aucassin's arrival. His injury upon dismounting from his horse and Nicolette's success in curing him suggest that a mimesis of death and rebirth is involved, at least for Aucassin. As for Nicolette, the centrality of the forest hut in her initiation drama is indicated by the fact that it has been built less as a shelter than as a way station, a place where Nicolette temporarily can establish her links with the forest and where she is destined to perform her healing mysteries in relation to Aucassin. Her skill in ministering to him by means of flowers, fresh grass, and green leaves is a demonstration of her newly acquired powers, quasi-magical from the masculine point of view, but consistent with her new status as an initiated woman. Our story leaves out the heart of the mystery—*how* Nicolette was transformed by her brief stay in the forest—but leaves no doubt that she had come into possession of impressive healing powers. Perhaps Aucassin's use of the term greyhound to describe the object of his quest to the stranger in the woods is indicative of a link between Nicolette and the hounds of Hecate. The setting of the forest at night-time and the reference to crossroads contribute to the impression—and it is hardly more than an impression—that Nicolette is briefly more-than-Nicolette, more than the frightened girl cowering in the fearsome woods.

I will return to Nicolette's bower at a later point and will indicate its relationship to the celebration of May Day. Within the context of the Maying festivities, it will be seen that Nicolette's initiation might well have included a sexual experience with Aucassin. Even the ride to the sea on horseback is replete

with sexual allusions: (Laced upon the saddle bow / There he
kissed her, chin and brow, / There embraced her, mouth and
eyes). By contrast, the passage across the stormy sea seems to
represent a phase of purification. The two lovers break decisively
with their past by entering upon the primordial waters, and, when
they come to rest on the remote shores of Torelore, they are ready
to assert themselves fearlessly.

The idyllic interlude in Torelore contains but one threat to
Nicolette, namely, the design of the king to take her away from
Aucassin and give her to his son because "she seemed a fair
woman of high lineage." It is curious that in the land of Beaucaire
Nicolette was regarded as unfit to marry a Count's son—Aucassin
—but that in Torelore she is sought after by royalty. This paradox
is heightened by the fact that even after Nicolette refuses to
accede to the king's wishes, she is permitted to live with Aucassin
in the royal castle for three years. What is the explanation for this
newly found status and independence?

An important clue is provided by the manner in which Nicolette affirms her commitment to Aucassin in the face of the king's
importunities. She simply declares that love-making with Aucassin is worth more to her than anything else on earth. This is the
sum total of her statement. Such a declaration leaves no doubt as
to the source of her newly found confidence: She has attained full
status as a woman. Although the status of adulthood would not
have conferred any special privileges upon Nicolette in the Middle Ages, it is necessary to view her situation outside the framework of history. Beyond the medieval framework, mythopoeisis
creates its own statuses and immunities and its own sacralities, of
which sexual power is not the least. Thus, Aucassin and Nicolette
in Torelore fulfill their libidinous wishes beyond the reach of
moral or rational persuasion and even beyond the reach of kingly
prerogative. Torelore is truly a land of make-believe; it is the
region where the sexual wish comes into its own. Characteristically, Aucassin's so newly acquired knightly aggression is out of
place in Torelore, where it is unnecessary for men to kill each
other in battle. In the absence of sexual frustration, there is
neither hostility nor guilt-feeling. I do not believe that the lovers'

guiltless acceptance of sexual freedom is a consequence of the licentious court life of the Age of Chivalry. It is rather that they have undergone the necessary rites of passage and have earned the right to full self-expression. Their union is as much mystical as carnal because, having completed their respective rites of separation through flight and isolation, they are ready in the sacramental sense to seek perfect unity.

Aucassin and Nicolette are removed from Torelore by the same magical power that brought them to that land of wish fulfillment. Aucassin is restored at once to Beaucaire, and Nicolette is taken back to her native city of Carthage. That she is the long-lost daughter of the king of Carthage is of no great significance. Instead, we must turn to several related elements that enter the narrative at this point. These features include:

1. Nicolette's assumption of male attire, ostensibly for the purpose of disguise;
2. the staining of her face with an herb;
3. Nicolette's bath in the house of her godmother, the Viscountess, and the removal of her stain by means of a plant called *Esclaire;*
4. Nicolette's reception of Aucassin, in which the heroine, richly dressed in silk and seated on a quilted coverlet of silk, seems to sit in state, awaiting her future husband.

To evaluate the above-mentioned features properly, it is necessary to de-emphasize the dramatic episode in which Nicolette, disguised as a *jongleur,* appears before Aucassin and his courtiers. This is a romantic conceit, apparently superimposed on the ritual substructure of initiation. More important, first of all, is Nicolette's assumption of male identity. We have an example here of a common feature of adolescent initiation rites, namely, a ritual of transvestism.[26] The psychological meaning of this practice is difficult to ascertain. Perhaps it represents a preliminary step to the solemn and definitive renunciation of the characteristic traits of the opposite sex. Thus, by performing a mimesis of maleness, the female novice establishes a baseline for defining her appropriate sex role at the conclusion of the initiation ceremony. A modern survival of this custom may perhaps be seen in the practice of addressing recruits in Marine boot camp as "ladies" or in the annual musical shows once staged by students in all-male Ivy League colleges in which young men acted the part of chorus girls.

The use of a plant by Nicolette to stain her face and hair black *(tote noire et tainte)* is again strikingly reminiscent of a primitive initiation rite. Eliade,[27] citing from a work by Berndt and Berndt on the Australian aborigines, describes a ceremony in which the girl novice is painted with ocher as a prelude to undergoing purification in a stream. It is obvious that this custom belongs to the more inclusive category of rites in which the initiate, by painting his body or covering himself with white clay, assumes a ghost-like identity. In effect, he dies in relation to his old identity and status and, drawing new strength from his sojourn among the dead ancestors, prepares himself to emerge as one reborn. This is the condition of Nicolette at the point where she retires to her godmother's house in Beaucaire.

Nicolette's bath and the removal of her dark stain are part of her rites of purification. The fact that she is sequestered in her godmother's house for eight days adds to the impression that the narrative has incorporated lustration rites connected with a girl's first menstruation. To be sure, the motifs of separation and purification appeared earlier in the story when Nicolette crossed the moat, but the full significance of this stage of initiation is revealed only in the closing scene of the tale. Only when Nicolette presents herself to Aucassin after having completed her ritual purification, and properly attired in ceremonial feminine clothes can the full meaning of her previous adventures be grasped.

There is a distinctly ceremonial and revelatory aspect to Nicolette's queenly appearance as she awaits Aucassin. This is the end of a mystery in which disguise and concealment figured prominently. Having completed her ordeal of initiation, Nicolette is ready, at last, to enter upon marriage to Aucassin. The narrative ends appropriately with marriage bells not because this is exclusively a romantic tale, but because it is also a narrative dealing with the rites of passage from adolescence to sexual maturity.

It remains now to draw attention to another facet of "Aucassin and Nicolette." I will deal briefly with the features of the story that appear to derive from folk customs associated with May Day. Of course, it should be said at once that a very close association exists between a variety of May Day celebrations, both ancient and modern, and rites of initiation. To this day, for example, the month of May is associated with First Communion in France. Well into the nineteenth century, it was the custom for girls who had entered upon the First Communion to be exhibited publicly under a leafy canopy during the month of May.[28, 29] These girls, dressed in white and crowned with flowers—especially lilies—could be seen here and there, often next to a church or at a crossroads (not unlike Nicolette), seated in a specially constructed bower and often holding a leafy branch in one hand.

The above practice is, of course, far removed in both time and in spirit from its pre-Christian origins, but the historical links are clearly evident. It is well known, for example, that the ancient Romans worshiped the tree spirit *Bona Dea*,[30] or Flora (eventually Diana), on May Day. This spirit was represented by the queen of the May, who sat in state in an arbor set up in a public place, near a Maypole. The contemporary secular practice of crowning a girl queen of the May is commonplace and can be directly traced back to the Roman custom, if not earlier, by way of traditional European and North American Maying festivities. These activities included the practice of gathering flowers and cutting fresh branches in the woods after midnight on the eve of May first. The young men and women who participated in these outings often engaged in sexual activities, if one is to believe contemporary accounts: "of fourtie, threescore, or a hundred maides goyng to the woode over night, there have scarcely the thirde part of them returned home againe undefiled."[31] Although the month of May is still considered unlucky for marriage by many people, it is not unreasonable to suppose that the amorous encounters on May Day eve were unofficial preliminaries to marriage in the more favorable month of June. In short, the woodland trysts reflect the persistence of the archaic custom of sexual initiation in connection with the month of May.

In seeming contradiction to this hypothesis is the fact that the mystery of the Roman *Floralia* excluded all men and that, indeed, effigies of men (in remote times, real men or boys) were thrown into a river by the officiating vestal virgins on this occasion.[32] How, then, can one speak of premarital sexual initiation of girls by their male partners in the Maying festivities?

This paradoxical situation is due, I believe, to the conjunction of Diana-linked initiation rites for girls with the complex of fertility observances connected with the phallic maypole. Although the maypole has ceased to serve as a blatant sex symbol, it has not lost its erstwhile relationship to the old vegetation cults. In this regard, Frazer notes that even in modern times, "May trees" covered with flowers and ribbons still were set up throughout Provence.[33] The maypole not only derives from vegetation cults; it is also inseparable from ancestor worship. It belongs to the realm of phallic symbols of the type associated in India with the god Siva. Today as in the past, the blue-faced Siva is both a phallic divinity and a frightening god of the dead, covered with ashes and given to haunting the precincts of the dead. A syncretic deity, he combines in his nature the procreative and life-destroying attributes often found in separate gods. Thus, it is no accident that the May tree, a symbol of the regenerative power of nature, was often carried around on May Day in the presence of one or more flower-covered, black-faced men variously called Jack-in-the-green, green George, etc.[34] These figures seem to represent death and potentially dangerous vegetation spirits. Their association with the life-giving maypole is a clear example of the cyclical character of vegetation cults, which view life and death merely as phases of nature. Now, then, to return to my question: How can one reconcile the exclusion of men from the mystery of female initiation with my thesis that the Maying festivities came to involve sexual intercourse between young men and women? Moreover, how does Aucassin's sojourn in the forest—an apparent intrusion into Nicolette's vigil beside her arbor—signify the presence of a motif of sexual initiation?

The missing link is the frightening, black-faced stranger in the forest who rebuked Aucassin for his frivolity and whose nature was surely demonic. With his totemic mask and his menacing club, he is clearly a representative of the underground gods who have assimilated the magical potency of dead ancestors. In nine-teenth-century Maying celebrations, the forest-stranger had his counterpart in chimney-sweeps[35] who accompanied the May queen while carrying a decorated May tree. In pre-Reformation England, his counterpart in the Robin Hood[36] celebrations on May Day was the terrifying Friar Tuck, who carried a huge club with which he threatened spectators and warned them to beware of purgatory. In the Netherlands today, the forest stranger is represented by Black Peter,[37] who accompanies Saint Nicholas on his rounds and threatens to punish naughty children. As was the case in the forest episode in "Aucassin and Nicolette," it was often necessary to placate these spirits of the dead with small sums of money, gifts of food, etc. How, then, does the forest stranger fit into the scheme of things? He tells us by his presence that Aucassin and Nicolette are not alone, but must come to terms with the ancestral totem, without whose blessing fertility cannot be vouchsaved. It is the forest stranger who gives Aucassin a license to proceed after he has been appeased and after he has taught Aucassin a lesson in filial piety. In his office of fertility charm, he legitimizes Aucassin's interruption of Nicolette's lonely vigil.

It can be seen from the various elements of the forest episode in "Aucassin and Nicolette" and from the typical features of traditional Maying activities in Europe that three distinct rituals are common to the medieval tale and the May Day celebrations: female initiation, ancestor worship, and fertility rites. In the light of the foregoing, the ancient Roman custom of drowning men or boys during the month of May would seem to have had little to do with hostility toward men, as much as it denoted a sacrificial rite to placate the dead. In "Aucassin and Nicolette" too the protagonists have a brush with death when Aucassin falls from his horse. This is his sacrifice to the ancestors, just as Nicolette's success in restoring him to health is her demonstration that she has been initiated into the secrets of life.

Finally, we can make a few observations on the strictly psycho-

logical implications of "Aucassin and Nicolette." I will not belabor
the point that the actions of the protagonists represent a successful rebellion against paternal authority and an affirmation of their
sexual rights. Nor is it necessary to dwell at length on the motif
of Oedipal rivalry that is reflected in Aucassin's thrashing of the
king of Torelore. It is reasonably clear that the appeal of the story
rests in part on its ability to satisfy vicariously the strong conscious
and unconscious needs for self-assertion mentioned above.

As was stated at the outset, "Aucassin and Nicolette" contains
certain features that are, in a sense, modern, side by side with the
extremely archaic, not to say primitive, motifs that have been
described hitherto. For example, the tale is frankly accepting of
sex, despite its veneer of romantic idealization. The storyteller's
efforts to sublimate sex along lines consistent with the medieval
code of chivalry are half-hearted at best, and one senses that the
love affair between the principals requires no validation other
than that of physical attraction. Aucassin and Nicolette are permitted by the mythographer to love each other physically no less
than spiritually, immediately as well as ultimately, guiltlessly and
without concealment.

Not only is the story pro-sex, but we see from the account that
it is pro-feminist as well, featuring a heroine who demonstrates a
very high level of adequacy. Nicolette is supremely capable on the
executive level and is a model of constancy. She is mobile, resourceful, musically talented, and not easily overawed by masculine authority. Instead of being cast in the traditional feminine
role of a vulnerable and dependent creature, Nicolette is indeed
the active principle, the *sakti*, of the narrative as she courageously
seeks out her lover, heals him, shares his misadventures, and
finally makes her way back to him from a distant land. What a
fine model Nicolette must have provided for the restless medieval
ladies who listened to the account of her exploits!

The treatment of religion by the storyteller is distinctly modern. The famous lines in which Aucassin states his decided preference for Hell as the place where one can expect to find the most
interesting people attests to the urbane and irreverent tone that
often creeps into the composition. This is no work of a village

curate, intended for the ears of devout provincial listeners, but a document that illustrates the nominal religiosity of a certain stratum of medieval society and does not fit our preconceptions about the "devout" Middle Ages.

Even the mythographer's attitude toward war and aggression is far removed from the single-minded ferocity associated with a warrior society. Aucassin is a reluctant warrior, and the author reduces the idea of war to scarcely more than a ceremonial mock battle. We are left in no doubt as to Aucassin's set of priorities: pleasure before pain, sensuality before heroics.

What is the meaning of these seemingly modern attitudes? They belong, I believe, to the realm of wish fulfillment. I do not think they are the product solely of an emancipated sensibility, although, to be sure, such license would not have been possible without the writer's special cast of mind. What we see as modern in "Aucassin and Nicolette" is precisely the basis of its appeal to readers, ancient and modern. If one equates modern with unrepressed, it is not difficult to see that the elements of the tale that seem most modern constitute the basis of its power to fulfil wishes. In other words, the appearance of sophisticated features in "Aucassin and Nicolette" is a derivative of a spirit of playfulness combined with defiance—defiance of adult authority, of sexual taboos, of religious conventions, and of the norms of a warrior civilization. The larger question remains: How to distinguish between the element of wish fulfillment and genuine expressions of critical thinking in fictional narratives? By the same token, what is the difference between humorous irreverence rooted in unconscious rebellion and genuine satirical humor grounded in a principled criticism of life? Systematic exploration of these questions can throw additional light on sophisticated narratives of the type of "Aucassin and Nicolette," as well as a broad range of imaginative works.

10

A Perspective on the Mythical Imagination

A SINGLE THEME runs through the chapters of this book. It is the idea that myth and ritual answer to the psychological and material needs of individuals and groups. In this context, the myths of Osiris, Jason and Medea, Rama and Sita, and other sacred dramas represent powerful, inescapable human preoccupations corresponding to unfulfilled hopes and half-forgotten disasters. In psychodynamic terms, myths communicate unconscious wishes or fears expressed as miraculous stories. These tales differ from mere legends insofar as myths are sanctioned by an entire community of the faithful and occupy a privileged and unassailable position. The myth itself is by no means a direct statement of its underlying motive. Instead, we are confronted by symbolic disguises and elaborations, as in the dream process. The purpose of these distortions is to defuse the emotional force of the wish or fear. Wishes that are productive of guilt, or fears that are potentially overpowering, would otherwise be experienced as threatening to the individual's security or the group's survival. At the same time, myths must symbolically satisfy insistent emotional needs without appearing to do so blatantly.

We can trace the myth-making function (more precisely, the process of myth renewal) by reference to the modern cult of Ramakrishna discussed in chapter 4. The starting point is, of course, the ancient Hindu belief that the god Visnu underwent a series of incarnations, revealing himself as one mythical hero or another. Future epiphanies are by no means ruled out. The most notable incarnations were those of Rama and Krsna. Ramakrishna came to be regarded as an *avatar* or reincarnation of Visnu; his assumed name is consistent with this identification. In effect, a modern myth was created by the followers of Ramakrishna, who saw in their master not only a saint, but a god-man. In chapter 4, I commented on the psychological needs that led the adolescent devotees of Ramakrishna to turn their leader into a living shrine. From a common sense standpoint, the reader may wonder if it was necessary to mythologize Ramakrishna. For example, why was Ramakrishna unable to see himself simply as a surrogate father to his spiritual sons? Why did the young disciples insist upon viewing their symbiotic relationship with Ramakrishna as a divine dialogue? The answers lie in the disciples' incapacity to consciously accept the facts of their emotional dependency, rebellion against parental wishes, and refusal to marry or pursue a conventional career.

In Erik Erikson's terms we might say the disciples were suffering from an identity crisis.[1] By attaching themselves compulsively to the service of the master, the youths magically blocked the forces that were pushing them toward adult status. In the name of the divine Ramakrishna it became possible for the disciples to stop the flow of profane time and to remain suspended in the dense atmosphere of the temple compound. In this traditional setting the disciples could act out their interim status as adolescents in the sense that Westerners understand this ambiguous term. To suppose that Ramakrishna's youthful followers could consciously acknowledge to themselves how poignantly they longed for dependency and nurturance is to underestimate the threat to their self-esteem. By the same token, the boys could assuage their guilt feelings by playing a nurturant role toward the frail Ramakrishna, identifying with his helplessness on the most profound level. In his sermons, Ramakrishna himself used the metaphor of "feeding" people when he spoke of giving them spiritual nourishment. It is conceivable, too, that his playing the role of a woman and living in women's quarters during an early period of his life reflected his self-concept as a mothering person besides indicating sex-role confusion.

The mythic or obsessive element, then, in the cult of Ramakrishna, consists of the transformation of a man into a god who provides spiritual sustenance to his followers.[2] This myth is reinforced in a variety of ways which fit into the category of ritual—devotional hymns, prayers, offerings of food and gifts to the goddess Kali, fasts, meditations, initiations, pilgrimages, sacred feasts—in short, a wide range of traditional Hindu religious observances. In the present instance, the dramatic myth of the god-man who has been reborn in a suburb of Calcutta overshadows the rituals, which are stylized expressions of fellowship and devotion. This distinction implies that the myth is being made to carry a heavier burden of need gratification than ritual, which serves as a vehicle for sustaining the myth through shared devotion on a daily basis. Nevertheless, the myth-making function cannot be understood apart from ritual, which, by strengthening the solidarity of the group and channeling the anxiety of the individual, provides a social basis for supporting the myth.

Sometimes the myth-making function seems to serve the goal of providing a rationale for important rituals. For example, the myths connected with initiation rites (see chapters 5, 8, and 9) may be more fluid than their associated rites, which are fixed by custom. The ceremonies may be more vivid for the celebrants than the myths, particularly because of their personal significance. Initiation rites, especially, are required to be intensely dramatic, since they are rites of passage. It is of paramount importance to the group no less than to the participating individual that the initiation ceremony be as memorable as possible, thereby guaranteeing that a new and vitally necessary role will be assumed and that expectations associated with the role will be fulfilled. In modern times, dramatic experiences of initiation continue to be provided by adult baptism among certain Protestant sects, confirmation among Catholics, bar mitzvah among Jews, and adolescent circumcision among Moslems. Though varying in emotional impact on the participants, these rituals far overshadow the sacred myths connected with them.[3]

It is uncertain whether the same can be said for ancient initiation rites such as those pertaining to the Greco-Roman mysteries described in chapter 6, or the initiation rites of preliterate societies. Unlike modern initiation ceremonies, archaic rites of passage appear to have been closely linked with a phase of esoteric instruction in the legends and traditions of the group. In effect, the novice who was initiated into manhood by means, for example, of the Plains Indians' Sun Dance, was simultaneously vouchsafed a glimpse of the spirit world.[4] The pain and suffering built into the ceremony (hanging suspended all day from a rope attached to skewers passed under the pectoral muscles) was intended to activate fantasies bound up with the spirit world. Although the Plains Indians were quick to identify and evaluate idiosyncratic fantasies induced by the Sun Dance, fasting, or other rituals, they routinely provided the raw materials for such fantasies through their oft-told sacred myths. These loosely standardized myths were transmitted orally from generation to generation, usually by informal storytelling. The personal significance of the myths was realized however only through participation in traumatic or otherwise emotionally heightened rituals. While it was important for a Sioux or Cheyenne brave to know the sacred myths of his tribe, it was far more important that he acquire the psychological traits appropriate for a warrior and hunter. This goal could be accomplished only by enduring a series of ritual ordeals that shaped the brave's attitudes toward danger and privation. The tribal myths, as such, apparently were less important in providing young men with legendary role models than the example of their stoical peers.

On the basis of the foregoing observations about initiation rites it might be hypothesized that the centrality of sacred myths depends on the viability of the role for which the novice is intended. If the role is still viable, and the novice's peers are eager to excel in it, there is no need to legitimize the role by citing legendary prototypes of the sort who figure in myths. By contrast, in the case of Ramakrishna's inner circle, it would appear that the monkish role to which the young disciples aspired was far from viable in late nineteenth century Calcutta and its environs. As a result, the mythical dimensions of Ramakrishna's life and teachings had to be enlarged to the utmost limits. Soon, the Plains Indians as well had to create a new myth once the traditional roles of warrior and hunter were rendered obsolete. I refer to the appearance of the Ghost Dance movement in the 1890s, with its promise of an Indian messiah and the expulsion of the whites.[5] This phenomenon spread rapidly throughout the Plains region and even to the west coast as a consequence of the final defeat of the Plains Indians and their forcible confinement to reservations. The dancing, viewed as a ritual enactment, undoubtedly strengthened intertribal solidarity, but the messiah myth was without doubt the justification for the ceremony. The messiah myth defended the vanquished Indians against unbearable anxiety at precisely the historical moment when their sacred rituals had lost their functional meaning due to the disappearance of the buffalo and the armed warrior. The new Ghost Dance was an attempt to undo a tragedy by the magic of frenzied dancing. Also, the Indians were able to deny the historical reality of the disaster that had overtaken them by allowing themselves to become obsessed with the imminent arrival of the messiah. Thus, repression went hand in hand with compulsive dancing as a form of ritual, and with the emergence of a powerful obsession in the guise of a new myth. The function of the repression-based ritual was to make rite (right) out of that which had been experienced as morally wrong, namely, defeat and humiliation. By imposing the *arithmos* of their repetitive dance step on the flow of profane history the Ghost Dancers also entered the region of sacred time, communing with the spirit world in which myths and reality are undistinguishable.

What I have said about rites of initiation has to be modified when applied to fertility rites and their associated myths, as discussed in chapters 3, 5, 6, and 7. Fertility rites and initiation ceremonies differ in a number of obvious ways, but there is an

underlying similarity. Both types of ritual are integrative in function. Initiation rites are designed to incorporate each new generation into society; fertility rites are an attempt to integrate the
human group with the forces of creation. The myths connected
with fertility rites revolve around personifications of the generative forces of nature. Hence, Rhea, Persephone, Demeter, Ceres,
Kali, Sita, and the host of Blanchettes, Rosettes, and Violettes
who appear in fairy tales in which initiation and fertility motifs
have been combined, as described in chapter 8. The function of
the fertility myth and its folkloric derivatives is no less integrative
than that of fertility rites. The legendary protagonists of fertility
myths enter upon a sacred union with nature spirits, thereby
renewing the natural order on a seasonal basis. Among agricultur-
ists, the desired end is the growth of crops; among hunters and
fishermen the aim is to increase the size of the catch. The integrative element common to myths and rituals is the affirmation of
group solidarity and the periodic restoration of the links with the
natural and supernatural world.[6] At the same time, the remem-
brance and recital of myths, along with the performance of rituals,
contribute to a reduction of anxiety associated with the prob-
lematic nature of farming, and, even more so, of hunting and
fishing. Anxiety is reduced either by the use of sympathetic magic
or by sacrificial acts.

It is necessary to ask why myths and rituals do not remain fixed
even though they are capable of drawing the community together
and renewing its covenant with the gods. I have already hypothesized that initiation rituals may disappear as a correlative of the
elimination of associated social and economic roles. Why myths
disappear, or are transformed, or even revived, is not known.
Here, too, one might speculate, as I did in chapter 1, that when
old gods are perceived as impotent, new gods or demons are
invented, and, along with them, new myths. But the laws that
govern the historic transformation of myths (if we could identify
them) would surely turn out to be political and economic, no less
than psychological. After all, it was only a generation ago that the
Japanese myth of the divine origin of the emperor had to be
abandoned for political reasons, namely, pressure from the victori-

ous United States. In more remote times, familiar Zeus-centered myths, mostly dealing with the seduction of nymphs and goddesses, replaced a wide range of matriarchal myths, reflecting the consolidation of a new social order in the Dorian Age.[7] Most intriguing of all is the question of why entire myth and ritual complexes, which we know as religious, appear in altered form or even change beyond recognition with the passage of time. Insofar as religions, or even sects, require institutional underpinnings, their mutations are bound up with the forces that generate social change on a broad front, as Tawney, Weber, and Marx have argued, each in his own way. The mechanisms that determine the direction of social change, including religious evolution, cannot tell us, however, why certain themes find their way into sacred myths at one point in history or another. Though historically conditioned, the content of sacred myths is also a function of the psychological needs of people rooted in distinctive cultures. Thus, Bultmann maintains that the sacred myths of Christianity were superimposed on the life of the historical Jesus in his Judean cultural context in order to imbue the new religion with a cosmic significance.[8] In this case, Bultmann argues, the resurrection motif became salient in order to provide a transcendent, messianic meaning to the life of the historical Jesus. Such an explanation is incomplete, however, because it ignores a central problem of early Christianity, i.e., the search for a broad institutional base. If Paul had not built such a foundation through his mission to the gentiles (who had their own fertility-based resurrection myths) it is uncertain whether the motif of the risen Christ would have come to occupy a central position in the structure of Christian beliefs. In a similar vein, the ritual of communion was incorporated into early Christianity as a means of winning wide support among gentiles long accustomed to analogous practices. As applied to the origins of Christianity, then, the history of the myth-making process illustrates the principle of multiple causation, in which obsessive ideas and institutional influences interact to produce new, or seemingly new, religious forms.

Religious sects provide similar evidence of the interplay of psychological and historical forces. The history of the Saint-

Simonian movement in France in the 1830s is instructive in this
respect.[9] Here was a mass movement based on a loose interpretation of the utopian teachings of Henri Saint-Simon, and shaped
by powerful economic, social, and political pressures channeled
into improvised religious myths and rituals. The eventual leader
of the movement, Prosper Enfantin, appealed to a wide audience
of secularized professionals and emerging middle-class entre-
preneurs who felt there was no place for them in the reactionary
France of the Bourbon Restoration. Enfantin and his disciples
hoped to build the foundations for an entirely new social order
somewhat along the lines of Saint-Simon's technocratic society.
This goal was to be accomplished by providing the movement
with a religious mystique combined with reformist socioeconomic
programs. Single-handedly (though with the unconscious collu-
sion of his young, hero-worshipping disciples) Enfantin manufac-
tured a complex of sacred myths in which he appeared in the light
of a savior. Describing God as androgynous and preaching a
doctrine of free love, Enfantin dispatched his disciples to Con-
stantinople to search for a female messiah to complement his own
redemptive role.

But the sacred myths invented by Enfantin—and the reasons
for their immense appeal to an otherwise sophisticated clientele
—would be incomprehensible without reference to the Saint-
Simonian blueprint for the society of the future. It was a plan that
envisioned bold and monumental undertakings by a new class of
capitalists, bankers, engineers, economists, and scientists who had
appeared for the first time in France. These plans did not remain
unfulfilled, and before the Saint-Simonian movement had died
out by the 1840s it had provided the capital and the leadership
for building the first railroad network in France. In addition, an
attempt was made to erect a dam at Aswan in Egypt, an undertaking in which Enfantin participated directly. His original plan had
been to dig a canal linking the Mediterranean with the Red Sea.
This proposal failed to receive official support, and it remained for
de Lesseps and his backers to build the Suez Canal two decades
later.

Nothing could have been more incongruous than the spectacle

of Enfantin's seventy bearded, long-haired disciples arrayed in their colorful holy vestments, marching and chanting in procession through the streets of Paris, while the leader and his closest advisers planned a French-style Industrial Revolution. Thousands of Parisians, as well as large crowds in the provinces, listened enraptured to Enfantin and his inspired apostles as they propounded their unique blend of economics and religious inspiration. Never was the connection between secular and spiritual goals more visibly demonstrated, or the utility of religious myths and ceremonies more clearly apparent. The myth-making process unfolded in accordance with profound psychological needs for emotional security on the part of Enfantin's followers, together with irresistible pressures for social and economic change.

Not unlike the history of the Ramakrishna movement, the story of the Saint-Simonian cult is at bottom the chronicle of a search to heighten the significance of life. In both instances the quest is formulated in religious metaphors, but involves unmistakable social and material objectives of a reformist nature. In addition, these religious movements provided new and viable roles for nascent social and economic classes. The connection between the transformation of religious forms and the phenomenon of social class mobility has long been recognized, of course, in relation to the rise of Protestantism.[10] The members of both movements had come to feel that their old lives were lacking in purpose and, accordingly, looked to charismatic leaders to provide them with objects of devotion. But it must be remembered that to achieve their spiritual and reformist goals it was essential for the followers of Enfantin and Ramakrishna to define and consolidate new social and economic roles for themselves.

Making allowance for the role of economic forces in generating religious growth and renewal, one should not lose sight of the element of disinterestedness in the invention or modification of religious myths, and of the ingenuous spirit that underlies the multiplication of rituals. Whether charlatan or self-deceived enthusiast, the myth-maker is a creator in a unique sense. The myth creates psychological distance between living creatures and the world of things, even as it integrates humanity with the natural order and the spirit world. There is a great paradox in this act of distancing because it combines alienation with integration. By calling to mind a fabulous history of past encounters between the human and the suprahuman, between the divine and the demonic, or between magical animals and the natural order (as in American Indian myths), the mythographer creates a special significance for all living creatures, saying, in effect, that the experience of living is memorable. Myths also tell us that the recorded history of the universe is not the whole story, but that an infinite number of vanished creatures, including the ancestors of the human race, lived and died under extraordinary circumstances. Moreover, myths project themselves into a no less glorious future, as in the case of messianic beliefs. It does not matter if we are talking about Navaho myths about primordial insects with anthropomorphic traits, Greek myths about gods who can assume many forms, Jewish myths about a lost Eden, Christian myths of an incarnate god, or utopian myths of our own time that look forward to a golden age of perfect justice and material well-being. These wide-ranging products of the imagination are much more than mere substitutes for scientific understanding or signs of a primitive mind. Myths are the story of would-be sins, of intended heroisms, and of a longing for perfection and harmony. These motives give rise to metaphors—sometimes beautiful, sometimes terrifying—for human experiences which cannot be expressed otherwise without impoverishing them. This is because the mind is not satisfied to remember past events, or to foretell the future, or even to understand the nature of causality. Myths express a deathless wonder at the visible and invisible forces at work in the universe and in the human spirit. Even destructive myths inspired by cruel impulses are an attempt to justify that baseness of spirit which is their source by appealing to some transcendent ideal. It is as if humanity needs to raise its eyes above its finite horizons by mythologizing the facts of its existence and the existence of all created things. One by one the traditional myths of the world have faded from consciousness or have been reduced to legends which one is free to believe or disbelieve for no compelling reason. It is the same with the ceremonial aspects of life, for we have entered upon an unceremonious age in which a fine line separates spontaneity from anarchy. Given the need for illusions, what will take the place of the old myths?

The secular myths of the twentieth century have proven disastrous. Fueled by malignant hatred, quasi-religious ideologies such as fascism and communism quickly destroyed the very illusions that they sought to foster. Their successors in the last quarter of this century—the myths behind virulent xenophobia, for example —appear to be a compound of nationalism and pure heartlessness, and are no less antihuman. The problem with myths is that it is difficult for people to generate illusions that are a genuine improvement over the actualities which have shaped their character. Only men of good will can create life-affirming myths; those whose character has been warped by generations of complicity in despotism and corruption can dream only bad dreams. Even their hopes for a bright future are shadowed by fear and malice.

Mythographers are like science-fiction writers who can imagine only a universe filled with conflict and grief with an occasional glimpse of peace and harmony. The grotesque shapes ascribed to extraterrestrial beings are nothing more than the mirror image of the human soul. It was the same with the ancients whose gods were as pitiless as those who invented them. But we must not ignore the hunger for transcendence. Our myths seem to say that human existence—indeed, all of creation—signifies something. Is it the fault of mythographers that thus far the mirror which they have held up to the human face has reflected back an ambiguous image, demonic as well as divine? No wonder the gods have demeaned themselves, acting the parts of men. But humans have the capacity to imagine suprahuman models and to be inspired by their noble deeds, even if those deeds exceed the capacity of mere mortals. Myths tell us that it is possible to be better than *Homo sapiens sapiens* has managed to be so far. No doubt when we succeed in mustering up enough nerve to act on this belief, we will at last be worthy of our most splendid myths.

Notes

Chapter 1

1. J. G. Frazer, *The Golden Bough*, abridged ed. (New York: Macmillan, 1939), pp. 264 ff.
2. Ibid., pp. 269 ff.
3. S. Freud, *The Basic Writings of Sigmund Freud, Book 5, Totem and Taboo* (New York: Modern Library (Random House), 1938), pp. 821 ff.
4. D. de Rougement, *The Devil's Share*, trans. by Haakon Chevalier (New York: Meridian Books, 1956), p. 139.
5. H. Zimmer, *Myths and Symbols in Indian Art and Civilization* (New York: Pantheon Books, 1946), p. 172.

Chapter 2

1. R.D. Laing, "Ontological Insecurity," in *Psychoanalysis and Existential Philosophy*, ed. by H. M. Ruitenbeek (New York: E.P. Dutton, 1962), pp. 41–69. Laing speaks of a type of person who is said to lack "ontological autonomy." He is someone who does not feel himself to exist in his own right, but only in the actual or symbolic presence of others, very much like Sartre's inauthentic type who exists only in the "gaze" of others. The would-be mystic who underestimates the strength of his emotional dependency needs cannot begin to transform his environment symbolically because he has yet to differentiate himself from the world around him, and to discover his unique identity.

2. Erich Fromm, *The Forgotten Language* (New York: Grove Press, 1957), pp. 241–49. Fromm argues that the Sabbath, viewed as a state of rest, adumbrates the mystical harmony of the Messianic age, just as the condition of work signifies the tension of unfulfillment. The state of Being may be compared perhaps to a kind of inner Sabbath. Nicolas Berdyaev, following Boehme's lead, assigns a negative value to the state of Being, equating it with the end of creative freedom.

3. The mystic's need, it seems to me, is more urgent and more particular than that felt by the celebrants of the ancient mysteries. Kerényi, in C. G. Jung and C. Kerényi, *Essays on a Science of Mythology* (New York: Pantheon, 1949) interprets the ritual use of an ear of grain in Eleusis as an affirmation of the unity of life. He rightly adds that the attitude of the devotee in such mysteries was essentially passive, not a search for redemption as much as a brief experience of "wordless wisdom." See particularly his chapter "Kore."

4. D. T. Suzuki, *Mysticism: Christian and Buddhist* (New York: Harper, 1957). Suzuki contrasts Oriental modes of experience with what he regards as the more analytical tendency of Western thought. The main distinction for him is that Western man, though fully capable of reverence for nature, is inclined to rearrange the world around him. He maintains that there is a marked tendency in Oriental thought to respect the "as-it-is-ness" of things. I would not presume to say which approach is more compatible with the attitude of mysticism, although it is clear that self-awareness plays a different role in Eastern and Western mysticism.

5. C. G. Jung, "The Phenomenology of the Spirit in Fairy Tales," in *Spirit and Nature*, vol. 1, *Papers from the Eranos Yearbook* (New York: Bollingen Foundation, 1954). It is precisely the conjunction of piety and unconsciousness, according to Jung, that prevents the human spirit from ridding itself of demonism.

6. Martin Buber, *Between Man and Man* (Boston: Beacon, 1955), pp. 65–66. Buber holds out hope that somehow the exceptional individual, the "Single One," can change the crowd by humanizing it. His point is that one must go on living in the world, in society, if he wishes to receive God for his companion. Buber does not minimize the coercive force of the community, but insists that if the man of faith peers directly into the face of the crowd he will discover the face of God.

7. Erich Neumann, *The Origin and History of Consciousness*, Part 2, *The Psychological Stages in the Development of Personality* (New York: Harper, 1962), p. 421ff. The mystic may be compared to Neumann's "Great Individual" who is among the few who can say no to society and its demands. The "Great Individual" possesses an ego which has successfully differentiated itself from its collective identity.

8. Nicolas Berdyaev, *The Destiny of Man* (New York: Harper, 1960), pp. 190–91. Berdyaev sees the love of God as a precondition for loving man. The problem is this: If God comes first, then one must be certain that it is God and not the Devil whom one loves in the beginning.

9. R. C. Zaehner, *Mysticism: Sacred and Profane* (New York: Galaxy, 1961), pp. 202–3. Zaehner is surely right in rejecting the assumption that the instinctive side of human nature is necessarily the same as moral evil. The integrated psyche may be said to embrace everything: man in nature, or man as he was before good and evil were capable of being distinguished.

10. Otto Rank, "Soul and Will," in *Psychology and the Soul*, trans. by W. D. Turner (New York: A.S. Barnes, 1961), p. 142 ff. I do not wish to imply in any sense that yogic willpower is ethically inferior to the mystical experience of powerlessness. Rank cautions against the tendency, especially in Western religious tradition, to assume a moral attitude toward the will and to interpret it as evil or sinful. It is sufficient, he says, to recognize that the central motivating factor behind man's spiritual strivings is the will to live,

which means struggling to overcome death. This is a natural rather than egotistical goal.

11. Mircea Eliade, *Cosmos and History: The Myth of the Eternal Return* (New York: Harper, 1959), pp. 3 ff. Not only do the myths overshadow the gods, but they seem to negate the uniqueness and poignancy of human experience, including the experience of the supernatural. Mircea Eliade, in analyzing the process of myth-making, has provided numerous examples of how man's historical experience is assimilated to the prototypical, thereby substituting archaic, traditional categories of thought for direct experience.

12. Evelyn Underhill, *Mysticism* (New York: Meridian, 1955), pp. 380 ff. discusses at length the experiences of desperation and lovelessness that often accompany a crisis of religious faith. Her treatment, essentially prepsychological, does not seem to recognize the guilt psychology of many mystics, and is representative of a vanishing romantic tradition.

Chapter 3

1. *Plutarch's Romane Questions,* trans. by Phelemon Holland and ed. by Frank B. Jevons (London: David Nutt, 1892), pp. 56–58.
2. J. G. Frazer, *The Golden Bough* (New York: Macmillan, 1960), pp. 152–53.
3. Ibid., pp. 157–58.
4. Ibid., p. 165.
5. Ibid., p. 679.
6. Robert Graves, *The Greek Myths,* vol. 1 (Baltimore: Penguin Books, 1955), pp. 298–303.
7. Frazer, *Golden Bough,* p. 167.
8. W. K. C. Guthrie, *The Greeks and Their Gods* (Boston: Beacon Press, 1955), p. 107.
9. Graves, *Greek Myths,* pp. 96–97.
10. *Ovid's Metamorphoses,* trans. by Dr. Garth (London: W. Suttaby & B. Crosby, 1807), bk. 6, p. 178.
11. Frazer, *Golden Bough,* pp. 403–13.
12. Ibid., p. 410.

13. Graves, *Greek Myths*, p. 78.
14. Ibid., p. 68.
15. See Martin P. Nilsson's *Greek Folk Religion* (N. Y.: Harper, 1961), pp. 42–64, for a detailed account of the Eleusinian Mysteries.
16. Frazer, *Golden Bough*, pp. 289–306.

Chapter 4

1. For a pertinent analysis of concepts dealing with religious change see "The Concept of Secularization in Empirical Research," *J. Sci. Study Relig.*, 6, 1967, pp. 207–20.
2. C. Isherwood, *Ramakrishna and His Disciples* (New York: Simon and Schuster, 1965), p. 324.
3. M. Monier-Williams, *Brahmanism and Hinduism* (New York: Macmillan, 1891), pp. 496–531.
4. The *Bhakti* movement in nineteenth century India, not unlike the revivalism of the American frontier, encouraged emotionalism as a means of expressing religious devotion. Ramakrishna's emphasis on the importance of suprasensuous experience was dictated by the wish to resist the false demands of worldliness, as well as the need to attain spiritual insight on a unitive basis.
5. See J. M. Yinger, *Religion, Society, and the Individual* (New York: Macmillan, 1957), pp. 262–64.
6. Isherwood, *Ramakrishna*, p. 225.
7. *The Gospel of Sri Ramakrishna*, trans. by Swami Nikhilananda (New York: Ramakrishna-Vivekananda Center, 1952).
8. Ernst Troeltsch's well-known distinction between church and sect involves, among other things, the distinction between the church with its efficient division of labor, and the sect with its intense, essentially indivisible focus on the struggle against practical compromises with the secular powers. Ramakrishna was by nature a sectarian, but tolerated role differentiation by his followers.
9. Ramakrishna's "bizarre" behavior must be judged within its proper cultural context. Because Ramakrishna was a Brah-

min priest who combined the performance of traditional religious functions with demonstrations of divine possession, especially in *samadhi*, he could appeal to a wide clientele. He was both an exemplar of Redfield's "great tradition" of Hinduism and of village shamanism, sublimated to a very high plane. Thus, Ramakrishna's trances and other dramatic manifestations, including, perhaps, even his psychotic behavior, were not truly aberrations from the standpoint of the non-Sanskritic popular culture. For an informative discussion of the respective roles of Brahmins and shamans in contemporary India, see Gerald D. Berreman, "Brahmins and Shamans in Pahari Religion," in *Religion in South Asia*, ed. by Edward H. Harper (Seattle: University of Washington Press, 1964), pp. 53–69.

10. Tillich, in one of his comments on Western man's search for immediate religious experience, compares the success of artists, such as Grosz, in capturing the "inner power of things," with the inadequacy of traditional religious symbolism in conveying spiritual insights. See J. L. Adams, *Paul Tillich's Philosophy of Culture, Science, and Religion* (New York: Harper and Row, 1965), p. 113.

11. E. E. Hagen, *On the Theory of Social Change* (Homewood, Ill.: Dorsey Press, 1962), pp. 55–85.

Chapter 5

1. G. Rawlinson, ed. and trans., *The History of Herodotus*, vol. 2 (New York: Appleton, 1859).

2. R. T. Rundle Clark, *Myth and Symbol in Ancient Egypt* (New York: Grove Press, 1960).

3. Ibid.

4. Mircea Eliade, *Myths, Dreams and Mysteries* (New York: Harper, 1960).

5. Theodore Reik, *Ritual: Four Psychoanalytic Studies* (New York: Grove Press, 1962).

6. Clark, *Myth and Symbol*.

7. M. F. Sciacca, "Death as a Non-Value in the Consciousness of Contemporary Man," *The Personalist*, 1959, 40: 152–64.

8. Eliade, *Myths, Dreams and Mysteries*.

Chapter 6

1. Jane Harrison, *Prolegomena to the Study of Greek Religion* (New York: Meridian, 1960), p. 288.
2. J. G. Frazer, *The Golden Bough* (New York: Macmillan, 1960), p. 338.
3. J. G. Frazer, *Studies in Greek Scenery, Legend and History* (London: Macmillan, 1917), p. 359.
4. Robert Graves, *The Greek Myths*, vol. 2. (Baltimore: Penguin Books. 1955), p. 253.
5. Mircea Eliade, *The Sacred and the Profane* (New York: Harcourt, Brace & Co.), 1959.
6. Ibid., p. 205.

Chapter 7

1. *The Ramayana*, trans. by R. T. H. Griffith, 5 vols., 1870–1875.
2. *The Ramayana*, as told by Aubrey Menen (New York: Scribner, 1954).
3. Norvin Hein, "The Ram Lila," in *Traditional India: Structure and Change*, ed. by Milton Singer (Philadelphia: American Folklore Society, 1959), pp. 73–98.
4. Mircea Eliade, *Yoga: Immortality and Freedom* (New York: Pantheon Books, 1958). Especially Ch.6, "Yoga and Tantrism."
5. Indera P. Singh, "A Sikh Village," in *Traditional India*, ed. by Singer, pp. 284–85.
6. Hein, *Ram Lila* p. 74
7. Ibid., p. 94.
8. W. J. Wilkins, *Hindu Mythology* (Calcutta: Thacker, Spink & Co., 1882), pp. 214–15.
9. Ibid., pp. 238–41.
10. J. A. Dubois, *Description of The Character, Manners, and Customs of The People of India; And of Their Institutions, Religious and Civil* (Philadelphia: M. Carey & Son, 1818), vol. 2, pp. 253–54.
11. Cited by Wilkins, *Hindu Mythology*, pp. 258–60.
12. E. W. Hopkins, *The Religions of India* (Boston: Ginn & Co., 1895), pp. 528–29.

13. Eliade, *Yoga*, p. 343.
14. A. L. Basham, *The Wonder That Was India* (New York: Grove, 1954), p. 321.
15. Wilkins, *Hindu Mythology*, p. 374–82.
16. H. Zimmer, *Myths and Symbols in Indian Art and Civilization* (New York: Harper Torchbooks, 1962), pp. 72–76.
17. Ibid., pp. 87–88
18. Ibid., pp. 82–88
19. Eliade, *Yoga*, pp. 326–30.
20. Cited in Wilkins, *Hindu Mythology*, p. 250.
21. Cited in Ibid., pp. 243–45.
22. Footnote in Ibid., p. 157.
23. R.C. Majumdar, ed., *The Vedic Age* (London: Allen & Unwin, 1957), p. 187.
24. Hein, *Ram Lila*, p. 97.

Chapter 8

1. P. Saintyves, *Les Contes de Perrault et Les Recits Paralleles* (Paris: Librairie Critique Emile Nourry, 1923).
2. Comtesse de Segur, *Old French Fairy Tales* (Philadelphia: Penn Publishing Co., 1920).
3. S. Thompson, *The Folktale* (New York: Dryden Press, 1946).
4. J. Harrison, *Prolegomena to the Study of Greek Religion* (New York: Meridian, 1960), pp. 595–97.
5. Ibid., p. 479.
6. Ibid., p. 593.
7. Ibid., p. 521.
8. A. van Gennep, *The Rites of Passage* (Chicago: University of Chicago Press, 1960).
9. Harrison, *Prolegomena*, p. 522.
10. E. Crawley, *The Mystic Rose* (N. p.: Meridian, n.d.).
11. Saintyves, *Contes de Perrault*, p. 340.
12. J. G. Frazer, *The Golden Bough* (New York: Macmillan, 1960), pp. 578 ff.
13. Harrison, *Prolegomena*, p. 155.

14. J. L. Weston, *From Ritual to Romance* (New York: Doubleday, 1957).
15. M. Eliade, *Patterns in Comparative Religion* (New York: Sheed & Ward, 1958), p. 292.
16. Ibid., p. 100.
17. Ibid., p. 281.
18. Weston, *Ritual,* pp. 52 ff.
19. Eliade, *Patterns,* p. 292.
20. M.P. Nilsson, *Greek Folk Religion* (New York: Harper, 1961), p. 46.
21. Harrison, *Prolegomena,* p. 627.
22. Ibid., p. 498.
23. H. J. Rose, *Ancient Roman Religion* (London: Hutchinson's Library, 1948), p. 86.
24. R. Graves, *The Greek Myths,* vol. 1 (Baltimore: Penguin Books, 1955), pp. 236–37.
25. Frazer, *Golden Bough,* p. 50.
26. W. K. C. Guthrie, *The Greeks and Their Gods* (Boston: Beacon, 1961), p. 95.
27. E. Neumann, *Amor and Psyche* (New York: Harper, 1962).
28. Frazer, *Golden Bough,* p. 21.
29. A. H. Krappe, *The Science of Folklore* (New York: Barnes & Noble, 1963), pp. 104 ff.
30. P. Radin, *The World of Primitive Man* (New York: Grove, 1960), p. 178.
31. Frazer, *Golden Bough* pp. 3–4.
32. Ibid., p. 145.
33. Ibid.
34. Ibid., pp. 139–56.
35. E. O. James, *Comparative Religion* (New York: Barnes & Noble, 1961), p. 90.
36. Neumann, *Amor,* p. 118.
37. Harrison, *Prologomena,* p. 304.
38. Eliade, *Patterns,* p. 164.
39. Frazer, *Golden Bough,* pp. 580–81.
40. Ibid., pp. 585–600.
41. Ibid., p. 594.

42. Ibid., p. 593.
43. Graves, *Greek Myths*, p. 92.

Chapter 9

1. H. Hallam, *View of the State of Europe During the Middle Ages* (New York: Harper, 1859), chapter 9.
2. A. Luchaire, *Social France at the Time of Philip Augustus*, Trans. by E.B. Krehbiel (New York: Ungar, Reprint of 1912 edition), p. 350 ff.
3. M. Eliade, *Rites and Symbols of Initiation* (New York: Harper, 1958), pp. 122–36.
4. F.W. Bourdillon, ed., *Aucassin and Nicolette: A Love Story* (London: Kegan Paul, Trench & Co., 1887).
5. F.W. Bourdillon, ed., *Cest Daucasi & De Nicolete*, reproduced in photo-facsimile and type-transliteration from the unique MS. in the Bibliotheque Nationale at Paris, fonds francais 2168 (Oxford: Clarendon Press, 1894).
6. Ibid.
7. A.J. Greimas, *Dictionnaire de l'ancien francais jusqu'au milieu du XIV siecle* (Paris: Librairie Larousse, 1969).
8. A.S. Waldstein, *English-Hebrew Dictionary* (Israel: Mizpah, n.d.).
9. Fauriel, C.C. *History of Provencal Poetry*, trans. by G.J. Adler (New York: Derby & Jackson, 1860), chapter 13.
10. L. Dheralde, *Dictionnaire de la Langue Limousine* (Limoges: Societé D'Ethnographie du Limousin de la Marche et des Régions Voisines, 1968), reprint of 1885 edition.
11. Ibid.
12. Ibid.
13. Ibid.
14. Eliade, *Rites*, p. 125. Eliade points out that "the function of sovereignty is generally bound up with an initiatory ritual. At the end of their quest, the heroes often attain sovereignty."
15. A. van Gennep, *The Rites of Passage*, trans. by M.B. & G.L. Vizedou (Chicago: University of Chicago Press, 1960), p. 82.

16. Ibid., pp. 65–115.
17. Luchaire, *Social France*, p. 305. Luchaire mentions the *chanson, Garin le Lorrain,* which contains a stereotyped description of a peasant, Rigaut, whose hideous appearance corresponds closely to that of the forest-stranger in *Aucassin and Nicolette.*
18. Eliade, *Rites*, pp. 126–27.
19. Fauriel, *Provencal Poetry,* pp. 283–84.
20. Bourdillon, *Aucassin* (see footnote 4), pp. 178–179, note g. Bourdillon notes that the practice of the *couvade* survived among the Basques of Biscay until the nineteenth century.
21. J. Brand, *Observations on the Popular Antiquities of Great Britain,* vol. 1 (London: Bell and Daldy, 1873), p. 222. Brand reports that "In honor of May Day the Goths and Southern Swedes held a mock battle between Summer and Winter, which ceremony is retained on the Isle of Man."
22. Eliade, *Rites,* p. 43. Eliade bases his interpretation on observations of Australian aborigines made by Berndt and Berndt in the 1950s.
23. J.G. Frazer, *The Golden Bough: A Study in Magic and Religion,* abridged ed. (New York: Macmillan, 1939), chapter 60. The author gives many examples of the seclusion of girls at puberty among preliterate peoples. Often, the girls were kept in dark cells for long periods of time, with old women ministering to their needs.
24. P. Sébillot, *Le Folk-Lore de France.* Tome Premier: *Le Ciel et la Terre* (Paris: Librairie Orientale et Americaine. Maisonneuve Freres, 1904). Perhaps Nicolette-as-animal had something in common with those forest-spirits who, not long ago, were believed by peasants to take the form of enchanted animals, as described by Sebillot. This author recounts the following "modern" superstition: "Le fantome de dame Nicole . . . habite le bois de la Pierre pres de Laigle, et se change souvent en loup et en chien. . . ." (p. 291).
25. Comtesse de Segur, *Old French Fairy Tales* (Philadelphia: Penn Publishing Co., 1920).

26. Eliade, *Rites*, p. 44.
27. Ibid., p. 43
28. Brand, *Observations*, p. 579.
29. J. Pouegh, *Le Folklore des pays d'oc; La Tradition Occitane* (Paris: Payot, 1952), p. 222.
30. Juvenal's reference to orgiastic activities associated with the worship of *Bona Dea* (Satire VI) leaves no doubt that this May-time festival was a fertility rite.
31. Brand, *Observations*, pp. 212–47. Brand quotes from Stubbs, in the *Anatomie of Abuses*, 1585.
32. Ovid refers to this custom, the *Compitalia*, in the *Fasti*. Also celebrated early in May was a rite called *Lemuria*, involving ancestor worship, as well as the sacrifice of human effigies. The connection between sacrifice and placating the spirits of the dead is evident.
33. Frazer, *Golden Bough*, p. 124.
34. Ibid., p. 121.
35. R. Chambers, ed., *The Book of Days, A Miscellany of Popular Antiquities in Connection with the Calendar*, vol. 1, (London and Edinburgh: W. & R. Chambers, 1869), p. 573.
36. Ibid., p. 581.
37. A. D. De Groot, *Saint Nicholas: A Psychoanalytic Study of His History and Myth* (The Hague: Mouton & Co., 1965).

Chapter 10

1. Erik H. Erikson, *Identity: Youth and Crisis* (New York: Norton, 1968).
2. The concept of loving a personal god is by no means foreign to Hinduism, as evidenced by the tradition of *bhakti*, dating back to the eleventh or twelfth centuries A. D. For a concise treatment of this motif in Hinduism see David L. Edwards, *Religion and Change* (New York: Harper and Row, 1969).
3. For an excellent discussion of the psychological significance of rituals, see Harold Fallding, *The Sociology of Religion* (Toronto: McGraw-Hill Ryerson Limited, 1974), chapter 4.
4. Thomas Rhys Williams, *Introduction to Socialization* (Saint Louis: C. V. Mosby Company, 1972), p. 69.

5. James Mooney, *The Ghost Dance Religion and the Sioux Outbreak of 1890,* ed. by Anthony F. Wallace (London: University of Chicago Press, 1965).

6. Emile Durkheim, *The Elementary Forms of the Religious Life* (New York: Free Press, 1965).

7. Robert Graves, *The Greek Myths,* vol. 1 (Baltimore, Md.: Penguin Books, 1955), pp. 55–56.

8. Rudolf Bultmann, *Primitive Christianity in Its Contemporary Setting,* trans. by R. H. Fuller (London: Collins, 1960).

9. Leo Schneiderman, "The Saint-Simonians: A Study of Religious Cult Formation and Dissolution," *Illinois Quarterly,* 1978, 40 (3):36–48.

10. Max Weber, *The Protestant Ethic and the Spirit of Capitalism* (London: George Allen & Unwin, 1930).

Index